REVIEW COPY
Publication Date: 17 Feb. 1986
Hb 0 86232 510 2 £ 18.95 $ 29.95
Pb 0 86232 511 0 £ 6.95 $ 10.95

Available from leading bookshops,
as well as Zed Books, 57 Caledonian
Road, London N1 9BU.

José Martí: Architect of Cuba's Freedom

José Martí: Architect of Cuba's Freedom

Peter Turton

Zed Books Ltd.

José Martí: Architect of Cuba's Freedom was first published by
Zed Books Ltd, 57 Caledonian Road, London N1 9BU, in
1986.

Copyright © Peter Turton, 1986.

Cover designed by Ian Hawkins.
Printed by The Bath Press, Avon.

British Library Cataloguing in Publication Data

Turton, Peter
  José Martí: architect of Cuba's freedom
  1. Statesmen — Cuba — Biography
  I. Title
  972.91'05'0924   F1783.M38

  ISBN 0-86232-510-2
  ISBN 0-86232-511-0 Pbk

US Distributor
Biblio Distribution Center, 81 Adams Drive,
Totowa, New Jersey 07512, USA.

Contents

Dedication

This book is dedicated to Mr J. T. Boorman, late of Corpus Christi College, Cambridge, much remembered by many generations of undergraduates for his kindness.

Acknowledgements

Acknowledgement is due to the British Academy, whose grant helped to fund the researching of this book. Thanks are also given to Dr Jorge Ibarra, of the Cuban Academy of Sciences, who looked over the typescript, and suggested several emendations. Any errors contained in this book are the result of my own judgement.

Introduction

The present book aims to give a basic introduction to the most important ideas and political struggles of the 'Apostle' and father of Cuban independence, José Martí (1853–95). To date there has been no book published in this country on Martí, and very little more in the way of articles, etc., whereas in Cuba itself, and to a lesser extent in the United States, there has been an enormous outpouring of materials on this complex man. In Latin America as a whole, again, the situation differs. There Martí is known, but insufficiently studied.

Martí was not only a political figure, but a poet, journalist and pedagogue. He even wrote a novel and published a magazine for children. However, his importance lies in his political activities and thought, and it is these with which this modest book is mainly concerned. Modest, yet necessary, since any serious student of Martí has to hack his way through a jungle of conflicting opinion and interpretation. The bibliography on Martí has now become so enormous as to bury the essence of the man himself, not least because he has been taken to be the forerunner of most shades of political opinion, and a spiritual mentor for both communist and anti-communist Cubans. Thus the Marxist regime of Fidel Castro heralds him as the ideological author of its revolution and accords him a veneration not second to that given the founders of Marxism-Leninism itself, whilst at the other end of the political spectrum Martí's name has been appropriated by a Florida-based radio station set up under the Reagan administration to churn out anti-Castro propaganda.

In my opinion, the way out of this labyrinth requires primarily an examination of the writings of Martí himself, in their true chronology, against the backcloth of his times. This may seem a truism, yet the temptation to pay too much attention to secondary sources and thus get bogged down in a welter of paradox has at all costs to be avoided, given the passions aroused by the figure of Martí and the witting or unwitting distortions of his ideology purveyed by the vast majority of those who have written or write on him, whether they be of the right or of the left. This book tries to present Martí in so far as possible through his own words – of which there is no lack. Someone once calculated that from the time Martí started to earn his living seriously as a writer he must have written for eight hours per day. But again, quotations from Martí's writings are produced to support the views of the right, left and middle, and it may seem that even direct quotation from Martí can make him appear as all things to all men. How could this come about?

In my opinion, this is because of the paradoxical ideology that fuelled Martí's vision of the world. Martí was at the same time an anti-imperialist and a non-socialist, however sympathetic he may have become to socialism towards the end of his life. Martí drew the basic premises of his world-view from the neo-Kantian movement known as Krausism (of which an appendix at the end of this book offers a summing-up), which held sway over the minds of Spanish intellectuals of a liberal bent from the mid-nineteenth century onwards, and which Martí imbibed in his first Spanish exile. Krausism was a strange mixture of moralistic idealism (Christianity filtered through Kant) and positivism. Its 'harmonic rationalism' held that the frugal and brotherly values of Christianity and similar religions, seen through a rationalist prism, could somehow be grafted onto a belief in the kind of material development of man as the positivists understood it. But when Martí discerned the true face of positivism in all its brutality in the United States of the 1880s and 1890s, he was horrified, and in consequence turned away from that nation, which in any case he had never taken as a model for a future independent Cuba. Yet he never really got round to providing an alternative blueprint for Cuba, beyond warning of the dangers of excessive accumulation of property by the minority and the evils of excessive industrialization, in the name of a 'balanced' society.

In point of fact, Martí hardly had the time to work out any really systematic world-view, taken up as he was so totally with the day-to-day politics of Cuban independence and, at a later stage, combating fiercely the onslaught being waged by the United States on Latin America as a whole with a view to unloading there its surplus production. Martí's daily bread at the height of his life was mainly earned by the stream of articles he wrote from the United States on these and other issues. He presents no synthesis of his thought in any one piece of writing, and his total world-view has to be gleaned and assembled from his complete *opus*, which was mainly journalistic. And journalism, of course, is not conducive to depth of thought.

The majority of those who have written on Martí have been concerned to extract from him whatever served their particular purpose, wilfully or lazily ignoring awkward contradictions and apparent paradoxes. But Martí's thought can be synthesized into a reasonably coherent whole, as long as one finds the key to it and takes his writings *in toto* and in their development. If one is not aware of the key (Krausism), one may mistakenly believe Martí to be a mere philosophical eclectic or, worse still, see his views as so shot through with contradictions as to possess little value as a general philosophy of life.

Chronology is paramount, because Martí evolved. It is for this reason that the chapters that make up this book are organized chronologically as regards their internal structure. It is possible to quote Martí on the United States, for instance, and by ignoring the time of writing make out a case for his being essentially enthusiastic, calmly critical or fired with a most un-Martí-like hatred of that nation. Likewise, his views on Karl Marx can be, and have been, presented tendentiously. It is downright stupid, or exceptionally perverse, to produce, as one Cuban exile in the United States has done, a dictionary (!) of his thought, as if he were the Delphic oracle, all of whose utterances contained an equal validity, despite their contradictoriness. But this leap into hagiography is an old tradition, or game, where Martí is concerned, and one of the objectives of the present book is to counteract this tendency, which in fact has the effect of devaluing Martí whilst claiming to do the opposite. Surely the intelligent reader does not want a plaster saint, and expects a few warts.

The three chapters of this book deal with key areas in Martí's thinking and socio-political activities. An examination of all the facets of his life would call for much more space than is available, and in any case the intention was to offer only an introduction to what is most significant about him. As stated, extensive quotations from Martí's writings have been made, in order to place the reader in as direct a contact as possible with the man himself. One of the problems arising from this tactic turns on the fact that Martí does not translate at all well into English, for the romantic exuberance of his prose seems rather heady to readers brought up in a more sober tradition. This is a great pity, for at its best Martí's prose can be extraordinarily vivid. One is always reminded, on reading him, that he was a figure of considerable literary interest, quite apart from his political and philosophical dimensions, in the manner of many eminent Latin Americans.

Lastly, two points which have to be made in the manner of confessions. The nearer this book came to completion, the more I felt the need to break fresh ground in Martí studies, in the sense that the question of *how* Martí expressed himself, if tackled in depth alongside *what* he says, would reveal more about him than this book does, concerned as it is with the *content* of his thought only. Martí's imagery, for instance, makes a fascinating topic which should not be abandoned to the literary specialists. Secondly, it will become apparent to the reader as he proceeds through the text that Martí's ideological evolution led him down paths that were far more radical than his early philosophical premises had catered for. At the end of his short life, Martí was hovering on the brink of a qualitative ideological change, of which he himself was dimly aware. He is, indeed, the forerunner of the present Cuban revolution, and the usurpation of his name for a radio station by the northern 'monster', as he termed it (and nearly a century hence the 'monster' has acquired powers that Martí would never even have dreamed of, to the detriment of the world as a whole), for the purpose of spewing out propaganda against a regime that Martí would surely have supported, is nothing short of ludicrous.

1: Martí and Cuban Independence

Early Formative Years. Cuban Imprisonment and Spanish Exile

Some of the complexities and apparent contradictions that all serious Martí scholars have to grapple with in order to understand this remarkable and complicated man may be traced back to the circumstances surrounding the early years of his short existence. Born in mid-nineteenth century Cuba (the exact date is 28 January 1853), a Caribbean country which, unlike the rest of the territories of the Spanish empire in the Americas, remained under colonial domination (the only other exception being Puerto Rico, likewise a plantation economy based on the production of sugar by slave labour), José Martí was the first child of Spanish parents of proven allegiance to the Spanish crown. The father, Mariano Martí, hailed from Valencia and at the time of José's birth was still a sergeant in the Spanish army, whilst Leonor Pérez, the mother, was a Canary Islander. The young José Martí, however, soon became an ardent supporter of Cuban independence.

This was partly due to the influence of the patriot schoolmaster and poet Rafael María de Mendive, who took the adolescent Martí under his wing, teaching him for a time in his own school and helping him financially. To a large extent Mendive served José as a surrogate father in that he supplied the lad with the affection and understanding that Don Mariano, a rough and ready, rather brutal parent, was seemingly unable to offer his son. In addition Martí's father, despite his rigid loyalty to the Spanish administration, found it difficult to hold down a steady job, and when in employment it was merely as a minor officer of the law in various localities usually in and around Havana. At times he found himself reduced to helping his wife sew army uniforms. The modest house where José was born, situated in the dock area of Havana and now carefully preserved, bears witness today to the family's relative penury.

Through the socially more acceptable and sympathetic Mendive, Martí was able to escape from this rather depressing background. His best friend, indeed, was Fermín Valdés Domínguez, the son of a wealthy slave-owning family. Curiously enough, although the two adolescents at first held different views on slavery – José being from the start totally opposed to the institution – it was Fermín who later on became the socialist. José's psychology led him to sympathize with people suffering under any form of oppression, not just that of a socio-economic or political nature, and had a quasi-Christian bias to it. Not for nothing was he to be known throughout Latin America as the Apostle. It was only after his experiences in the economic depression of the eighties in the United States and his later close contact with Cuban emigré workers (mainly those employed in the Florida tobacco industry, at the beginning of the 1890s) that Martí began seriously to occupy himself with the specific problems of the working class as such. He then became much more radical vis-à-vis the question of social class, and his thinking acquired a more materialist hue, whilst never quite freeing itself from the kind of romantic idealism that had constituted part of his nature from very early on.

The relative importance of the many different influences on Martí's thinking, over the whole of his life, makes a fascinating subject for speculation, as does the question of the exact extent of his late radicalization. Suffice to say, for the moment, that his earliest years provided him with an intense hatred of injustice in general.

In 1866, not long after Martí had come under the influence of Mendive, the Spanish government had been forced to set up a *Junta de Información* (Board of Enquiry), including representatives from Cuba itself, for the purpose of defusing a situation which had become explosive. The Board was to discuss reform in Cuba, but the Spanish government carefully gave it no executive status whatsoever. Although a whole range of options were set before it, from integration into Spain as an overseas territory to Home Rule for Cuba, the Board was mere window-dressing for a situation which the Spanish authorities had no intention of changing in any meaningful way. Even years later, a Spanish deputy to the Madrid *Cortes* (Parliament) was to ask what a colony was for, if not exploitation, in a specific reference to Cuba. The Board was disbanded in 1867, having seen through a few minor reforms.

The following year saw war break out, led by a representative of the creole planter class, Carlos Manuel de Céspedes. Quite apart from the question of political rights for Cubans, the revolt was a protest at the dire economic situation which the native bourgeoisie was facing, in that taxation was levied mainly on its members. The war was actually sparked off when taxation suddenly increased in 1867, as if in mockery of the interests of people like Céspedes.

This happened against a background of press censorship, the subordination of civil authority to that of the Spanish army, the terrorization of suspected Cuban subversives by the Spanish Volunteers (groups of paramilitaries concerned with the strictest defence of the *status quo*) and, to cap it all, a cholera epidemic.

Events in Spain itself also precipitated the Cuban war of 1868. On 17 September that year, the ramshackle regime headed by the licentious

Queen Isabel II was toppled by the 'Glorious' Revolution of General Prim which demanded 'Spain with Honour'. An uprising in Spain's other American colony, Puerto Rico, quickly followed, known as the Rebellion of Lares. Then, on 10 October Carlos Manuel de Céspedes took the field from his sugar-mill La Demajagua, in Cuba's Oriente province, freeing his slaves and initiating what was to become the Ten Years' War.

Clubs of supporters were formed in secret all over Cuba, and many people left home to join the armies of the *mambises* or independence fighters. The fifteen-year-old José Martí penned a sonnet in honour of the insurgents entitled the 'Tenth of October', and circulated it amongst his fellow secondary-school students.

Early in 1869 the Spanish authorities replaced the repressive Captain-General Lersundi by his predecessor, the liberal and relatively popular General Dulce, who lifted the ban on meetings and withdrew the press censorship. Martí's bosom friend Fermín Valdés Domínguez took the opportunity to publish a satirical newspaper, *El Diablo Cojuelo* (The Lame Devil), of which only one number appeared. However, this number was sufficiently forceful. It asserted that in Cuba one had to take sides: either Yara (where Céspedes had declared independence) or Madrid. The idea was in fact Martí's, and he himself brought out a newspaper (also restricted to one issue), called *La Patria Libre*. Martí's main contribution was a long dramatic poem entitled *Abdala*, 'expressly written for the fatherland' and in which a country called 'Nubia' (Cuba) was struggling for liberation.

Later on Mendive, whose views were well known and whose house was used as a meeting-place for supporters of independence, was arrested, to be subsequently deported to Spain. Whilst in prison in Cuba he received visits from his wife, accompanied by his young disciple José, who thus furnished the authorities with further indications of his subversive tendencies, in case they were not already aware of these. Don Mariano accompanied verbal disapproval of his son's views with thrashings that so humiliated José as to make him contemplate suicide. But much worse lay in store for him.

On 4 October 1869 a group of Spanish Volunteers forced their way into the affluent home of Fermín Valdés Domínguez, provoked by laughter coming from it which they took to be directed at themselves. In the house they found a letter, signed by the two friends and addressed to a former schoolmate, also a Cuban, accusing him of 'apostasy'. On investigation this turned out to refer to his enrolment in the Volunteers, and José and Fermín were arrested and courtmartialled. Each declared himself the sole author of the letter, but José insisted so vehemently on his responsibility that he was sentenced to six years' hard labour (at the age of sixteen!), whilst Fermín received only six months' imprisonment.

Martí began his sentence on 5 April 1870, but served only six months of it, since in October of the same year he was pardoned, sent to the Isle of Pines (off the south coast of Cuba) to recover, and eventually, in January 1871, deported to Spain. The six months' hard labour he had served marked him for life, both physically and psychologically. Most of this time was spent in the quarries of San Lázaro, only a mile or so from his family's house in Havana, although he also worked in a prison cigar workshop. In the quarries he had to hack out blocks of stone and cart them to the top, wearing a chain that led from waist to ankle and left him with a groin lesion from which, despite several operations, he never recovered. The prisoners were regularly maltreated both verbally and physically, whippings and beatings occurring frequently. The suffering that Martí shared with his fellow jailbirds, coupled to the sadism of the warders, shocked him to the core.

All this he later described in a tract, *Political Imprisonment in Cuba*, published in Spain in the year of his arrival there. The pamphlet was an attempt to move the Spanish public to do something about its government's brutalities in Cuba and even the issue of Cuban independence itself. The inferno of the San Lázaro quarries is well depicted, mainly by focussing on the horrifying cases of certain individual prisoners: the suppurating wound into which beatings had turned the back of a seventy-six-year-old man; the smallpox contracted by a boy of twelve serving ten years' hard labour; the death from cholera of a Chinese; the induced insanity of a black convict; the attempted suicide of someone else, etc.

The political point was made that in Spain even those who dreamed of a 'universal federation, of free atoms within a free molecule, and respect for other people's independence as the basis for one's own strength and independence'[1] did not countenance any change for Cuba, and indeed supported the war against the insurgents. Martí was not exaggerating: the brief Spanish Federalist Republic of 1873, which professed to espouse precisely the libertarian notions quoted above, was to change nothing.

Whilst studying (mainly law) at the Central University of Madrid, Martí threw himself into open polemics on the Cuban question, using the Spanish press as one debating medium. In November 1872 he circulated a document protesting at the execution of eight medical students in Havana the previous year for supposedly having desecrated the grave of a reactionary Spanish journalist. Fermín Valdés Domínguez himself had received a prison sentence at the same trial, and on release joined his friend in exile.

After the proclamation of the First Spanish Republic by the Cortes on 11 February 1873, following the abdication of King Amadeo of Savoy, brought in by Prim to replace Isabel II, one of the Spanish deputies to the new parliament, a man later to become Leader of the House, reaffirmed the status of Cuba as inseparable from Spain. Martí responded with *The Spanish Republic and the Cuban Revolution*, which he sent five days later to Prime Minister Figueras. He argued that it was a great anomaly for a freely elected body of deputies that had just proclaimed a republic based on democracy to fail to grant Cuban freedom, which was desired by the majority of Cubans. A republic could not countenance colonialism, and Cuba was obviously not part of Spain itself, the two countries being separated by the Atlantic Ocean. Martí went on to define his concept of the *patria*, or fatherland, the nexus of his political thinking:

> Fatherland is something more than oppression, something more than pieces of land without freedom or life, something more than the right to possession by force. Fatherland means a community of interests, unity of traditions, unity of goals, the sweetest and most consoling fusion of loves and hopes (. . .). Cubans do not live as Spaniards live (. . .). They are nourished by a different system of trade, have links with different countries, and express their happiness through quite contrary customs. There are no common aspirations or identical goals linking the two peoples, or beloved memories to unite them (. . .). Peoples are only united by ties of fraternity and love.[2]

The Spanish Prime Minister indicated vague approval of the general principles expressed in Martí's letter, and proceeded to shelve the issue. Martí had copies printed and circulated in Madrid, and took part in many debates with his opponents. With touching naivety he even stated, in an article called 'The Cuban Question' (26 May 1873), that it was Cuba's very prosperity, in contrast to the decadence, economic backwardness, demoralization and administrative corruption of a thoroughly divided Spain, that gave Cuba a title to independence. Reforms had been tried, and had failed: the proof was that Cuba found itself at war. The only solution was independence. These arguments remained the basis of Martí's case against Spain right up to his death.

Later on, in Zaragoza, to whose university Martí and Valdés Domínguez had transferred, the two friends saw the fall of the weak First Republic, swept away by a military coup. This provided Martí with another early piece of evidence for his dislike of military methods. The question was to haunt him all his life.

The Restless Years. Martí in Spanish America, the *Guerra Chiquita* and First Experiences of the United States

Having left Spain for Mexico, where he resided in the period 1875–76 (see the next chapter), Martí did what he could for the Cuban cause. For example, in the press he excused the tactic employed by the *mambises* of burning canefields as a legitimate economic weapon. More reluctantly, he condoned the shooting of Spanish prisoners, because this was done in reprisal for similar and worse actions taken by the occupying army. He underlined his total opposition to slavery, and noted with bitterness the Spanish Republic's past refusal to abolish the infamous institution. He commented with hope on the invitation sent to pro-insurgent Cubans by the United States' authorities for the official celebrations marking the centenary of that country's independence.

After Porfirio Díaz's November 1876 military coup, Martí left Mexico, a nation he had come to love second only to Cuba. In January of the following year he arrived in his homeland, the bearer of a Mexican passport made out in the semi-bogus name of Julián Pérez (Julián being his second Christian name and Pérez his mother's maiden name). In 1877 the war was still going on, with enormous losses to both sides in lives and property. The Cuban insurgents were additionally weakened by the great acrimony that had arisen between the military and civilian leaders of the Republic in Arms. With the arrival of the Spanish General Martínez Campos, sent to conclude peace, it was clear that, given the degree of demoralization of the insurgent forces, the war would soon be over. Martí stayed in Cuba for not quite two months, after which he made his way to Guatemala, where he stayed for a year and a half until his departure in mid-1878 (see the next chapter).

We find him back in Cuba in September of that year, peace having been made and formalized by the Pact of Zanjón (19 February 1878). The two main *mambí* leaders, Céspedes and Ignacio Agramonte, were dead. However, not all the rebel commanders recognized the Treaty. An amnesty was in force, and the slaves already freed by the Republic in Arms were to retain their liberty. There was, nonetheless, no question of granting Cuban independence. Cuba was too potentially lucrative for that. In the meantime, the hostilities had meant the loss of some 200,000 lives and huge economic damage. Both sides were well-nigh exhausted. Cuba was promised the same rights as those obtained by Puerto Rico in 1870, i.e. representation in Spain and assimilation as an equal part of Spanish territory, with the limited democratic rights that this supposed. However, on enquiry it was found that Puerto Rico had had those rights annulled in 1874, after the restoration of the Spanish monarchy. The Restoration Constitution held no proviso for major changes in Cuba.

Antonio Maceo, one of the two foremost rebel generals of the Ten Years' War – the other being Máximo Gómez, who hailed from Santo Domingo – saw the Zanjón Treaty as all but worthless for Cuba, and took up arms again, only for his revolt to peter out after a short time. Both Maceo and Gómez, along with other prominent insurgent leaders, went into exile.

Notwithstanding this fact, Martí, in the year he spent in Cuba following his return from Guatemala, publicly voiced his pro-independence views and conspired rather less openly. It was at this time that he met the young mulatto lawyer Juan Gualberto Gómez, who was later (during the preparations for the 1895 war) to be Martí's main agent inside the island. Meanwhile, only two months after the February Treaty, a revolutionary committee headed by General Calixto García had been set up in New York. It was a measure of Martí's standing that just two years later he was to be appointed its interim president, whilst Calixto García embarked for Cuba to take part in the *Guerra Chiquita*, or Little War, in 1880. Martí had already been proposed as a possible deputy to the Madrid Cortes –

Cuban representation having been made possible by a royal decree in 1878 – but he had declared that he would only take his seat in the Cortes in order to plead the cause of Cuban independence.

Eventually, his abrasive and open opposition to Spanish rule, along with his conspiratorial activities, led to another deportation. Martí arrived in Spain on 11 October 1879, but this time left fairly quickly for France. Finally he made his way to New York, setting foot on North American soil on 3 January 1880, and soon joining Calixto García's revolutionary committee.

His first public utterances on the Cuban issue in the United States were delivered in a speech to Cuban immigrants in Steck Hall, New York, the following 24 January. He told his audience that the war against Spain had to continue, and reminded it of the sufferings, heroism and creativity of the rebels during the Ten Years' War. He attacked those Cubans who wanted peace with Spain. The war had proved that Cuba was a real nation, and had therefore a right to independence. The Spaniards had reneged on their promises made in the peace treaty, manipulated the elections provided for by the agreement and falsified their results. Excessive taxation was continuing, the countryside was in ruins and crawling with Spanish agents. Where was the prosperity promised by Spain? Why were the incomes of emigré Cubans still being seized by the authorities, contrary to assurances given. Slavery had not ended over the whole of Cuba. (Later on that year, the Spanish parliament did agree to abolish slavery completely, by phasing it out under an interim system whereby ex-slaves would still be required to work for their former masters for a few years, but as wage-labourers. This system was known as the *patronato*, and came to an end in 1886, leaving Brazil as the only slave state in the Americas.)

Martí was also concerned to combat Spanish propaganda that alleged that Antonio Maceo and other mulatto and black rebels of the *Guerra Chiquita* had the secret intention of setting up an independent black republic in Oriente. Martí gave the lie to this rumour, and affirmed that the war aimed at uniting Cubans of all colours and social classes against the colonialists. He also pointed out that the Cuban deputies to the Spanish parliament has just been informed that there was no question of further concessions to Cuba. Home Rule, for example, was deemed not to be a topic for negotiation.

Martí was the author of Calixto García's war proclamations of May 1880. In these he made it quite clear that García had not gone to Cuba to set up a military dictatorship, but rather to lay the foundations for a future democratic republic. The war was one of liberation, and stood above the interests of particular classes, groups, colours or regions. Martí never in his life swerved from these basic aims, although to uphold them, as we shall see, he had many struggles with his Cuban compatriots.

The *Guerra Chiquita*, as it turned out, could not sustain itself for long, mainly due to the lack of coordination between its military leaders, and in October of that year 1880 we find Martí writing to the last of the insurgent chiefs in the field, Emilio Núñez, to lay down arms. Significantly, in this letter Martí voiced his disappointment at the lack of agreement between the military men, and voiced his fear that a continuation of the campaign would only lead to the emergence of a new military supremo engaging in a 'selfish and personal war' which moreover was unwinnable. The prolongation of the campaign would be 'probably stained by impure desires, and hampered by jealousies, unworthy, when all is said and done, of those who think and act in an upright way'.[3] This would occur if, as was the case, popular support was not forthcoming.

Having called off the war, Martí believed that for the time being nothing more could be done in that direction, and he left New York, which he did not like, for Venezuela. Armed with a letter of introduction from his landlady (and probable lover) Carmen Mantilla, whose cousin had connections with the Venezuelan President Antonio Guzmán Blanco, Martí's first act on disembarking at the Caracas port of La Guaira was to hurry to pay homage to the statue of the Liberator Simón Bolívar, even before finding himself lodgings. It was in a speech to the Caracas Chamber of Commerce that he later announced his intention of writing the last stanza of the glorious poem of 1810, that is, putting the last touches to the independence of Spanish America by freeing Cuba and Puerto Rico. Nevertheless, as related in the following chapter, Martí's democratic consciousness fell foul of Guzmán Blanco's very autocratic methods, and August 1881 found him back in New York, where he was to live permanently until 1895 and the start of the final anti-Spanish war.

Early Skirmishes in the United States.
The Break with Gómez and Maceo

In New York Martí renewed plans for the overthrow of Spanish rule, meeting with such Cuban patriots as Flor Crombet and Enrique Trujillo. On 20 July 1882 he sent two letters, one to Máximo Gómez and the other to Antonio Maceo, introducing himself and setting out his ideological position on Cuba. The letters are remarkable for the fact that they showed Martí to be politically far in advance, as early as 1882 and at the tender age of 29, of any other Cuban leader. He had already laid down in his own mind the main planks in the political platform for the war of 1895.

Writing to Gómez, he stated that he had deliberately avoided the temptation to 'renew those pernicious cliques of previous wars, or those spontaneous acts of assuming command which do so much to encourage rivalries and rancour'.[4] He did not think the time ripe for another war. Rather, what was needed was unity, and patience. He also warned Gómez against those Cubans who desired annexation to the United States. This constituted, he said, the greatest threat of all to independence:

11

In Cuba there has always been an important group of cautious men, proud enough to abominate Spanish domination yet timid enough not to put their personal well-being in danger by fighting against it. These kinds of men, helped by those who would like to enjoy the fruits of liberty without paying for them at their bloody price, are vehemently in favour of the annexation of Cuba to the United States. All the timid people, all the ones lacking in decisiveness, all the superficial observers, all those attached to wealth, have marked inclinations to support this solution, which they believe to be cheap and easy. Thus they flatter their patriotic consciences, as well as their fears of being true patriots.[5]

Further light on Martí's attitude to annexationism is shed by his 1881 notebook, where he commented that whereas the annexationist current had been born 'in order to speed up the enjoyment of freedom' – he meant the campaigns waged in the late 1840s and early 1850s by such as Narciso López (whose flag in fact became that of the later Cuban Republic) – in 1881 it signified only 'the desire to avoid revolution'.[6]

In the same letter to Gómez we have quoted above, Martí proposed the formation of a *revolutionary party*, without which, he believed, once all hopes in a Spanish solution had been exhausted, Cuba would turn to the Home Rulers. Although there is some doubt here about what Martí meant by revolutionary party, it does seem possible that he had in mind the kind of party he was to found in 1892. In fact, until this party (the Cuban Revolutionary Party), with its extremely democratic structure and multi-class composition, came into being, no serious anti-Spanish campaign got off the ground. Martí knew already that this kind of organism was necessary to weld together the various pro-Independence groups and win support amongst the Cuban population in general, whether resident in the United States, Cuba itself or neighbouring countries. The party had to have the broadest possible base and a political and social (not merely military) programme. Otherwise the new Cuba would sink into the old Spanish American bog of military dictatorship in the wake of a successful anti-colonial war.

The Home Rule Party (*Partido Autonomista*) was merely the old Liberal party which had tacked Home Rule onto its aims and adopted the idea as its title. It was made up mainly of professional people who had stayed out of the Ten Years' War and who desired a peaceful transition to economic and political autonomy, stopping short of outright independence. In its midst there were a few tired war veterans, plus some others who were still committed to independence, yet could not publicly agitate for this.

Martí's radicalism showed itself better in the letter to Maceo than in the one Gómez received. To the former he wrote:

I have no time to tell you, General, how in my eyes the Cuban problem needs, rather than a political solution, a social solution, and how the latter cannot be achieved except through mutual love and forgiveness between the two races, and that always dignified and generous prudence by which I know your noble heart is moved. For me, the person who whips up hatred in Cuba, or takes advantage of those hatreds already present, is a criminal. And the person who tries to put down the lawful aspirations to livelihood of a good and prudent race which has already seen enough misfortune, is another.[7]

Martí was seeking, he said,

the way to create, by means of a quick and winnable war, a country where, despite its having had great experience of hatred, all its diverse elements will begin, from its founding, to enjoy real rights, amongst real conditions for attaining a long and peaceful life.[8]

Although in these quotations Martí was primarily focussing on the race problem in Cuba – it will be remembered that Maceo was suspected by some of aiming for an independent, non-white republic in eastern Cuba – it is also quite clear that he had in mind the avoidance of *any* kind of strife amongst his compatriots in the free fatherland. His position on race was extremely radical for the 1880s, whilst the implication that it was possible to achieve a harmonious post-Spanish Cuba in those times bordered on the utopian.

The break with Gómez and Maceo which occurred a couple of years subsequently, in 1884, and which was never completely patched up, shows how Martí always tended to understate the differences between even those Cubans sincerely striving for independence. A harmonizer himself, he felt wounded when others were not so selfless. The quarrel of 1884 occurred because of Gómez's high-handed conception of his own pre-eminence in the independence struggle. Gómez and Maceo had come to the United States from Honduras, where they had settled, in order to coordinate plans for another invasion of Cuba. It had been agreed that a governing junta was to be set up which would allow the military ample powers in the conduct of the war. Martí himself agreed to this (despite his bitter experiences of military despotism in Cuba, Spain, Mexico, Guatemala and Venezuela), but an incident which happened in mid-October that year between himself and Gómez so humiliated and disgusted him that he withdrew from the enterprise and, for a time, into the political wilderness.

It had been decided that Martí and Maceo should go to Mexico to drum up support for the Cuban cause. Martí was waxing enthusiastic about the trip to a country which he loved second only to Cuba and outlining his ideas for it when Gómez curtly interrupted him with the peremptory order that he limit himself to following instructions, and that Maceo would be the man in charge. Martí, who was extremely sensitive to personal slights – the frequency with which the words 'honour' and 'dignity' appear in his writings and speeches is an indication of his rather knightly conception of personal relations – sent a letter two days later (20 October) informing Gómez that he was resigning from the enterprise on the grounds that Gómez was conducting himself as if preparing to set up a military dictatorship. Martí told Gómez that he would never be party to a tyranny of that kind, and launched a ferocious verbal attack on the old hero:

A people is not founded, General, in the same way as one commands a military camp; and when in the preparatory tasks for a revolution which is more delicate and complex than any other, the sincere desire is not shown to become acquainted with and conciliate all the labours, desires and elements which will make the armed struggle possible – this desire being the mere form of the spirit of independence – but rather the intention is stated and brusquely expressed at each step, or barely concealed, to put all the resources of faith and war that the spirit gathers together at the service of the calculating and personal objectives of the justly famous leaders who come forward to conduct the war, what guarantees can there be of public liberties, which are the only goal for which a country should be launched into struggle, being respected on the morrow? What are we, General? The heroic and modest servants of an idea which warms our hearts, the faithful friends of a people fallen on bad times, or the brave and fortunate military leaders who, whip in hand and spurs on their feet are preparing to lead a people into war, only to lord it over this people in the aftermath? (. . .) The man that uses a great idea to serve his personal aspirations to glory or power, although he may be putting his life at risk for them, is to be abominated. To sacrifice one's life is only a right when it is sacrificed disinterestedly.[9]

Martí was shocked, he continued, at the idea that Gómez considered the Cuban war as his own personal property. *This* was not patriotism.

In a letter to Enrique Trujillo, the editor of *El Avisador Cubano*, dated 6 July the following year, Martí made his position even more explicit, declaring that

those who do not make war in order to wreak desolation, but rather to act as founders; not to set alight, but rather to bring redemption; not to exclude, but rather to include; not to strike terror, but rather to join together, these are the only people who deserve to aspire to triumph in a people weary of hatred.[10]

This was a dilemma which pursued Martí all his life: the contradiction between his basic ideology of conciliation, respect, dignity, balance, etc., (in short, a quasi-Christian set of tenets founded on love), and the need to go to war to achieve Cuban freedom. In addition, he believed that with the establishment of the *patria* (and good government), Cubans of all social classes and colours could live in harmony. War was necessary, unfortunately, because the Spanish could never be ejected in any other way. But once this brief and 'generous' war was over, the free fatherland would be a scenario for what Marxists would term essentially 'non-antagonistic' disputes, resolvable through the conciliatory measures of enlightened statesmen thrown up in the democratic process, the *pater-familias*, so to speak, of a nation tempered in struggle and respectful of the 'dignity' (a favourite Martían word) of each and every Cuban. The concept of fatherland, founded on these principles, is paramount to the political thinking of Martí: it is its very core. Let us quote a few more words from his letter to Trujillo:

> I cannot say or do anything which is not for the benefit of my fatherland. That is my whole reason for living. If I think, it is to defend it. If I put up with an offence in apparent silence, it is because I am serving it in this way. I will do anything, anything noble will I do on this earth, to create in my father-land a people of men, to save my compatriots from the danger of not being men. And I would not want for them fanatical wars or nominal freedoms. I would not wish them to rest on rancour. (. . .) If we go where our people wishes to go, we shall win; if not, not. (. . .) We must fight, if we are brought to this, so that when we unbuckle our weapons, a people emerges. If not, we do not deserve the honour of bearing arms for our fatherland's sake, nor do we have the right to stir it up.[11]

The forced break with Gómez and Maceo was all the more painful for Martí in that he genuinely admired them as heroes whose military prowess he could not emulate. Martí's enemies were quick to attack him on this point, and did so throughout his life. It is probable that his death on the battlefield in Cuba came as an indirect consequence of these attempts to insinuate that Martí was a mere intellectual with oratorical gifts who did not bear comparison with the military veterans of the past. Martí was determined to face enemy fire, and rode recklessly forward, contrary to Gómez's orders in a skirmish with Spanish troops, who killed him.

This occurred some ten years after the first recorded insult of this type. In autumn 1885 Antonio Zambrana, using Martí's refusal to back the plans of Gómez and Maceo, suggested that persons like him should be wearing skirts and petticoats. Although Martí's name was not actually mentioned, the allusion was clear, and into the bargain was made in public in front of veterans such as Maceo and Crombet, who had to pull Martí away from his adversary. Martí had already publicly vindicated his position that summer, at the Clarendon Hall, New York, but evidently was still regarded in some circles with suspicion, and until he became once more part of an organization to liberate his country spent some bitter years. Nevertheless he never attacked the Gómez-Maceo expedition in public forum, and let it be known that he had withdrawn from it purely over questions of detail. In private he was willing to be more frank, as a letter to J.A. Lucena, who had invited him to the Philadelphia 10 October commemoration for 1885, demonstrates. He stated here that a people being led into war needed to know exactly what objectives were being pursued, and in addition, had themselves to be the masters of a liberated fatherland. Martí always stuck by these principles, and he was proven right, since the expedition never got off the ground, hampered by lack of funds, a sure sign of lack of public support. Martí himself had been chairman of its finance committee, and his eloquence was sorely missed.

During his time in the political wilderness Martí busied himself with sending chronicles of North American life to *La Nación*, the great Buenos Aires newspaper, and other organs of the press in Spanish America. He also tried his hand at novel-writing, none too successfully, as the book entitled *Amistad funesta* (Fateful Friendship), or alternatively, *Lucía Jerez*, bears witness.

In May 1886 Martí felt it necessary to clear up another misunderstanding about himself, refuting in a letter to Ricardo Rodríguez Otero, a resident of Sagua la Grande (Cuba), the latter's misconception that Martí was willing to accept a Spanish solution for Cuba as long as this was the wish of the majority of Cubans. Martí denied this, and went on to clarify his position. He compared Cuba under Spanish colonialism to a steam engine with an insufficient number of valves to prevent it from exploding. Let the Spaniards continue with their reforms: it was beneficial to receive these without having to fight for them. But war was inevitable, albeit abominable. A premature war, however, would do immense harm to the Cuban cause, and for the moment Spain was still capable of holding on to her colony.

This was so because Spain was able to divide Cubans in several ways: by encouraging fears about the blacks (although the blacks, wrote Martí, because they had fought and suffered alongside patriot whites in the wars, were in fact the latter's natural allies); by provoking premature uprisings so as to have an excuse for further curtailment of liberties; and by encouraging corruption and vice to the extent that it was no longer possible to think of 'the cities that should be our pride without shame hiding our features'.[12] The parallels between this last point and the situation in Cuba prior to the 1959 Revolution are evident. One of the main drives of the 26 July Movement headed by Fidel Castro was against precisely those evils. Fidel Castro himself had belonged to the *Ortodoxo* Party, whose leader Eduardo Chibás committed suicide over the radio in protest against corruption under Batista.

Spaniards as individuals, continued Martí, were nonetheless not to be harmed or hated because of their nationality. Many had strong roots in Cuba and even (like Martí's own parents) brought Cuban patriots into the world. It was the Spanish state that had to be fought and eliminated in Cuba.

Martí's greatest worry was the possibility of Cuba's being annexed by the United States. To this, he informed Rodríguez Otero, he was totally opposed. 'Only he who is ignorant of our country, or of this one [the US], or of the laws by which peoples are formed and brought together, may honestly think of such a solution; or he who loves the United States more than Cuba'. Anyone who has lived in the United States and knows it well, its 'lawful glories' as well as its 'subordination of politics to questions of money', its 'real tendencies', is aware that 'never, except as an idea hidden away in the depths of some generous souls, was Cuba anything more to the United States than a desirable possession, whose only inconvenience is its population, which it considers to be unruly, lazy and worthy of scorn'. Martí then cited opinions expressed on this subject by prominent United States citizens, starting with the 'odious letter of instruction' written by Henry Clay in 1828, in which the United States expressed its satisfaction that Cuba had remained, after the Spanish American Wars of Independence, in Spanish hands. The North Americans thought of themselves as the Romans of the continent, and any sympathy for Cuba was really only the outcome of the vagaries of United States party politics. Some people wanted to buy Cuba, some wanted to go to war over it, so as to block a bill to lower taxes. Perhaps, added Martí, the fate of Cuba was to be left to bleed to death until such time as the United States could grab it with its 'selfish and disrespectful hands'. Finally, Martí warned Rodríguez Otero to be wary of the ambitions of those people who saw Cuba as a stepping-stone for their own ambitions: 'The fatherland is an altar, and not a pedestal. One serves it, but one does not take it to put at one's own service'.[13]

Later on in that same year 1886, as related in the next chapter, Martí began his series of articles on the Cutting affair, involving a chauvinistic North American journalist who had been jailed in Mexico for insulting that nation. This had provoked a furious public anti-Mexican backlash, especially in the regions of the United States' southern frontier. The episode had the effect of reinforcing Martí's belief in the impossibility of reconciling the interests of the two halves of the American continent. Martí's anger at North American jingoism and overt contempt for the nations to the south was to grow until reaching the proportions indicated in the famous letter he wrote to Manuel Mercado on the eve of his death. His one aim in life, as he told Mercado (18 May 1895), had always been to free Cuba and in so doing stop the United States from falling on the nations of Latin America. By 1895 he had become so disgusted with the United States as to ignore certain favourable impressions he had received of that country prior to 1886–87, which are the watershed years for his general view of the 'colossus of the north'.

Martí Ends His Isolation.
Laying the Ground for the Revolutionary Party

By the time Martí broke his public silence on Cuba (when he presided over the 10 October commemoration held for 1887 in New York's Masonic Temple), he had behind him the shocks of the Cutting affair, the Charles Dudley Warner articles on Mexico (further proof of North American scorn for Latin America – see the next chapter), and the Chicago Haymarket trials and executions. The latter events, detailed in a special chapter of their own at the end of this book, and involving bloody confrontations between workers and police leading to the framing of several anarchists who were hanged with no genuine proof of guilt, destroyed Martí's last shreds of faith in the United States. No longer could he remain on the sidelines of Cuban politics, and when requested by a group of Cuban artisans to preside over the yearly October commemoration, he agreed to do so. It was from this time onwards, notably, that Martí began to pay more attention to the specific problems and possibilities of the working classes. He suggested, in a letter to José Dolores Poyo in Key West (November 1887), that his intention was to win Cuban freedom 'to benefit the lowly, who are the ones that have most known how to defend it'.[14] There is no doubt that the Chicago Martyrs' case was, at least in part, responsible for this ideological shift.

As far as Cuba went, however, Martí still counselled prudence. This was the tenor of his Masonic Temple speech, and ten days afterwards he was writing to Juan Ruz, a veteran of the Ten Years' War who was proposing another invasion of Cuba, that Ruz should hold back, because the situation in Cuba was ripening of its own accord, due to increasing hunger and unemployment.

In conjunction with certain other Cubans resident in New York, Martí started to draw up plans for future action. A report was produced stressing the need for a democratic organization as the basic structure for the campaign. Only when this had been achieved were the military to be called upon to join in. This was a significant break with the past, when Cuban military leaders (improvised or not) had been the initiators of anti-Spanish wars and, rather like the *caudillos* of Spanish American independence movements of the first quarter-century (Bolívar, San Martín, O'Higgins, etc.) had ruled the roost over civilian elements, with harmful results for democracy in the new Republics. An important part of the report stressed the need for unity in the face of the aspirations to hegemony of any one particular group, whether military or civilian, or claiming leadership on behalf of a specific social class, race or region.

In December Martí wrote to Máximo Gómez, on behalf of pro-independence Cubans resident in New York, Philadelphia and Key West, requesting his support. Martí pulled no punches about the kind of organization he was asking the old hero to join and to which Gómez would have to subordinate himself:

> Cuba is no longer the infant, ignorant people that took to the countryside in the Yara Revolution [he informed Gómez]. We must (. . .) organize the approaching war according to the spirit of the country, because if we do not we cannot carry out the war. It is a crime to use the glorious aspirations of a people to promote one's own interests or satisfy personal hatreds. (. . .) The revolution is surging forth, and we can organize it with our honesty and

prudence, or strangle it with useless bloodshed by our clumsiness and personal ambitions.[15]

The military would have to declare willingness to subordinate themselves to the general interests of the fatherland in order to dispel the (doubtless unjust, Martí was careful enough to add) suspicion of them harboured by the nation. A political plan was needed to thwart 'the argument that the war will only be a battlefield for the hatreds and ambitions of rival leaders'. The military chieftains had to 'show by their union abroad and submission to the public good that, instead of being a scourge to the country, they are its hope'. Martí and his fellow signatories of the letter wanted to be able to say

> that you, like ourselves, believe that the war waged by a people for its independence (. . .) cannot be the private undertaking of someone who owes to the work of the whole country the part that heroism gave him in the common glory; (. . .) that you (. . .) understand that the war in Cuba must be organized and carried through (. . .) for the good and peace of Cuba, and not for the rise to power of those who, because they have won honour in her service, try to use this honour to exploit Cuba for themselves, or serve their own passions, or lead her astray; (. . .) that you (. . .) would not help the war with the impure aim of giving victory to a vengeful and arrogant party, but rather to give liberty to the entire Cuban people.[16]

Things could not have been put plainer, and in this Martí showed great courage, in view of his own relative lack of experience, his not having fought in the previous wars and the great difference in age between the two men (Gómez was his senior by seventeen years), coupled, of course, to the fact of the previous quarrel and break with Gómez in 1884. Martí, despite the harshness of his arguments, won Gómez round, which itself is evidence of the older man's patriotism, although there were signs that Gómez was perhaps not being entirely sincere in agreeing with Martí's plans. In his diary, for example, he expressed doubts about the project in the sense that the authors of the letter appeared to be trying to 'eliminate the military element'. In addition, an entry made just one month after Gómez's reply in the affirmative expressed joy at a decision to settle in Panama.

In the meantime, the pressure on Martí and his collaborators to push ahead with their plans increased, due to a growing threat from the United States, which needed new markets to place the glut of its industrial products, and thus alleviate its economic crisis and the attendant social turmoil (see the next chapters). Martí's letter of 19 February 1888 to Manuel Mercado, quoted more extensively in our chapter on Martí's ideas about Latin America, speaks of a general 'onslaught' on the nations of Latin America from public and private interests in the United States, which were often interlocked, as Martí well knew. The letter refers to the 'declaration, already almost official, that it [the US] is attempting to propose to Spain the purchase of Cuba'. 'I do not know,' added Martí in desperation, 'if that were to happen, how I should stay alive'.[17]

Very similar sentiments were being expressed one year later by Martí in a letter to his Uruguayan diplomat friend Enrique Estrázulas (15 February 1889):

> I am beside myself, because what I have been fearing for years and announcing is bearing down, and that is the United States' policy of conquest, for they are already declaring officially through Blaine and Harrison a desire to behave high-handedly towards all our countries, as if these were natural dependencies of this one, and to purchase Cuba. (. . .) If it were possible for me to die from a piece of bad news, I should have died from that one.[18]

In view of the alarming menace from the United States, Martí resolved to found an English-language newspaper in New York to defend the interests of Latin America and show that its inhabitants were 'good, hard-working and capable peoples', as he put it in a letter to Mercado of 21 March 1889. This project, nonetheless, never came to fruition.

The Philadelphia *Manufacturer* Article

Shortly before his last letter to Mercado, the Philadelphia *Manufacturer* had published an article in its 16 March issue asking whether the purchase of Cuba by the United States from Spain was desirable. Scandalized by the scornful characterization of the Cuban population in the article, Martí replied the following 21 March, sending his rejoinder to the New York *Evening Post*, which printed it on 25 March.

The *Manufacturer* had stated the arguments for the purchase of Cuba as follows: Cuba's strategic position in the Gulf of Mexico, very near Florida; its great productive capacity; the quality of its tobacco (the world's best); its sugar cane and tropical fruits; its potential as a market for US manufactures. The United States could reactivate Cuba and double its population. Its disadvantages were: its non-English-speaking population, whose character was undesirable, since if the Spaniards in Cuba were corrupt and unendurable, the Cubans were not much better and into the bargain effeminate and lazy, naturally incapacitated and lacking the experience necessary for becoming citizens of a free country; their attempts at rebellion had been farcical. Cuban blacks were barbaric, worse than Georgia negroes. Cuba thus was not suited to becoming an equal state of the Union, although it might perhaps become an associate territory or dependency (this was what actually occurred in the case of Puerto Rico, after United States' intervention against the Spaniards in 1898). Cuba's only hope, continued the *Manufacturer*, was an influx of North American settlers; however, even these might become degenerate there in time. The conclusion reached, therefore, was that the United States should not purchase Cuba.

Five days later, the New York *Evening Post* chimed in. Its 21 March number broadly backed the point of view set out in the *Manufacturer*, and added that the negro problem in the United States would be compounded by the annexation of Cuba, since then a million Cuban blacks would also be US citizens. According to the last Spanish census of Cuba, made in 1887, its total population was 1,600,000, of which under a third were classified as 'coloured' (i.e. black, mulatto, etc.), in other words roughly half a million. Comparison of these two sets of figures throws a sharp light on the attitudes to race of the ruling circles in the United States, whose phobias about racial purity were commonly shared by the general populace. All believed that the slightest negro admixture was enough to define an individual as 'black'. The *Evening Post*, therefore, concurred with the *Manufacturer*'s conclusions: annexation would do more harm than good.

Little wonder that Martí was outraged. In his reply, he castigated the gross ignorance and boastful expansionism of the United States. It was preposterous to deny the capability of Cubans, insult their virtue or scorn their general character. There were, he conceded, Cubans who desired annexation, but the worthiest Cubans did not want it, because Cuba had no need of it. Martí turned his letter into a seething indictment of the United States itself, a nation, he said, which Cubans admired as the greatest ever built by 'liberty', but whose blood contained elements of destruction. These elements were, principally, 'excessive individualism, (. . .) reverence for wealth, and the protracted exultation of a terrible victory', plus an immoderate appetite for power. The victory alluded to was that of the North over the South in the American Civil War, which allowed a great expansion of ruthless capitalist enterprise into a world which, for all its faults (the principle and unforgivable one being the institution of slavery), nevertheless seemed to Martí to preserve some of the courtly values he admired. Martí (ever a dualist in his thinking) affirms that there are two United States: one good, the other (which predominated) evil. Cubans, he declared, loved the fatherland of Lincoln as much as they feared that of Cutting. They themselves were by no means the wretched vagabonds or 'immoral pigmies' described in the *Manufacturer*. Nor should they be seen as an impractical and verbose nation which shunned hard work and was incapable of action, a characterization which North Americans tended to extend to all the peoples of Latin America.[19]

Cubans had suffered greatly under Spanish tyranny, and had fought bravely against it. They were not effeminate or politically inept. In fact, and Martí was at pains to stress the point, Cubans had the happy faculty of uniting good sense to passion, moderation to exuberance. The average Cuban knew as much about politics as the average North American. Cubans were not religious fanatics. They would defend their property acquired through hard work (and it was Cubans who had built up Key West and other thriving communities in the United States). In addition, they were well acquainted with the laws and practices of freedom. Thus they had proven themselves quite fit to rebuild Cuba into a prosperous and democratic nation after the ejection of the Spaniards. Martí declared indignantly that the Ten Years' War had been anything but the farce some North Americans made it out to be, and mentioned casualty figures of 200,000.

Martí's speech at the 1889 10 October commemoration emphasized the joint sacrifices of blacks and whites in that war. He also attacked the Home Rule Party for drawing off support for full independence, and cited the words he had heard in audience with a prominent Spanish politician who had been thought favourable to Home Rule. According to this man, it was true that Home Rule was merely a stop-gap, since Spaniards and Cubans could not live together. It was question, he told Martí, of either 'you or us'. However, Martí warned against a premature war and declared that what was needed was to prepare 'with everybody, for the good of everybody, the definitive and invincible war' in which there would be no scope for military or political adventurism, or a 'class revolution'.[20]

The Washington Interamerican Congress
In the meantime, an Interamerican Congress had been summoned in Washington, starting on 2 October of that year (see the next chapter). Martí viewed this as 'dangerous for our America, or at least of no use',[21] as he wrote to Gonzalo de Quesada, secretary to the Argentinian delegate Roque Sáenz Peña and later on to be Martí's own amanuensis. The only possible advantage to be wrung from this conference would be an assurance from the United States that it would back the idea of Cuban independence. Nevertheless, US Secretary of State Blaine, who had organized the Congress, wanted annexation, and there was even a rumour that he was negotiating with Martí over this. Martí denied this last allegation, and reiterated his constant position: full independence, nothing less. The interests of Cuba and the United States, he said, were diametrically opposed, and Cuba's future lay with its sister nations of Latin America. But if nothing were done to the contrary, Cuba would inevitably fall into the hands of the United States, and somehow that nation had to be persuaded of Cuba's right to independence before the final war versus Spain got under way. The trouble was that the United States, 'the nation which by geography, strategy, economics and politics, needs us',[22] would not countenance any Cuban independence contrary to its interests. If the United States did intervene, it would be with the main objective of preventing Cuba from falling into foreign hands.

And if the Spaniards withdrew from Cuba with economic compensation, who but the United States could guarantee payment? And with this foothold in the island, who could remove the United States? Cuba would become a kind of 'artificial nationality, created for strategic reasons'. Martí went on: 'I want a firmer base for my people. (. . .) A sacrifice made in time is preferable to final destruction'.[23] A bill had actually been presented to the United States Congress in which, were it to become law, the US President would be authorized to negotiate Cuban independence in return precisely for payment to Spain by Cuba.

Martí was quite correct in seeing the strategic importance of Cuba for the United States, and what he feared did in some way come to pass, i.e. through intervention in the anti-Spanish war the United States did secure a foothold, which it consolidated through the Platt Amendment, written forcibly into the Cuban Constitution of 1901 and giving the United States ample scope to intervene even militarily in Cuban affairs, plus military bases and coaling stations, along with the Isle of Pines. Although eventually (in 1934) the United States signed away all the concessions it won by the notorious Amendment, excepting the Guantánamo military base, which it still possesses, by 1934 its economic and political domination of Cuba had so increased as to render these losses almost meaningless. Martí was quite right to believe that it needed a successful revolution to prise Cuba away from the United States. This of course was not to happen until 1959, and the survival of that revolution was only achieved at a crippling economic price (after the United States removed Cuba from its economic orbit) and with the backing of another superpower (the Soviet Union).

Martí wrote to Serafín Bello, some two weeks after his letter to Gonzalo de Quesada, voicing similar anti-annexationist sentiments, and fears lest the majority of the Latin American delegates to the Washington Congress should support United States' attempts to seize Cuba. This would be a disaster for their nations as well, since Cuba was the key to the 'other' America, and with the acquisition of Cuba it was only a matter of time before the United States extended its dominion over the entire rest of the continent. Martí thus saw Cuba as a test case. Whereas Thomas Jefferson had suggested that the limits of US territory might embrace Cuba, Martí, on the other hand, viewed Cuba, if independent, as a stumbling block to US expansion southward. This has indeed proven true politically, in the sense that the present anti-capitalist revolutionary movements of Latin America do derive much of their psychological impetus from the 1959 Revolution of Fidel Castro, which has survived in the teeth of enormous hostility from the United States.

In the same letter to Bello, Martí outlined his ideas for the future internal workings of Cuba. Not only was a political revolution necessary, social reforms had to be made. 'Social matters are implicit in political matters in our country, as everywhere', he informed his correspondent. The rich would not be allowed to lord it over the poor in the new Cuba, for 'riches are generally accumulated by sacrificing one's honour and through abuses, although I well know that, with patience and hard work, an honest fortune can be made'. Notwithstanding this tolerance of 'honest' wealth, he added: 'My heart goes out to a worker as to a brother'.[24] Until his very death, as we shall see, Martí maintained precisely these views on socio-economic matters, regarding inequalities in this area as inevitable, although hinting at times that socialism might be possible at a future date. This is implicit in his characterization of Karl Marx and the Cuban Marxist leader Carlos Baliño as men who wanted to go 'too fast'. Thus whilst disliking the concept of class struggle and believing socialism to be, at least, premature, he is able to praise Marxists for their aims, if not their methods. In view of the complexities involved in unravelling Martí's views on these matters, it is worthwhile quoting extensively from his letter to Serafín Bello:

> It is necessary to pay attention to the social elements, and satisfy their just demands, if one desires to study the real problem of Cuba, and set it right in a realistic way. The coloured man has the right to be treated for his human qualities, without reference being made to his colour; and if there is to be any yardstick, it has to be that of excusing him his mistakes, of which we have been the cause, and to which we have incited him by our unjust disdain. The worker is not an inferior being, and he must not be fenced off and ruled by force, but rather the considerations and rights which ensure happiness in peoples must be opened up to him, as from brother to brother. The man in him would stop him overstepping his limits, and no others are necessary. Clean living is the real nobility, and filthy living the plebs. The man who cultivates his intelligence goes in one direction, and the one who does not cultivate it goes in another. My circle consists of honest men, and the crooks belong to another. I want to know who does not want to be counted amongst the noble! For that reason, natural proclivities must be the basis, and the conditions for happiness must be made sincerely available, and with thorough-going equality, to everyone. And I do not even imagine that one may think otherwise. But people do. And the well-being of men is set back, and, through stupidity and injustice, that of our fatherland.[25]

This letter, in part a response to a Cuban workers' strike in Key West, makes Martí's position, with all its innate idealism, quite clear. Whatever the defects of these views, they had the advantage of making Martí the most suitable leader for the Cuban national liberation struggle, at that particular time.

To underline his stance on the race question, Martí had sent an invitation for the 1888 10 October celebrations in New York to a prominent black Cuban, Rafael Serra, with whom he later founded *La Liga* (22 January 1890), an association aimed at helping and educating non-white Cubans and Puerto Ricans. Martí became its honorary president, and devoted much time to giving classes to its members.

As the Interamerican Congress drew to a close, Martí felt increasing alarm at the expansionist truculence of US politicians and businessmen. He decided to return to Washington in order to do some secret lobbying, and one month later, on 15 May 1890, he contacted Emilio Núñez to arrange a meeting in New York with the latter and other Cubans to make plans for action. The following August he revealed almost a sense of despair to Juan Bonilla, saying: 'Never were there worse elements for embarking on a war for independence, nor was there a greater need for war'.[26]

A major problem in this pressing situation seemed to be the lack of unity amongst the Cubans. Martí had made unity the key-note of a speech given two months previously (16 June) at Hardman Hall, New York, for a benefit organized by the only constituted Cuban revolutionary organization, the club *Los Independientes*. Unity, likewise, was the theme of his 10 October speech of that year. After stressing this, and the urgency with which Cubans had to prepare for a 'probable' war against Spain, Martí stated that in the course of organizing for the struggle, the foundations for the future society in Cuba had to be laid down. Moreover, certain mistakes had to be avoided, for example the attempt to 'apply to a people (. . .) institutions born of different antecedents and possessing a different nature, and already discredited because of their ineffectiveness where they had most promised salvation'. Martí advocated 'scientific politics', which for him meant 'leading the country with its real elements towards the possible'. This kind of political empiricism was to be the major plank in the platform of arguments around which his most influential political utterance (the article 'Our America', published on 30 January 1891 in *El Partido Liberal*, the Mexico City newspaper) was constructed. As indicated later on in this book, the manner of thinking was part and parcel of the neo-Kantian philosophy known as Krausism which lies at the root of Martí's ideology.

Another major theme of the 10 October speech, and originating in the same corpus of concepts, was the need to harmonize the diverse entities which constituted the Cuban nation (its 'real', as opposed to 'apparent' elements, to employ neo-Kantian ideology). The question was to 'gradually effect shifts, through cordiality and justice, in those elements which were at loggerheads with each other, and transform them, insofar as possible, into elements of amalgamation'.[27] At a national level, therefore, Martí subscribed to the politics of conciliation, in the manner of many nineteenth century liberals. The authoritarian tendencies which had emerged in previous wars had disfigured the enterprise of Cuban independence, affirmed Martí, and had to be checked. War was 'probable' because its causes could not be eliminated (i.e. Spanish exploitation) and were even on the increase. But this war had to be brief and final. At the same time Cuba must not be turned into 'a forum for inept legal hacks or a herd of jealous generals, or a heap of ashes'. Free Cubans were not going to become mere 'saddles for a military tyrant to parade himself from, after a triumphant war, over a tribe of submissive demagogues'. And lest anyone should feel himself offended by these remarks, Martí was quick to add that only those who 'do not know many of our military people, who [themselves] know that a man dishonours himself when he dishonours everybody else' could believe this to be on the cards. In any case, Cuban reality, 'the hidden and real fatherland', would prevent it.[28]

The time had passed when military *caudillos* (as in the aftermath of Spanish American independence) could make and unmake governments at will. Having said that, Martí tried to soften his implicit criticism of such as Gómez and Maceo by inveighing against the civilians who without purpose or character (. . .) because of their pusillanimity in action awaken the just scorn of those who are capable of action, and with their petty jealousies and tolerance of indulgence, luxury and flattery, made possible in the new republics the predominance of a daring and skilful military man'.[29]

He then launched into a high-flown peroration which must have concealed his own fears about being unjustly placed in the category he had just castigated:

The man of action only respects the man of action. The man who has faced death a thousand times does not respect, nor can he respect, the authority of those who fear death. The politician who reasons is defeated, in times of action, by the politician who acts; defeated and scorned, or used as a mere instrument and accomplice, unless, when the hour comes to mount [a horse], he does not gather up his reason and mount. Reason, if it desires to lead, must become part of the cavalry! And it must die, so that those who know how to die may respect it. It is not the blind admirers of military prestige who are the most fearsome enemies of the republic, but those who, when it is time to be soldiers, refuse to be soldiers.[30]

Reading this passage makes it easier to understand Martí's death on the battlefield of Dos Ríos, which deprived the Cuban cause, in a seemingly senseless way, of its most valuable organizer and ideologue, who might well have prevented Cuba's being turned into a corrupt fief of the United States. As far back as 1879, Martí's qualities had been denigrated by certain of his compatriots. The first well-known instance of this was perpetrated in that year by Ramón Roa, a veteran of the recently-concluded Ten Years' War who was sailing on the same ship that was taking Martí into his second Spanish exile, Roa himself had given up the struggle and, into the bargain, was trying to procure for himself a job in the Spanish colonial service. The two men had a violent argument, and Roa called Martí a 'useless Christ'. Later on, in 1891, Roa was to publish a book which, because of its pessimism, Martí deemed deleterious to the Cuban cause.

Martí's biting criticism of Roa's book *A pie y descalzo* (On Foot and Without Boots) was answered with considerable venom by Enrique Collazo, another veteran of '68, who heaped insult after insult on Martí, referring in scornful tones to his illnesses, accusing him of wanting, in 1879, a seat in the Madrid parliament, and alleging that Martí's law practice in Havana was for the purpose of enriching himself (when it was really a front for conspiratorial activities). Collazo portrayed Martí as a cowardly and self-serving fop. If we add to these slanders Zambrana's insinuations of 1885, the humiliating scene with Gómez one year before that, and the invective that Antonio Maceo directed at Martí in the notorious Mejorana interview (5 May 1895) during the final campaign in Cuba (Maceo saw in Martí the meddling non-combatant heir to the legalistic civilians of the Ten Years' War, argued for a military junta to be in charge and had also been upset by Martí's replacement of him as commander of the expedition which set sail from Central America), it seems no wonder that Martí insisted on placing himself in danger at the Dos Ríos battle.

Martí's later writings sometimes evidence a growing attraction for the repose that only death could bring, and in some quarters it has been suggested that his death had a suicidal element in it. After all, the aforementioned trials, coupled to the always precarious state of his health, his wife's desertion and his political disappointments in Mexico, Guatemala and Venezuela, might give force to this supposition. Martí's own use of Biblical imagery to describe himself (a Latin American David facing a Northern Goliath, Moses leading his people to the Promised Land, etc.) certainly helped others to manufacture the image of Martí the Apostle and Martyr. But there is no evidence that his death at Dos Ríos was a kind of blood sacrifice born of despair. For one thing, the cause of Cuba was *the* driving force behind all Martí's activities, and having come so far in the teeth of innumerable problems it was extremely unlikely that he would throw his life away. There is concrete proof, also, that he was planning to go to Camagüey to convoke, along with Gómez the military commander-in-chief, an Assembly of Delegates which would work out the structures of a future Republic in Arms. Neither must one exaggerate the importance of the hostility shown to him at various times by certain individual compatriots, for pro-Independence Cubans in general accorded Martí massive support from the time of the founding of the Cuban Revolutionary Party (in April 1892) onwards.

As for his problems with Gómez and Maceo, it seems that Martí and Gómez had no serious differences after they landed together in Cuba on the final expedition (11 April 1895). Gómez, faced with Martí's determination to be part of the military campaign, acceded after some doubts, and henceforth showed great cordiality towards the latter, who was even made Major-General of the liberating army. Martí, for his part, probably realized that he had done Gómez a disservice by suspecting him previously of dictatorial ambitions. The fact is that Gómez was primarily a military man who had little time for politicians or politics. A small farmer in civilian life, he apparently harboured no ideas of climbing to the top of the political tree. Martí's own *Campaign Diaries* quote Gómez as believing that the vast majority of Presidents in the Americas had become corrupted.

With respect to Maceo, it seems that even the very harsh words that the mulatto veteran directed at Martí in the acrimonious Mejorana meeting of 5 May had only a relative effect, since Maceo later apologized for his peremptory conduct. Thus one may conclude that when he rode to the front line in the battle at Dos Ríos, against Gómez's orders, it was not as a despairing gesture, as some writers have made out, but because Martí felt it his duty to face the enemy fire.

To return to the October 1890 commemoration speech after this lengthy but necessary digression, it stressed the need for unity, particularly between the civilian and military elements in the future campaign in Cuba. Martí pointed out that this struggle would enjoy a certain advantage over the previous Spanish American independence movements of the first quarter of the century insofar as, unlike the creole elites of those days, anti-Spanish Cubans had not acquired the habit of living as lords and masters on the back of the working population. The 'social problem' existed, but Martí denied that Cubans now imagined 'cruelly and ungratefully' that the only way to solve it was by making it 'more acute' (through the rich exploiting the poor). What was the use, he asked, of 'having Darwin on our tables if we still carry the plantation overseer in our habits?'[31]

The admiring reference to Darwin should not be misinterpreted. Martí was sufficiently a nineteenth century progressive to see Darwin as a bringer of enlightenment, but he did not share the latter's scientific materialism. He allowed himself to wonder why Darwin had not written, alongside his famous works, a history of the spirit! Again, one sees all too plainly the influence of Krausist dualism on Martí's thought. Writing of Darwin, back in 1882, he had castigated the latter for not seeing that 'life is twofold', for all monists (including Darwin) were wrong.[32] On the other hand, he never had any truck with that vulgar distortion of Darwin known as 'Social Darwinism', which Latin American elites were using (and still use), under the mask of positivistic 'progress', for choking democracy and the aspirations of the working class to a better life. The times were those of equality and democracy, asserted Martí, here in this speech as elsewhere. Quite apart from the moral evil of exploitation of the majority, a system based on privilege (like Spanish rule in Cuba) bred revolt, and not necessarily fruitful revolt. The downtrodden lower classes, who were the majority, 'have the strength born of ignorance and suffering, and if justice favours them can overturn the seigneurial carriage'.[33] This had already happened in Latin America, and had led to the dictatorship of pseudo-populist tyrants such as the Argentinian Juan Manuel de Rosas. Conciliation was also to be extended to the Spaniards in Cuba, who had strong blood ties to the creole population and even stronger ties to the land. There was no reason why Spaniards should not become good Cuban citizens.

As for the annexationist question, Martí had been delving into the history of the United States, and had found much to abhor in that nation's independence movement. How could a nation that

> on the day following its independence, tarred and feathered its defeated adversaries in the public square, created with its military men a secret order of nobility, marched with the army bearing weapons on the national Congress, disobeyed it and turned its members out of their seats, raised up one state against another, through petty jealousies and self-interest, became

so passionately involved in its disputes as to decide the assassination of the founding fathers of the Republic, and signed without compassion the charter of its freedom on the backs of its slaves,[34]

ever be suited to ruling a free, democratic Cuba? Moreover, Cuba did not need the help of the United States to beat the Spaniards. After all, Benito Juárez, with 'thirty madmen', had ejected the French from Mexico, having previously refused aid from the United States, which would have led to ignominious concessions. Now Mexico was free, and being courted for its intellectual genius and industrial assets by the powerful peoples of the planet. Martí made the point that Mexico, with its 'one million whites and seven million Indians', was, like Cuba, a racially hybrid nation, and that the great Juárez himself had been an Indian.[35]

Martí summed up his oration with the following words:

> Neither childish feats, nor vain promises, nor class hatreds, nor strivings for authority, nor blind opinion, nor village politics, must be expected from us, but rather the politics of cementing and embracing, in which the feared ignorant man rises to a level of justice through his culture, and the haughty cultured man respects, in repentance, the brotherhood of man.[36]

This speech has to be seen in the context of Antonio Maceo's rapturous reception in Cuba in the summer of that year, and the failure of the uprising planned by him for the following September. Maceo, Crombet and Amador Guerra found themselves deported when the Spaniards got wind of their plans. Martí obviously considered the whole undertaking premature and lacking a correct political basis. Maceo's failure, of course, only served to enhance Martí's own standing amongst patriotic Cubans.

By the end of 1890, Martí had been delegated as the representative of Uruguay at the International Monetary Conference in Washington. As is shown in the next chapter, he used this opportunity to frustrate US plans for tying the nations of Latin America economically to their northern neighbour. In October 1891 he relinquished his consular posts in New York (he had acted on behalf of Uruguay, Argentina and Paraguay) and gave up his columns in Spanish American newspapers, in order to devote himself entirely to the new campaign against Spain. He also found himself free from the urge to publish any purely literary works, having in the previous June brought out his *Versos sencillos*, whose preface itself contained a political diatribe against the United States.

Martí in Florida amongst Cuban Tobacco Workers

Invited by the *Ignacio Agramonte* club of pro-independence Cubans to take part in fund-raising celebrations, Martí arrived in Tampa, Florida on 25 November 1891. This was the first time he had been to Florida, where so many expatriate Cuban tobacco workers lived. The two speeches he delivered in Tampa (on 26 and 27 November) were greeted rapturously, and furthered his reputation to an enormous degree as the most significant leader of the Cuban cause. In December he was to visit the other large Florida centre of Cuban tobacco workers, Key West. From this time on, the two communities were to constitute important bases for the new Cuban campaign and the greatest sources of support for Martí himself as a revolutionary leader, although he had still to deal with some opposition.

Tampa and Key West were for Martí the proof, to be held up before scornful Yankees, that a future Cuban Republic would be founded on intelligent industriousness. From what he had seen in Tampa, he told the audience in his first speech there, he believed even more in 'the republic of open eyes, neither over-bold nor timid, neither dressed in a toga nor in a collarless shirt, neither overcultured nor uncultured'.[37] If he valued one thing among all others for the new Cuba, it was, he stated, 'the Cuban cult of the full dignity of man',[38] a phrase echoed countless times in the socialist Cuba of today, which still retains much of Martí's political vocabulary. What Martí envisaged at that time for Cuba was a multi-class democratic republic based on

> the whole character of each one of its sons, the habit of working with one's hands and thinking for oneself, the integral exercise of one's whole being and the respect, as if it were that of family honour, due to the exercise of the whole being of others, the passion, when all said and done, for man's decorum. (. . .) We are working to free Cubans, and not to shut them up in a pen. We are working to bring together in peace and equity the interests and rights of the loyal inhabitants of Cuba, and not to erect, at the mouth of the continent, the frightened overlordship of Veintimilla, or the bloody *hacienda* of Rosas, or the lugubrious Paraguay of Francia.[39]

These last were bywords, in Martí's time, for backward and ruthless dictatorships (in Ecuador, Argentina and Paraguay), although modern anti-imperialist historians are engaged in establishing more progressive credentials for Rosas and the Paraguayan Supremo. 'Dignity' and 'decorum' were key concepts for Martí, although to us they have an old-fashioned ring. One notes, also, the reference to the nation *qua* family. Not for nothing did this speech become remembered for its main theme: the building of a society 'with all and for the good of all', for Martí wanted, as he insisted here, to ensure 'the welfare and prosperity of all Cubans',[40] independently of class, occupation or race.

The whole edifice would be held together by pride in being Cuban amongst fellow-Cubans:

> One says Cuban, and a sweetness as if from gentle brotherhood spreads through our bodies, and our savings-boxes open by themselves, and we press together to make another place at the table, and our enamoured heart sprouts wings in order to give shelter to the one who was born in the same land as ourselves, even though sin lead him into confusion or ignorance send him astray, anger make him furious or crime bloody him.[41]

The new Cuba was here in Florida, facing the corrupt colonial territory some ninety miles away. This corruption would be cleaned up, but 'novelties of Yankee cut' would not be introduced in place of the 'colonial spirit'. Instead, Martí sought 'the essence and reality of a republican nation of our own' which would guarantee freedom of expression and the rule of law.[42] The attainment of these goals would not be easy or free of harshness. He promised no demagoguery feeding on the sufferings of the poor, but neither would the well-born be allowed to serve exclusively their own interests. All would have to work together.

Cubans would not look to England or France for political structures, because the Cuban spirit of freedom was already strong enough and sufficiently in tune with Cuban realities to need no model, asserted Martí. 'We are men, and we are not going to want governments resembling paper cutouts, but rather the labour peformed by our own hands, taken from the mould of our country'.[43] He then painted an almost idyllic picture of Cubans working together in harmony:

> Only a person who is very ignorant of our fatherland does not observe in it how, running parallel with this native impetus which raises it up for war and will not let it sleep in peace, has grown up with experience and study and a kind of clear knowledge which our beautiful land gives us, an accumulation of forces of order, humane and cultured – a phalanx of full intelligences, fertilized by the love of mankind, without which intelligence is only a scourge and a crime – such an intimate harmony, with its origins in common pain, between the Cubans of natural law, without history and without books, and the Cubans who have put into study the passion they could not put into the formation of the new fatherland – such a fervent brotherhood between the most humble slaves of life and the slaves of a devastating tyranny.[44]

And, as is usual in Martí's elucubrations on society, the idea of balance is stressed. Here we see again the influence of Krausist thinking, with its emphasis on the universe as harmony:

> It is just as necessary for peoples to be held in check as to be pushed forward: it is just as necessary in the house of one's family to have a father, always active, as to have a mother, always fearful. There is a male politics and a female politics. What use is a locomotive with a boiler to drive it, but without a brake to hold it back in time? It is necessary, in the affairs of peoples, to have one hand on the brake and the other on the boiler. And it is there that peoples come to grief: through too much brake, or too much boiler.[45]

Faith in the cause would not die, Martí went on, and neither would the Cuban military men overreach themselves and try for domination. It was at this juncture of his speech that he made his tempestuous attack on Ramón Roa's book, which described the daunting trials faced by the insurgents in the Ten Years' War, and which Martí thought ill-timed and too pessimistic. Martí asked rhetorically whether Cubans were going to be deterred by

> fear of the tribulations of war, a fear whipped up by impure people who are in the pay of the Spanish government, the fear of going barefoot, which is a very common way of going about in Cuba, because amongst the thieves and those who aid them, only accomplices and thieves have shoes in Cuba.[46]

This unwise and exaggerated outburst provoked, as noted, a vicious and slanderous attack on Martí from Enrique Collazo, and awoke bad feeling about him in other veterans. One of these was Fernando Figueredo, president of the Cuban Convention of Key West, who probably felt that Martí was also alluding to him, since he himself had found a job in the Spanish administration following the Great War. Other prominent Cuban fighters, like the black soldier Guillermo Moncada, whose patriotism could not be questioned, had done likewise. Martí had overstepped the mark, and Figueredo and his Key West comrades tried to block Martí's election as Delegate (i.e. Leader) of the Cuban Revolutionary Party, and only ceased their formal opposition to him in July 1892, three months after the formation of the Party.

Continuing his 26 November speech in Tampa, Martí assured his mainly working-class audience (where blacks and mulattoes were in a majority) that there would be no race problem in Cuba, because in the process of the struggle for liberty, in which blacks had played an equal part, the latter had learnt to forgive their white masters for having enslaved them. The Spaniards remaining in the future Republic would pose no problem, since the ones who had the closest ties to Spain would have left, and the rest would settle into the new state. Indeed, some Spaniards had benefited little from Cuba's colonial status. Some loved liberty, and had shown this by helping persecuted Cubans.

Rich and poor, ex-slavemasters and ex-slaves, had all been united in the Great War. The future war would not be the product of resentment, or the cavorting of an unemployed general, or yet the revolt of a mob whipped up by an ambitious or despotic individual. The fact was, declared Martí characteristically, that nobody could live happily without a *patria*. In the case of Cuba its banner would be inscribed with a 'formula of triumphant love': 'With all and for the good of all.'

On the following day, 27 November, in homage to the eight medical students shot in Havana in 1871, Martí pronounced a speech known thereafter as *Los pinos nuevos* (the new pines). Cuba's dead heroes were not forgotten, he stated, and indeed provided the life-force for her new heroes, just as in the vicinity of some dead pine-trees Martí had glimpsed on his way to Tampa, new pines were growing up. 'That is what we are: new pines!' he exulted.[47]

One day later, on 28 November 1891, the following resolutions were made in Tampa by the leading Cuban emigrés in conjunction with Martí. The unification of all honest revolutionaries 'in a free and republican common action' was to be brought about, to prepare a war leading to a popular, 'frank and selfless' republican government. No particular group or class was to be favoured in this enterprise, and the Republic would be set up, 'with the participation of all and for the good of all'. Lastly, the revolution would have as its organic basis freely constituted emigré associations.[48] Martí wanted the maximum participation of all pro-independence Cubans, and knew that this could only happen under the umbrella of a genuinely democratic movement which allowed no one sector to predominate. None of the old antagonisms between rich and poor, blacks and whites, emigrés and people living inside Cuba, veterans and new revolutionaries, civilian and military elements, would be permitted to hamper the movement. The Tampa resolutions constituted, in fact, the germ of the future Cuban Revolutionary Party.

The Cuban Revolutionary Party

A week later, Martí wrote from New York to José Dolores Poyo in Key West that now was the 'hour of the furnaces',[49] a phrase much remembered in Latin America. On 25 December he arrived in Key West, where the Tampa resolutions were amplified into a set of basic points for the formation of the Cuban Revolutionary Party. These were approved formally by the local Cuban revolutionaries on 5 January the following year (1892), and by 5 February twelve organizations (from Tampa, Key West and New York) had accepted them. Finally, on 8 and 10 April (the latter date being the anniversary of the Constitution of the Republic in Arms, ratified in 1869 in Guáimaro during the Great War), the first internal elections of the CRP were held. In these, thirty-four clubs took part (thirteen from Key West; seven from New York; five from Kingston, Jamaica; five from Tampa; and one each from Philadelphia, Boston, Ocala and New Orleans). Martí was elected to the Party's highest office, that of Delegate, the term President smacking too much of dictatorship, whilst Benjamín Guerra became its first treasurer.

 The 'Bases and Statutes' of the CRP may be resumed as follows: they aimed at 1) winning absolute independence for Cuba and aiding that of Puerto Rico; 2) ordering a 'generous and brief war' that would ensure peace and happiness for all Cuba's inhabitants; 3) organizing this war so that it should be 'republican in spirit and methods', and lead to a society fulfilling 'in the historical life of the continent, the difficult duties which its geographical situation gives it' (an obvious allusion to North American expansionism); 4) ensuring that in the new Cuba the 'authoritarian spirit and bureaucratic make-up of the colony would not be perpetuated' and with the objective, instead, of 'founding (. . .) a new people based on a sincere democracy, capable of overcoming, through real work and the balance of social forces, the dangers of sudden liberty in a society moulded for slavery'; 5) preventing any one particular group from lording it over the nation, since the free fatherland would be for all; 6) creating a harmonious fatherland with economic prosperity ensured by allowing outlets for the economic activities of all its inhabitants; 7) not provoking 'the peoples with whom prudence or affection counsels the maintenance of friendly relations' (i.e. some *modus vivendi* with the US had to be found); and, lastly, 8) bringing about the above intentions through a set of 'concrete aims'. These were: to unite all Cubans living abroad; to bring together all factions inside and outside Cuba; to prepare inside Cuba the knowledge and spirit of the revolution; to collect funds; to establish relations with friendly peoples so as to accelerate the success of the war and create the 'new Republic indispensable to the balance of America'; and finally, to organize the CRP according to the secret rules agreed upon by the founding organizations.[50]

The 'secret statutes' of the Party were to do with its internal workings, and may be summarized in turn. All associations of pro-independence Cubans who accepted the party programme and carried out their duties could belong to the CRP. These freely-constituted organizations would set up in each locality a council made up of their respective presidents. A Delegate and Treasurer for the Party would be elected annually by the associations, which had to agree to carry out the tasks set them. Members would be informed by their association's president of these duties. They would also have to collect funds for the war and pay regular contributions into an action fund. They had to unite for the cause all those people it was possible to unite, and prevent actions harmful to the revolution. The Delegate had to be kept informed, by the local councils of presidents, of all pertinent occurrences. These local party councils were the formal intermediary organisms between the associations and the Delegate, and had to coordinate the activities of the former and transmit their suggestions to the latter. They also had to oversee and authorize elections in each locality, report to the Delegate on the activities of the associations, and receive from the Delegate an account of his own actions.

For his part, the Delegate was obliged to: carry out the aims of the party programme; spread the organization abroad, but more specifically within Cuba itself; increase funds; inform the local party councils of news; administer thriftily the funds collected; submit to the Treasurer for approval all payments made from the action fund; work assiduously for the cause; render an annual account of the funds received and their use, at least one month before the annual elections. The Treasurer had to: approve payments authorized by the Delegate; keep accounts; distribute funds; account for the funds handed over to the Party by the Delegate; and, in conjunction with the latter, draw up annual accounts.

Each local council had to elect a secretary and president who would receive the communications of the Delegate and pass them on to the various associations. It had, also, to authorize the communications that the presidents of the associations wished to direct to the Delegate. If the president of a local party council resigned, new elections were to be held.

If the Delegate died or disappeared, the Treasurer was to inform the local councils, and new elections would take place. If a local council, through a majority vote, wished to dismiss the Delegate, it could put this resolution before the other councils, and if their votes so decided, the Delegate would have to resign. The bases and statutes of the Party might be changed after a request to the Delegate, who would organize a vote on this. Associations had to have at least twenty known and active members in order to vote for Delegate and Treasurer. In these elections, each association would have one vote per 20–100 members.

This scheme, whilst allowing the individual associations total autonomy in their internal workings, concentrated power in the hands of the Delegate, who could only be dismissed if the local party councils so willed it. A great check on the Delegate and Treasurer was their obligation to present themselves each year for re-election. The system in fact combined grass-roots democracy with efficient executive action. The contemporary Cuban historian Jorge Ibarra has called it 'democratic centralism', i.e. the forerunner of the present (communist) Cuban party organization. Martí, in fact, due to his growing prestige, was easily able to maintain himself as Delegate. This did not necessarily mean that he would become the President of the future Cuban Republic, although some Cubans he met inside Cuba once the 1895 military campaign had got off the ground greeted him with this title. Rather, and this followed the previous *mambí* practice during the 1868–78 war, the idea was that a Republic in Arms would be set up in liberated territory, governed by a parliament of delegates elected from within that territory. The President of the Republic in Arms would be chosen by these delegates. When this had come to pass, the CRP would lose its leading role and confine its activities to propaganda and fund-raising, etc.

As to the question of who would be in charge of the military operations, Martí, once elected Delegate in April 1892, ordered elections to be held amongst all the military veterans belonging to the new Party. This had the effect of simultaneously binding the military to the democratic statutes of the CRP and reconciling to a large extent those veterans such as Fernando Figueredo of Key West who were hostile to Martí's being the Party leader. The military commander chosen, inevitably, was Máximo Gómez, and Martí immediately wrote to Gómez setting out before him the terms of his post, to which Gómez assented. This represented a great step forward in the cause of Cuban democracy, since it meant that the military had become, theoretically at least, an arm of the Party, and not vice-versa.

By July 1892 the Cuban Convention of Key West (Figueredo, José Francisco Lamadriz, Juan Arnao and their associates) had swallowed its pride and affiliated to the CRP. Martí had thus become the undisputed leader of the Cuban independence movement, which was only just, since most of the new theoretical and organizational premises of this democratic entity had emanated from Martí in the first place. Moreover, he had done more than anybody else to bring together Cubans in exile, some of whom were living as far away as Central America (Gómez and Maceo) or Jamaica.

Martí had already publicly refuted Enrique Collazo's slanders, in a waspish letter published in the 20 January number of *El Porvenir*. Undoubtedly the two allegations that most wounded Martí were those of cowardice and immorally relieving Cuban emigrés of their savings. Martí pointed out to Collazo that he had not been able to take up arms for Cuba because he had spent most of the Ten Years' War in prison or exile in Spain. Theoretically he might have joined the insurgents after leaving Spain, in the period (1875–78) when he lived in Mexico, (briefly) Cuba and Guatemala. But there was really no good reason why he should, given the fact that during these years only the tail-end of the war was being fought out, by two demoralized armies. Neither were expeditions prepared from the United States. Of course, Martí's temperament, it is true, led him away from warfare: his bent was clearly political and conciliatory, as long as fundamental freedoms were observed. To accuse him of cowardice was patently absurd, in view of the great courage with which he publicly voiced his anti-Spanish ideas in the very face of the Spanish authorities. And what of his outspoken opposition, also, to the disguised dictatorships of Mexico, Guatemala and Venezuela? (See the next chapter.) As for his fund-raising activities amongst emigrés in Tampa and Key West, Martí reminded Collazo of his popularity in those localities, mentioning as evidence the donation by workers in the latter community of a cross to the very person supposedly emptying their money-boxes. The open squabble between the two men abated when Martí challenged Collazo to a duel and the latter ignored the challenge.

One of the bitter contradictions of Martí's short life was that, disliking war, he had to become the leading figure in the final anti-Spanish insurgency. He tried to reconcile these tensions by stressing that although war was inevitable, it should be conducted in a spirit of love and reconciliation. This was, he pointed out, in harmony with the elevated sentiments he had noticed in the tobacco workshops of Florida.

> Let others speak of castes and hatreds, I did not hear in those workshops anything save the eloquence which founds nations and sets souls alight and improves them, and scales the heights, fills in dividing moats and adorns academies and parliaments',

he told his audience in New York's Hardman Hall that February.[51]

Even before the first elections of the Cuban Revolutionary Party in April 1892, Martí had founded *Patria*, a newspaper largely written by him and used to promote the coming struggle. The first number appeared on 14 March 1892, by which time Martí had given up all his other obligations apart from those to the revolutionary cause. In this number, in an article entitled 'Our Ideas', he explained the nature of the movement and the kind of nation he saw as arising from it, a 'state of full decorum where, once the tools of daily labour had been locked away, one man would only be distinguished from another by the warmth of his heart or the fire in his forehead'.[52] It would be a nation for all Cubans, democratic and in tune with the 'real' (i.e. essential) spirit of the country. 'The son of the Antilles, because he has been patently favoured by Nature, is a man in whom moderation of judgement equals the passion for liberty',[53] he wrote, after having made his usual diatribe on the perils of class warfare:

> It makes one sad to see men reduce themselves, through the exclusive labelling of themselves as workmen, to a narrowness which is more harmful than benign; because this isolation of men of one particular occupation, or of a certain social circle, outside the proper and sensible agreements between people of the same interest, provokes the grouping together and resistance of men of other occupations and other circles.[54]

The Final Years: 1892–95

This period – between the founding of the Cuban Revolutionary Party and Martí's death – was naturally devoted to organizing as secretly as possible the anti-Spanish war. *Patria* constituted a key instrument of this design, and it was there that Martí set out his final ideas on Cuba. Many of these writings contained nothing new, and there is no need to repeat views already stated, except insofar as one must see them as a backcloth for fresh points. The key areas to be examined are: Spanish colonialism; Home Rule; Annexationism; United States' policy towards Cuba; and finally, the future Cuban Republic.

Spanish Colonialism

Martí's main writings on this topic from 1892 to 1895 are contained in two articles published in *Patria*, 'The Cuban Revolutionary Party' (3 April 1892) and 'The Revolutionary Party to Cuba' (27 May 1893), plus a letter dated 2 May 1895 which he sent to the *New York Herald* from the war zone in Oriente, Cuba.

Martí believed that between Spain and Cuba there were irreconcilable contradictions, the major one of which being, of course, Cuba's colonial status and consequent exploitation. Significantly, Martí felt that Spain itself had never been a real nation, but was rather a conglomerate of 'original and diverse' nationalities (Basques, Catalans, Galicians, etc., as well as Castilians) occupying 'harsh and jealous' regions that had been artificially brought together in the Reconquest against the Moors and whose uneasy union had been temporarily strengthened by the exploitation of America. Spain, in fact, was a nation at war with itself. (It was not the diversity of nationalities that Martí objected to for constituting Spain as a political entity, but rather the way in which they had been brought together, as far as one can make out.)

The Conquest of America had been harmful for Spain, since it led to dependence on easy wealth, obtained by plunder and oppression, draining the metropolis of its boldest and most capable talents. The feudal mentality which sought to avoid labour for itself and exploit that of others was thus prolonged. When Spain lost its other American colonies (except Puerto Rico) in the Spanish American Wars of Independence, it was all the more determined to hang on to Cuba for its wealth and obligatory markets for otherwise unsaleable Spanish goods. Spain's debts were being paid by Cuban-created wealth and Cuban-paid taxes. Corruption was such an integral part of the Spanish colonial system that in Cuba 'One either eats the bread of corruption, or there is no bread to eat'.[55] Spain was doing nothing to alleviate Cuba's ills; on the contrary, it was fuelling them. Taxes rose incessantly and were employed, ironically, to maintain a military stranglehold on the very people who paid them. A further irony was that Cubans had to bear the burden on their backs of hordes of Spanish functionaries and merchants, non-productive, rapacious and privileged. Moreover, hungry Spanish workers were taking Cuban jobs and land. Spain was a 'starving nation of no account whatsoever in the modern world', and would no longer be permitted to use Cuba as a 'latrine' for its 'sterile and exploitative population'.[56] Spanish politics reflected the national decay, being mere Madrid café intrigues, where cheap trickery passed as statesmanship. Martí's views on this subject found an echo in the writings of the brilliant Spanish novelist and playwright Ramón del Valle-Inclán, whose satire, produced a generation later, aimed at the very same target.

The 'tortured Island of Cuba', continued Martí, 'in the historic time when this whole planet is opening up and the seas are coming together in an embrace at her feet' was being prevented from 'opening wide its harbours and gold-bearing bowels to the world full of idle capital and unemployed masses, that in the warmth of the steady Republic would find (. . .) the calm of property and a friendly meeting-point'. As Jorge Ibarra has noted, 'idle capital and unemployed masses' meant for Martí, as far as their application to Cuba went, 'workers and holders of modest resources who desired to invest in low-level economic activity'. The large-scale export of US capital to Cuba, which Martí did not want, only began later.[57]

The Home Rule (Autonomista) Party
Martí also had to wage a determined ideological struggle against the Cuban Home Rule Party, whose aims fell considerably short of full independence from Spain. The origins of this party are to be found in the Reform Party which flourished in the 1860s, with encouragement from the Spanish Captain-General Serrano (1859–62), a relatively moderate ruler of the colony who saw the need for Cubans to have some representation in government and constitutional guarantees. In 1865 the Reform Party was asking for tax reform, an end to the (technically illegal) slave

trade, plus political representation in the Spanish parliament, as a prelude for a general programme of reforms in Cuba. As a result of this pressure, the Spanish authorities set up a *Junta de Información* (Board of Enquiry), to study possible changes in the administration of Cuba (and Puerto Rico). In March 1866, sixteen Cuban representatives were elected on to the Board, fourteen of these being Cuban-born and belonging to the Reform Party. The Board started its deliberations in Madrid in October of that year, and these continued until the Board itself was dissolved only eight months later, in April 1867.

Whilst still functioning, however, the Board had heard Cuban requests for the gradual phasing-out of slavery itself, consequent on the immediate abolition of the slave trade. Absolute free trade was another demand, plus tax reform. Spain should also separate civilian from military government in Cuba (the island had been since the twenties under a virtual military dictatorship), and Cubans should be able to deliberate formally on Cuban affairs. The only result of all these proposals was minor tax reform. The Board had been merely Spanish window-dressing. After the Board was dissolved war was inevitable.

After the end of the Ten Years' War, with both sides exhausted, the Reform Party reorganized itself into the Liberal Party, now (in 1878) including amongst its affiliates a greater proportion of professional middle-class people as well as some small plantation owners, to swell the ranks of its traditional members (the Cuban bourgeoisie whose interests were being harmed by Spanish interests). In 1881 it added the word 'autonomista' to its title and was thereafter known as the *Partido Autonomista*, or Home Rule Party. A small number of patriot veterans, some of whom secretly supported total independence, joined the Party.

With the 1878 peace treaty, a modified form of the Spanish constitutional regime was applied to Cuba, allowing Cubans to sit as deputies to the Madrid parliament, and at provincial and local council level. The Home Rule Party was thus able to agitate publicly in electoral campaigns, the Spanish *Cortes* itself, and the press. Electoral practices in Cuba, however, were heavily weighted in favour of Spaniards, both by legal and illegal means. Consequently, out of over one and a half million inhabitants of Cuba, only fifty-three thousand had the vote, and native-born Cuban deputies to the Madrid *Cortes* formed only one per cent of its members.

Martí had always been opposed to any measure falling short of full independence for Cuba, and hence was in permanent disagreement with the Home Rulers. In *Patria*, on 19 March 1892, he wrote that 'the movement for Home Rule had not been born in Cuba as a child of revolution, but rather in opposition to it'.[58] However, he was forced to tread carefully so as not to alienate members of the party who might be won over to the cause of independence. Moreover, it contained such prestigious figures as the pedagogue Enrique José Varona (who in fact was later to become editor of *Patria* when the 1895 war broke out and then Vice-President of the Republic), and the influential orator Rafael Montoro. The party had a sizeable following inside Cuba, and was the main legal propaganda organ for liberal Cubans. Of course, given the dominance of Spanish interests, it was overshadowed by the reactionary pro-Spanish *Unión Constitucional* Party, which even managed to block a plan for a mild form of Home Rule proposed by the Spanish Overseas Minister Antonio Maura in mid-1893.

When a crisis arose in 1894 over a tariff war with the United States (to which most of Cuba's exports went), crippling the country's trade and therefore the economy as a whole, the weakness of the Home Rule position was made manifest. The Home Rule Party could only survive, Martí pointed out in view of the fact that the economic power of the creole oligarchy had been broken, in two ways, both unacceptable: 'through the hidden link to Spanish power, or the handing over of the country to an alien civilization [i.e. the United States], which denies Cuba the proven capacity for free government.'[59] He declared the demise of the Home Rule interest, and exhorted its followers to go over to the revolution. Later on that year (December 1894) Martí stated that as Cuban Home Rule had been hissed out of the Spanish parliament, and threatened with the bullet, there were no more Home Rulers in Cuba.[60]

This last assertion was a piece of rhetorical exaggeration for the readers of *Patria*, since only two months later (February 1895), Martí was writing to his secretary Gonzalo de Quesada that the Home Rulers, whom he termed 'the tacit Cubans', were in no way to be harmed in the struggle.

Martí's last statement on this question appears in the famous last letter to Manuel Mercado, penned just one day (18 May 1895) before his death. Here he lumped Home Rulers together with annexationists, as people who only desire 'a master, whether Yankee or Spanish' to allow them to lord it over the 'pressing mass – the clever and touching mass of mixed-bloods of the country – the intelligent and creative mass of whites and blacks'.[61] By then, the annexationists were also supporting Home Rule.

Martí was quite correct in seeing Home Rule as just one more way of avoiding a final confrontation. In desperation, the Spaniards themselves granted it to the Cuban population, in November 1897, when the last war had been fought for more than two years, and then only after pressure from the United States. A Home Rule government was set up in March 1898 in Cuba, after elections, but it barely managed to hang on until the final defeat of Spain in December of that year. As Martí had predicted, most of the rank and file of the Home Rule Party deserted it to join the insurgents, or else abandoned politics altogether, once the war began (in February 1895). The Home Rule government in Cuba only controlled half of the island, and even for that had to rely on the Spanish military and its system of concentration camps. Martí's stance on this question had been totally vindicated.

Annexationism

In mid-1892 Martí asserted that very few people, whether Cubans or North Americans, were in favour of annexation of Cuba by the United States.[62] The whole issue had been defused by the abolition of slavery in the latter country, and the few Cuban annexationists that remained were people who held the absurd view that Cubans were incapable of self-government. In any case, annexation, in Martí's eyes as in those of a Cuban intellectual of the previous generation, José Antonio Saco, would led to the death of things Cuban, since the country would become swamped by North American settlers, rather as Texas had been. Ruling circles in the United States, as has been shown, had come out against annexation. The issue was a dead duck.

Cuban-United States Relations

United States attitudes to Cuba had always been conditioned by two main concerns: the island's economic potential (as a source of cheap sugar, tobacco and other crops, and as a market for US manufactures), and the need to control Cuba because of its strategic position a mere ninety miles away in the Gulf of Mexico. The relative weight of these two factors has varied throughout history: whereas nowadays the strategic factor is paramount, it was originally commercial interest for the United States that led to contacts between the two countries. There had been trade as far back as the French Revolution, and in the early years of the nineteenth century Thomas Jefferson even urged his successor in the US Presidency to negotiate with Napoleon with a view to incorporating Cuba into the United States, of which it would form the southernmost territory in that nation's expansion. However, the United States faced continued British and French hostility with regard to its acquiring Cuba, and decided to pursue a policy of encouraging Spain's hold over the island, in the knowledge that in time it would drop off into the lap of the United States once Spain's ever-weakening colonial power made this inevitable.

The United States bought Florida from Spain in 1821, and proclaimed the Monroe Doctrine in 1823, which served to formalize its policy on Cuba, in that it publicly declared its opposition to European interference in America at the same time as it sanctioned *de facto* European colonies there. Little wonder that Cuban patriots were aggrieved at what they saw as an act of selfish treachery on the part of the world's first free nation.[63]

The annexationist plans of the 1840s and 1850s were not supported by the US government, which continued its policy of trying to acquire Cuba peacefully from Spain by purchase. Thus the Cuban-Venezuelan Narciso López went to his death unaided, and even impeded by the US government in his annexationist designs. No official recognition was conceded to the Cuban insurgents in the Ten Years' War, although in 1868–69 President Ulysses Grant had given them some encouragement and suggested purchase to the Spaniards. Spain rejected this proposition, and Grant, influenced by his Secretary of State Hamilton Fish, went as far as to ban Cuban expeditions from the United States to the island.

As the nineteenth century advanced, the US received an ever greater share of Cuban exports: by 1884, 85% of Cuban products was going to that nation. This involved especially sugar and its by-products, of which it was taking virtually the entire Cuban output: 94%. Spain was thus hardly consuming Cuban sugar, although its merchants were making fortunes from it and its government was using the tax revenues generated by it to shore up the tottering home economy. Moreover, Spain needed Cuba as a market for its own manufactures, and in consequence erected high tariff barriers against foreign imports into its colony. However, Spanish merchants also enriched themselves by circumventing these tariffs, passing off foreign imports as Spanish. The general economic picture emerges in a remark by the US consul in Havana, in 1881, to the effect that from the point of view of trade, Cuba had become a dependency of his country, although politically still subservient to Spain.

Obviously, the United States had an interest in breaking down these Spanish tariff barriers, and in 1890 a counter-measure was approved by President McKinley, allowing Cuban sugar free entry into the United States as long as US goods were allowed the same access to Cuban markets. The sugar and tobacco interests in Cuba pressed hard for a treaty of reciprocity, backed by the Home Rule Party and even a splinter of the pro-Spanish Constitutional Union. Thus opposition to Spanish policies was significantly growing, as the contradictions between colony and parasitic metropolis became more and more glaring. A treaty was in fact signed in 1891 allowing free entry of Cuban sugar into the United States and preferential treatment for its tobacco and certain other crops. This had the effect of boosting sugar production, which between 1890 and 1894 doubled to one million tons. Sugar became thus even more crucial to the Cuban economy, and tied it even more closely to that of the United States. Any measure taken subsequently by the United States to limit these privileges would have a devastating effect on the Cuban economy. On the other side of the picture, US imports into Cuba (especially manufactures) were beginning to swamp the Cuban market, thus laying waste to the hopes of Cuban industrialists, who could not possibly compete. This situation, indeed, obtained right up to the Castro Revolution of 1959.

In 1894 the Reciprocity Treaty was annulled, when certain new customs duties were introduced in the United States. The Cuban economy was plunged into chaos, which greatly aided Martí's war plans, and by January 1895, when a new treaty was signed, the momentum built up by the Cuban Revolutionary Party could not be gainsaid.

By this time, also, direct investment by US companies in the Cuban economy had grown, especially in the sugar area, but also in those of chrome, iron, manganese and tobacco. According to US statistics, by 1895 US investments in Cuba added up to some 50 million pesos (dollars).

It is against this background that we must now examine Martí's ideas on US-Cuban relations. We have seen how the public debate conducted in the US press around the possible purchase of Cuba from Spain, and the scorn which was heaped on Cuba and its population by influential US public figures, shocked and embittered Martí. The 1889–90 Panamerican Congress and its sequel, the Monetary Conference of one year later, likewise, represented a dire threat to the whole of Latin America, including Cuba. Martí's one hope was that the United States could be persuaded to back Cuban independence. However, he did not want US help in the coming anti-Spanish war, fearing that this would mean a continued US presence in the island. In fact, later events (after Martí's death) proved the correctness of his views, since although the United States rejected outright annexation of Cuba, for the reasons we have seen, it did intervene in the anti-Spanish war, after the mysterious explosion on the US battleship *Maine*, in Havana harbour in February 1898, and used this intervention to tie Cuba even more closely to itself. This was done during the US occupation (1898–1902) by the notorious Platt Amendment, which was forcibly written into Cuba's first Republican constitution, and granted the United States bases, coaling stations and the right to intervene more or less at will in Cuban affairs, if US citizens or property were deemed to be in peril. The Platt Amendment was actually invoked several times in the first two decades of the Republic, and US troops sent in. A Treaty of Reciprocity was also signed, giving Cuba a preferential sugar quota on US markets in return for easy access to those of Cuba for US products, thus renewing (definitively now that Spain had withdrawn from the scene) the economic ties of the 1890s. Thus any major industrialization of Cuba was prevented, and the new Republic made increasingly dependent on the giant to the north.

Had Martí survived the 1895–98 war he would certainly have bitterly opposed the Platt Amendment as an insult to Cuba's political sovereignty. The economic problem, however, was more difficult, and it was here that the root of Cuba's future ills lay, since in a world of capitalist economics Cuba was bound to become a mere appendage of its huge neighbour. The high price of sugar, in the nineteenth century, masked a basic economic weakness of the nation. Martí spoke optimistically of Cuba's 'gold-bearing' bowels – the expression was a figure of speech, and really alluded to the fertility of Cuba's soil and its capacity for producing cash crops like sugar and tobacco – but the future belonged to the industrialized nations, of which the United States, by the 1920s, was to become the leader. The myth of a paradisiacally wealthy Cuba, dating from the time of Columbus, was to be cruelly exposed as the twentieth century advanced. Sugar prices dropped catastrophically in the wake of the First World War, never to recover. But far more serious (quite apart from the basic question of Cuba's small size) is the fact that Cuba has a very poor potential for industrialization, having no native sources of energy to speak of (like oil, coal or large, fast-flowing rivers) and no large deposits of industrial metals (except nickel). It is evident that Martí, who in any case would never have claimed for himself any importance as a thinker on economics, only partially foresaw these problems. Let us, in the light of this, examine one of his relatively few statements on economic matters, one, nonetheless, that is oft quoted:

> Economic union means political union. The country that buys is the one that commands. The country that sells, obeys. One must balance trade out, in order to ensure freedom. The people that wishes to die sells to a single people, and the one that wishes to be saved, sells to more than one.[64]

The above statement was made in the context of the 1891 Washington Monetary Conference, in which the United States was attempting to break Latin American trade links with Europe by foisting on its neighbours a common silver currency, unacceptable to European nations. Martí himself played a major role in preventing this, as is related in the next chapter. Nobody could quarrel with the first sentence of this quote, or with the idea that a nation needs to balance out its trade. But as a general *dictum*, the whole statement gives the wrong emphasis in the selling-buying equation, because surely it is the selling, or producer countries that have ruled the roost in modern times. A quick look at British and then North American domination of the world over the last two hundred years makes this clear. And, more recently still, of course, one must talk no longer of the nation-state as the main accumulator of capital, but rather the transnational company. Martí's error comes because he always underestimated the importance of man's economic activities as a determinant of history, and hence played down the image of man as producer, in favour of him as a moral entity, in accordance with his neo-Kantian creed.

On matters to which Martí's mind responded more readily, his thinking penetrated deeper. For instance, he was correct in seeing the political independence of Cuba (not fully realized, of course, after the Cuban-Spanish-American war ending in 1898) as a check on the expansionist ambitions of the United States. This notion appears as a corollary to the statement, made in Martí's third article on the Panamerican Congress of 1889–90 (see the following chapter), that the true independence of Latin America held the key to the world balance of power. Cuba came thus to be seen by him as the 'fulcrum' of the entire globe, because it was a test case for United States' behaviour towards Latin America. Cuba, thought Martí, by achieving its independence without 'help' (read 'interference') from the United States, would block that nation's expansion. If it failed, it would serve as a 'pontoon' towards other nations. In the end, of course, Cuba's political independence from the United States was only gained in 1959, and that revolution had to consolidate itself by becoming a socialist one, a fact that Martí did not foresee, for obvious reasons. However, there is no doubt that he would have been delighted to see his idea vindicated by the effect of the 1959 Revolution on the rest of Latin America.

Throughout the last three years of Martí's life, his diatribes against the United States grew in virulence. The 'democratic and universal Yankee' of the early years of North American independence, he wrote in July 1892, had been transformed into 'the authoritarian, greedy and aggressive Yankee (. . .) drunk on the ill-fated victory over his very brothers and the easy credit that followed it', adding that everybody in the United States respected just one thing: strength.[65]

One year later, in August 1893, he made a fuller and even more scathing indictment of the United States:

> The North has been unjust and greedy; it has thought more about ensuring the fortune of a few than about creating a people for the good of all: it has transplanted to the new American land all the hatreds and all the problems of the old monarchies (. . .). In the North the problems are getting worse, and the charity and patriotism which could solve them do not exist. Here men do not learn to love one another, and neither do they love the soil where by chance they were born, and where they toil without respite in the animal struggle, full of tribulation, for existence. Here a more hungry machine has been constructed than can satisfy the universe saturated with products. Here the land has been badly shared out; and the unequal and monstrous production, and the inertia of the soil held by the monopolizing few, leave the country without the safeguard of shared harvests, which feed a nation even if they do not make a profit for it. Here the rich pile up on the one hand and the desperate pile up on the other. The North is closing itself off and is full of hatreds. We must start leaving the North.[66]

One week later, writing in *Patria*, Martí took up the same theme: Cubans were being corrupted by living in the United States, and they should leave before 'the habit of a purely material existence in foreign countries takes away from the creole character the gifts of disinterestedness and brotherhood of man that make life firmly based and agreeable'. Continuing, he characterized the United States as

> this North where we came to live out of fantasy and imprudence, and through the deception arising from taking peoples at their word, and assuming that the realities of a nation are what its Sunday sermons and books tell us about it (. . .) this barbed and anxious country which, at the first clash of its interests, since it has no other bond than that of interest, shows without shame its deep splits, a sad country where are neither alleviated nor forgotten (. . .) the naked struggles between satisfied appetites and those that wish to be satisfied, or the interests that give priority to one locality over the balance of the nation in whose shade they were born, and the well-being of a greater sum of men (. . .) the sordidness and animality which surround us (. . .) the greatest of all dangers for man, which is the blind and exclusive cult of the self (. . .) a hotchpotch of beings with no means of support, who divide and flee at the moment when the community of profit does not bind them together; where have come, without the

intimate communion with the soil that softens them, all the problems of hatred of the old human continent (. . .) this agitated pack of hounds, of rich versus poor, Christians against Jews, whites against blacks, farmers against traders, Westerners and Southerners against people from the East, of voracious and despised men against everything which is refused to a man, and to his thirst (. . .) this furnace of angers (. . .) these sharp jaws (. . .) this smoking crater.[67]

A black (and faithful) picture indeed, of a society lurching into monopoly capitalism, a society light years away from Martí's idea for Cuba, which was more akin to the Greek *polis* of the fifth century BC, described by the Hellenist H.D.F. Kitto as 'the family writ large'. The voracious and seething monster had to be treated, meanwhile, with prudence. Martí had already remarked on the need for a

> policy of friendship and work between Cuba and the North, which will replace the antiquated and rudimentary dream of annexation, nurtured in good faith by our fathers in the idyllic times, now past, of the North American Republic.

The United States was 'the foreign country with which we have to continue after freedom in a friendly and preferential relationship'. Not from affinity, of course, but from necessity. This relationship had to be one of 'independent and virile friendship between the Cuban and Northern peoples', and was 'necessary for the honour and peace of both'.[68] This respect would be ensured, on the North American side, by the latter's regard for Cuban capability and industriousness. In reality, to expect 'honour' or 'friendship' from the nation which Martí himself only four months later was to revile as a ravenous beast (see above) seems disingenuous. But Martí had no alternative to presenting the picture in a rosier light than was warranted to a nation about to enter a bloody conflict for its very right to exist.

Fidel Castro himself followed Martí in hoping for some kind of *modus vivendi* with the United States: that was the reason for his visit to that country in 1959, shortly after the defeat of Batista. Cuba was still, it will be remembered, a capitalist country, but that did not stop him being spurned by Nixon and Eisenhower. The fact was that the goal of the 1959 Revolution (a more socially just nation *à la Martí*) clashed of necessity with North American capitalist interests. To implement Martí's ideas only, Cuba was forced to become socialist and align itself with the nations of that camp, who afforded protection (and economic aid) against United States belligerence. The question is: what would Martí have done in his time (had he survived the war) to stop the enfiefment of Cuba by its neighbour? What could he have done? We do not know, but one thing is certain: he would have abhorred the corruption and servility to the United States of the pre-1959 Republic.

Returning to the 1890s, one must underline the dilemma in which Martí found himself when dealing with the United States. Whereas privately he could voice his extreme abhorrence of that nation, in public he had to express a more accommodating attitude. His official position may be seen in a letter he wrote from the Cuban *manigua* to the *New York Herald*, dated 2 May 1895 and handed over to the newspaper's correspondent Eugene Bryson (the Herbert Matthews of his day). His private views were set out just sixteen days later, in the oft-quoted letter he wrote one day before his death to his Mexican friend Manuel Mercado.

The letter to the *Herald*, signed by both Martí and Gómez, stressed the efforts of Cubans to emancipate themselves from Spain and found an independent people, worthy and capable of self-government, a people that would 'open up the stagnated wealth of the Island of Cuba'. Spain was closing off 'the island bursting with natural forces and the creative character which releases them, from the production of the great nations'. It was preventing, anachronistically, Cuba from 'opening up wide her harbours and gold-bearing bowels to the world full of idle capital and unemployed masses, which in the warmth of the steady Republic would find in the island the calm of property and a friendly meeting-point'. Martí added that 'Cubans recognize the urgent duty imposed on them, vis-à-vis the world, by their geographical position and the present time of universal gestation', and continued:

At the mouth of the oceanic channels, in the knot joining the three continents (. . .) and at the gates of a people disturbed by the plethora of products which she could acquire in this people, and today buys from her tyrants, Cuba wants to be free, so that man shall realize in her his final destiny, so that in her the whole world may work, and so as to sell her hidden riches in the natural markets of America, where the self-interest of her Spanish master forbids her to buy today (. . .). The United States (. . .) would prefer to contribute to the solidity of freedom in Cuba, by its sincere friendship for her independent people that loves it, and will open up for it all her doors, to being the accomplice of a pretentious and no-account oligarchy. (. . .) It is certainly not in the United States that men will dare to seek the sowers of tyranny.[69]

Earlier on in the same communication, Martí had taken care to point out the error of believing that

the Cuban revolution is the insignificant desire of an exclusive class of poor Cubans in foreign countries, or the uprising and preponderance of the black race in Cuba, or the immolation of the country in a dream of independence which cannot be sustained by those who will conquer it.

It was a question of freedom which would 'open up for the United States the Island which today is being closed off to it by Spanish self-interest'.[70]

The letter to Mercado, on the other hand, constituted a violent indictment of the United States. Its very first sentence informed Martí's 'dearest brother' of Martí's duty and determination to 'prevent in time by Cuban independence the United States from spreading itself over the Antilles and falling, with that additional strength, on our lands of America'. The second rammed home the message: 'Everything I have done up to today, and everything I shall do, is with that goal in mind'. Then comes the explanation of the divergence in Martí's utterances on the United States, at this late stage of his life, according to whether he was addressing himself to North Americans or his 'brothers' of Latin America.

> It has been necessary to do this in silence [he confided to Mercado], and as it were, indirectly, because there are things that, if one is to achieve them, must be hidden, and that, if proclaimed out loud, would raise too formidable difficulties for the goal to be attained.

The annexation of the peoples of Spanish America – 'our America' – 'to the turbulent and brutal North that despises them' had to be stopped, and Cubans were doing this now with their blood (on the battlefield). 'I lived in the monster, and know its innards, and my sling is that of David', stated Martí, in a phrase which, slightly adapted, has become famous.[71]

The divergence in attitudes towards the United States, however, is not the only contradiction in these last two documents quoted. Martí told Mercado that the people he most relied upon in Cuba were 'the pressing mass – the clever and touching mass of mixed-bloods (. . .) the intelligent and creative mass of whites and blacks'.[72] This contradicts the impression that he was at some pains to convey to the readers of the *New York Herald* that nothing like a social or racial revolution was on the cards for Cuba. What Martí's aims were for the Cuba of the future we shall now discuss.

The Future Cuban Republic
Martí believed that Cuban independence, once attained, would be free from the major problems that had plagued – and continued to plague – the Spanish American nations which had won their emancipation in the 1820s.

> Other Republics were born seventy-five years ago: ours, now. What has happened in other republics will not happen in ours. We have the marrow of the republic, nurtured in war and in exile; and the habits and healthy vigilance of republican government. The Cuban, sometimes untamable because he was born of rebelliousness, is as harsh towards despotism as he is courtly towards reason. The Cuban is independent, moderate and proud. He is his own master, and does not want masters over him. Whoever tries to saddle him will be thrown off. Other peoples of America are about to fall, because liberty rested with the powerful who did not love it, or understood it only for their own, higher, caste; because the masses did not know liberty, nor did they know how to defend it, nor did they understand the means to

propagate it and maintain it; because the national majority, which is that which ensures liberty, understood of it only the spirit of independence versus the foreigner, which has been enough to save it, again and again, from the betrayal of the lettered classes and the despots. But in us, there is a public mass that knows and adores liberty, that speaks and writes it, that reasons it and adjusts it to the truth, and will defend it tooth and nail; and there we shall be, all of us, defending it.[73]

Cubans were quite capable, Martí declared in the *Montecristi Manifesto*, the programme signed by Martí and Gómez on 25 March 1895 and addressed to the Cuban people as the CRP's war manifesto, because of the experience of the Ten Years' War ('the first years of sublime fusion') and of 'the modern practices of government and work', of 'saving the fatherland from its very beginnings from the maladjustments and tentative practices, necessary at the start of the century, without communications and preparation in the feudal or theoretical republics of Spanish America'.[74] These Spanish American nations had experienced upheavals through mistaken attempts to impose 'foreign moulds' on 'the ingenuous reality of countries whose only knowledge of liberties were the strong desire that conquers them and the sovereignty that is won by fighting for them'.[75] Martí then detailed the various malaises affecting them:

> The concentration of a culture which is merely bookish, in the capital cities; the erroneous attraction (. . .) for the lordly customs of the colony; the imperfect relations between the distant regions; the rudimentary state of the sole industry, whether this involved agriculture or stockbreeding; and the abandonment of and scorn for the fertile Indian race in the disputes over belief or locality.[76]

These problems were in no way the problems of Cuba in the 1890s, which was 'going back to war with a democratic and educated people, which jealously guards its rights and those of others' and whose 'humblest strata' were far more 'cultured' than 'the cowboy or Indian masses, with which, urged on by the great heroes of emancipation, the silent colonies of America turned from roving herds into nations'.[77]

More than rivalry and suspicion, inherent in man, the main difficulty in Spanish America was to find structures to channel the spirit of freedom from warfare into viable, harmonious national entities. Thus the present war in Cuba had to be organized and carried on in such a way as to be a prelude to democracy. 'From its roots the fatherland must be constituted with viable forms, born from itself, so that a government lacking reality or sanction does not lead it into partialities or tyranny'.[78] The democratic organization of the Cuban Revolutionary Party had proven the capacity of Cubans for working together: 'Doctors and workers, factory owners and mechanics, tradesmen and generals, unite to vote and elect their representatives'.[79]

Universal suffrage, in fact, would be a keystone of the future Republic, for 'with plenty of political discussion, and a free and frequent vote, there is no war to be feared, or a tyranny from above or below, in democracies'.[80] Voting would be obligatory, for this was a way to 'educate the public and balance out classes'. Two points in Cuba's favour, in comparison with the newly liberated nations of the 1820s, were its small size and lack of 'personal *caudillaje*', which was foreign to Cuba's 'nature and character'.[81] To sum up,

> Cuba arrives at American life, because of her habits of work, liberal discipline, extensive pilgrimages, modern improvements, public aspirations and happy geography, with elements that are certainly very different from the indolent patrician caste, the false or theocratic constitutions and the uneducated and inaccessible countryside that disturbed, with conflicts mostly foreign to Cuba, the development, in an unenlightened era and one that was uncharted, of the first American Republics.[82]

Let us examine more closely Martí's sketches for this future democratic republic, based on universal suffrage, to see whether a coherent picture of the special nature of this society can be drawn. For this purpose, a good starting point is one of the first articles to appear in *Patria*, entitled 'The Economic Assembly' (26 March 1892), where he stated:

> Freedom has as its roots lawful self-interest, which is defended in it; and the first thrust of freedom in Cuba would be, on the day after victory, to go out and sow workers. The fool scorns public wealth; or tries to maintain the wealth of some over the wretchedness of the many. The war must be waged so as to put an end, at one stroke, to this uneasy state of affairs; to place the products of the Island, without hindrances or entanglements, in their natural markets; to give Cuban industries a permanent territory of their own.[83]

By lawful self-interest Martí appears to mean the right to make a profit, but not at the expense of an economically downtrodden working class. Everybody would be encouraged to work, but extremes of wealth and poverty would be frowned upon. Moreover a full development of Cuba's productive resources allied to the placement wherever it was most profitable of the commodities thereby created would be arranged. Spanish restrictive practices had led to the mass emigration of tobacco workers to Florida, and prevented the free flow of trade between Cuba and the United States.

As for the question of democracy, Martí was determined to 'continue the democratic revolution in the spirit of the constituent assembly of Guáimaro',[84] i.e. that of the 1869 Cuban Republic in Arms. Political leaders would not become dictators, for 'peoples are not like herds of cattle, where an ox carries the bell, and the rest follow him'.[85] Yet universal suffrage, as Martí knew because he had seen dictatorships operating behind democratic facades in Guatemala, Venezuela and

Mexico, was not sufficient to safeguard the democratic process. Although his speeches and public writings do not touch on this problem in any practical way (rather, Martí relies on exhortations to harmony in the name of patriotism), recent research has shown that Martí was in fact addressing himself to this matter. In his late notebooks, for example, appears a sketch for democracy based on proportional representation. According to these jottings, he wanted a government where 'all the diversities of opinion in the country are represented, according to the number of votes polled in their support'. 'The minority will always be in a minority', he adds, because that is just. But 'let it not be obliged to be the opposition (. . .) or influence the government as an obligatory enemy, as a standing opposition, but rather let it be close to it, expressing its daily opinion, as it must have the right to do. A guarantee for all. Power for all.' Then, just below: 'On purely political jobs. – Non-transferable posts'.[86] Jorge Ibarra, whose invaluable book *José Martí, dirigente político e ideólogo revolucionario* (José Martí, Political Leader and Revolutionary Ideologue)[87] first drew our attention to these notes, believes that Martí had become so disgusted with the pluriparty system in the United States (where rewards for party political, financial and other support often consisted of government posts and sinecures after electoral victory) that he determined to avoid this for Cuba. Certainly Martí wrote enough on the subject of both Republican and Democratic corruption in the United States, and sincerely believed that Cuba could be run as a kind of large family (the interests of its members being essentially non-antagonistic). One thinks also of the Greek *polis* (minus slavery, of course). Whatever the merits and demerits of this possible scheme, history was to prove that the pluriparty system adopted in Cuba under the Republic after Martí's death and modelled on that of the United States was a disaster, turning Cuba into a byword for corruption and vice, quite the antithesis of all that Martí stood for.

The key concept in Martí's thinking on society, we repeat, is his idea of *balance*. 'The world is balance, and it is necessary to make peace in time between the two weights in the scales', he remarked in 'Poor and Rich' (*Patria*, 14 March 1893).[88] This comment merely reflects a general philosophical view, the product of Martí's neo-Kantianism. Specifically applied to Cuba (and Puerto Rico), we read:

> The republic, in Puerto Rico as in Cuba, will not be the unjust predominance of one class of Cubans over the rest, but in the open and sincere balance of all the real forces in the country, and of the free thoughts and desires of all Cubans. We do not want to redeem ourselves from one tyranny to enter another (. . .). We will die for true liberty; not for the liberty that serves as a pretext for maintaining some men in excessive pleasure, and others in unnecessary pain. People will die for the Republic afterwards, if it is necessary, as they will die first of all for independence.[89]

The last sentence clearly indicates that Martí knew there would be a struggle to maintain the kind of society he wanted. 'The task,' he had remarked just two months previous to this last utterance, 'is not to get Spain out of Cuba, but to get it out of our habits. (. . .) Independence is one thing, and revolution another.'[90] The cement that would hold the new Cuba together would be, basically, 'the religion of love in which the Cuba soul is melting down its elements of hatred', as Martí told José Dolores Poyo nearly one year afterwards, adding: 'About the evil that we may meet on the way, it is not necessary to speak. Evil is punished by allowing itself to be shown. Evil is suicidal'.[91] And just ten days later, he was telling Alejandro Gómez of 'the human and friendly revolution, made with all, and with the soul of the poor, for concord between the poor and the rich'.[92]

Here speaks Martí the Apostle and Redeemer, the utopian spirit that infused the tireless political organizer. The weaknesses of Martí's world-view as applied to the realm of politics are obvious, and led him to reject concepts like the class struggle. But although the whole cast of Martí's mind is idealist, quasi-Platonic, his strictures on Marxism are very far from being total, as might be expected. We have seen that he characterized both Marx and Carlos Baliño, a member of the CRP and future founder of the Cuban Communist Party, as people whose intentions were praiseworthy, but who tried to go 'too fast'. This fits in with Martí's own kind of Kantian moralism and also with the need to *unite* Cubans at that moment in their struggle for national identity. Martí shared the Marxian belief in progress because Krausism had taught him to believe in this, but he differed from Marx in thinking that progress was really the result of a gradual spiritual purification in each individual man. He did not think this would be achieved only after the triumph of the working classes over all others. For both Martí and Marx the goal was the same: a society where each individual would be able to cultivate his talents to the maximum of his desires. Martí had seen too much of the United States to believe that the latter nation, with its rapidly growing inequalities and ferocious jungle morality, was the proper starting-point leading to the classless society that he, like Marx, desired. But for Cuba, at least in its immediate post-revolutionary stage, he wanted a free-enterprise system, albeit, as has been shown, with curbs against the grosser forms of economic exploitation.

Thus it is logical that he should write, in an article entitled 'The Cuban Worker' (*Patria*, 2 July 1892), 'Our lips are made to burn, by these unnecessary words about "workmen" and "class",'[93] and that he should praise *El Proletario*, the Key West workers' newspaper which 'because of the total absence of hatred in its frank columns, wins one over and is proving itself a real factor in the cause of the country's independence', despite its name, 'that casts shades of mourning over one's thoughts and grieves one's heart'. Martí went on to explain that 'in our generous and abundant fatherland a cause for this newspaper will not be able to exist'.

We have already seen in our people the equitable adjustment of existing interests and the reason which will be brought to bear on the economic agreements between the factors of production when the lawful aspiration of the worker to be respectfully treated and justly paid is not irritated, as it is today, by the systematic degradation of man around him.[94]

The economic basis for such a regime seems to imply, for Martí, a more equitable distribution of land.

Wide is the land in uncultivated Cuba, and dear is the justice in opening it up to the person who will use it, and in directing it away from the one who will not; and with a good land system, easy in the beginnings of a country of abundance, Cuba will have a home for many a good man, balance for social problems and the root for a Republic that, rather than being one of disputes and names, must be that of enterprise and work.[95]

The idea seems to be that everybody willing to work should be at least guaranteed a piece of land (Cuba had roughly one-sixth of its present population). Martí certainly had a bias against life in the big city, and work in the large factory. And it is quite in keeping with the Krausist influence he had absorbed that he should believe in the need for man's constant contact with Nature. Perhaps, as Jorge Ibarra has indicated, Henry George and his book *Progress and Poverty* (which Martí had read) also steered his mind in this direction. George believed in the nationalization of land and its renting out to all those who wanted it, as a means of absorbing the surplus population of the cities. Only those renting land would pay tax, and hence the high cost of city life would be brought down. Whatever Martí's exact ideas on George's system, there is no doubt that he wanted for Cuba a society of small and medium producers, having been increasingly appalled by the tremendous industrial crisis of the beginnings of monopoly capitalism in the United States of the 1880s. There is much that is appealing in Martí's vision for Cuba, but it is also open to the kind of criticism that Marx levelled at Proudhon for the latter's *Philosophie de la misère*, which advocated a similar type of society. Marx pointed out that the laws of capitalism would soon destroy its equilibrium. And of course this would be even truer in the case of tiny Cuba, swirling around in the economic vortex of the United States.

Martí's ideas on government found their most detailed expression in an article written for *Patria* in April 1894 called 'The Third Year of the Cuban Revolutionary Party'. Again, good government is seen as a process of balancing out the real (i.e. living) forces in society.

Every public political party must adjust itself to the people of its nation, and politics is, or should be, only the art of guiding, with self-sacrifice, the diverse or opposing factors of a country so that, without undue favour being given to the impatience of some, or the unjust denial of the need for order in societies – which is only ensured when the rule of law prevails – the various elements that have an equal title to representation and happiness in the fatherland may live without clashing, and with freedom to pursue their aims or resist those of others, in the continual peace provided by the recognition of law. A people is not the will of a single man, however pure that will may be, or the childish insistence on realizing, with a human group, the pure and innocent ideal of a celestial spirit, some blind man who has graduated from the tottering university of the clouds. Peoples are made up of hatred and love, and of more hatred than love; it is only that love, like the sun it is, consumes and melts everything; and what greed and privilege have been accumulating over centuries is thrown off, along with their natural consequence, oppressed souls, by a single shrug from the indignation of a pious soul. With these two forces: expansive love and repressive hatred – whose public forms are self-interest and privilege – nations are gradually built. Pity for the unfortunate, for the ignorant and dispossessed, cannot go so far as to put itself at the head of their mistakes or encourage these. The recognition of the hidden and malignant forces in society, which under the name of order cover up rage at seeing those whom the day before they had at their feet raise themselves up, cannot go so far as to join hands with impotent pride, to provoke the sure anger of powerful freedom. A people is made up of many wills, vile or pure, frank or venomous, blocked by timidity or spurred on by ignorance. It is necessary to relinquish much, to restrain much, to sacrifice much, to climb down from fantasy, to set one's feet on the ground in the midst of the turbulence of the fatherland, by picking up sinners by the neck, whether their sin wears fine or coarse cloth. It is necessary to raise them from out of the depths, without falling into the error of ignoring them because they come in humble clothing, or denying them because they are accompanied by wealth and culture.[96]

Of course, for such a society to function, its politicians must be enlightened and virtuous, in the manner of those ruling Plato's Republic. Martí no doubt would have fulfilled Plato's requirements, but who else did? Such people were certainly few and far between in the venal Cuban Republic. The problem with Martí's view of politics, obviously, is that it is too bound up with moralism, and thus has to rely too heavily on example and exhortation, in the manner of a religious creed. Not for nothing is Martí known in Latin America as the Apostle: concepts like redemption were ever to the fore of his mind. Apostles do have an influence disproportionate to their number, but Martí exaggerated their importance. The weakness of this kind of political thinking stands fully revealed in the first sentence of the long passage we have just quoted. Martí states: 'politics is, or should be', as if the world were at fault for distorting the Platonic archetype. Then, lower down, there comes an attempt to rectify excessive optimism by a seemingly frank admission of the preponderance of evil and selfishness in society. Martí felt, however, that love would win out in the end, because it was the prime mover in the universe, a belief that his Krausist teachers had taken over from Christianity. One sees Martí, in such passages, at his worst as a political ideologue, yet if one had to choose between such semi-religious moralism and the mechanical economism of so many who call themselves Marxists, one would have to prefer the first. And it must be stressed that Martí's political praxis was always streets ahead of his theoretical musings, probably, in part, because he was always involved in the concrete struggle and had little time to think his ideas through. Certainly Martí pulled Cuban nationalists together in the late 1880s and early 1890s as nobody else showed signs of doing.

Martí's 'equitable' (i.e. multi-class and multi-race) society enshrined the rule of law as a cardinal principle, but Martí believed that the disparate elements which would make up the future Cuban nation-state would not tend to infringe the law, since in war and exile they had all already fused their divergent interests for the sake of the *patria*. (At times, it is true, he shows less optimism, and admits that the real battle will come after the defeat of the Spaniards.) The *patria* was the cornerstone of Martí's political creed, and his nationalism shows great similarities with that early nineteenth century liberal romantic nationalism of small European nations like Italy and Germany, which were trying to throw off the yoke of large imperial powers. Much of Martí's political vocabulary harks back to those times. His insistence on 'dignity', for example, derives from the Kantian concept of man as an end in himself and the possessor of a certain area of individual inviolability. The recognition of the 'dignity' of each individual subject makes for what Martí calls a society of 'decorum'.

> The hope for a harmonious and decorous life today encourages to an equal degree the prudent seigneurial elements of yesterday, who see a danger in the unmerited privilege of non-productive men, and the Cubans of humble origin also, who in the creation of themselves have discovered an invincible nobility. (. . .) Frank and possible, the revolution has today the strength of all clear-sighted men, of the productive ruling classes and the cultivated masses, of generals and lawyers, of tobacco workers and peasants, of doctors and traders, of masters and freedmen. The revolution will be victorious with this spirit, or defeated if it lacks it. (. . .) Cuba and Puerto Rico will come to freedom with a very different make-up and at a very different time, and with far greater responsibilities, than the rest of the Spanish American peoples.[97]

Despite the 'balanced' (and therefore possibly rather static) society he advocated for Cuba, Martí was nonetheless a believer in human history as progress. This belief he derived from Krausism, and therefore the contradiction one sees here comes (as usual) from Martí's ideological source. Krausism stated that moral and material progress went hand in hand, which was palpably not true in a nation so familiar to Martí as the United States. Martí became increasingly aware of the evils of life in the United States, but did not really get to the root cause of these. What he perceived there was the predominance of evil over good, but he offered no remedy for the United States beyond pointing out that in that nation men did not love one another and that it had become too 'masculine' (i.e.

aggressive). Part of the problem, of course, was the sheer size and variety of that country. Cuba's difficulties appeared less daunting.

Martí came to believe the Cuba and Puerto Rico were test cases, both from the point of view of their future internal politics and foreign relations, for the triumph of the kind of 'dignified' freedom and democracy he espoused. They had to take their places amongst the free nations of America 'before the disproportionate development of the most powerful section of America turns into a theatre of universal greed the lands which may still be the garden of their inhabitants and, as it were, the fulcrum of the entire world'.[98]

> The Antilles are at the fulcrum of America, and they would be, if enslaved, a mere pontoon for the war fought by an imperial republic against the zealous and superior world which is preparing to deny it this power – a mere fort of the American Rome; and if free – and worthy of being so through the order of equitative and hard-working freedom – they would be on the continent the guarantee of balance, the guarantee of independence for Spanish America which is still threatened, and that of honour for the great Northern Republic, which in the development of its territory – unfortunately now feudal, and split into hostile sections – will find a greater certainty than in the ignoble conquest of its lesser neighbours, and in the inhuman battle in which the possession of them would be its opening shots against the power of the globe in the fight for world predominance (. . .). It is a whole world which we are balancing out: it is not just a question of liberating two islands. (. . .) An error in Cuba is an error in America, is an error in modern humanity. (. . .) the Cuban Revolutionary Party is convinced that the independence of Cuba and Puerto Rico is not just the only way of ensuring the decorous well-being of free man in the just toil of the inhabitants of both islands, but the historic event which is indispensable for the salvation of the threatened independence of the free Antilles, the threatened independence of free America, and the dignity of the North American republic.[99]

And just two months prior to his death, Martí reiterated this view, telling Federico Hernández de Carvajal, in a letter sent from Montecristi, in the Dominican Republic, that the 'free Antilles will save the independence of our America and the already doubtful and injured honour of English America, and perhaps accelerate and fix the balance of the world'.[100]

Postscript. The Final Years: A Resumé of Events

Martí spent the time between the founding of the Cuban Revolutionary Party in April 1892 and his death on 19 May 1895 organizing first of all the invasion of Cuba and then, once he had arrived in the island (11 April 1895), travelling in the bush as part of the politico-military expedition and debating with Gómez and Maceo as to the exact role he would play and the structures to be forged for the new Republic in Arms.

Before his definitive departure for Cuba via Haiti and the Dominican Republic, he journeyed to the various Cuban communities in the United States, and also to the Dominican Republic (to see Gómez), Haiti, Jamaica, Costa Rica (to see Maceo), and Mexico. He survived an attempt to poison him (and, typically, won his would-be assassins over to the cause), and dealt as best he could with the problems posed by certain premature uprisings, such as that of the Sartorius brothers, which were to the advantage of the enemy. He also managed to get the United States government to declare illegal the importation of blackleg labour from Cuba into Key West, after a strike by Cuban tobacco workers over the closing down of a factory.

In January 1895 the Party's first secret expeditionary plans were discovered, due to the negligence, or worse, of a Cuban collaborator. This failure, of the so-called Fernandina Plan, called after the Florida port from which one of the expeditions was to sail, paradoxically acted as a stimulus to the revolutionary cause, since it convinced many hitherto sceptical people that Martí and his comrades were in earnest.

Later on that same month, the revolutionary leaders inside Cuba gave the go-ahead for the uprising to begin, and Martí left New York for the Dominican Republic, where he joined Gómez. There, in Montecristi, the two men drew up and signed the *Montecristi Manifesto*, publicizing to the world the aims of the Revolution. Eventually, after many problems, Martí, Gómez and half a dozen others landed in Cuba (Playitas, Oriente). These experiences, and others which continued right up to Martí's death, are narrated in his *Campaign Diaries*, written in a cryptic prose quite unlike Martí's other forms of literary expression and conveying in a most moving way all the tensions accompanying a guerrilla army roaming about the bush.

Martí's joy at being once again in Cuba is made patent, but sometimes the Diaries make harrowing reading, as when Martí relates how one of their band was court-martialled and shot for robbery and rape, or when he gives his version of the acrimonious 5 May meeting with Maceo at La Mejorana. Martí, and, it seems, Gómez, insisted on an Assembly of Delegates being convoked as the nucleus of a future government. Maceo wanted the liberated zones to be ruled by a *junta* of generals, but was overruled and went off in a huff, although, as recorded, the dispute was later patched up. Later on, the Diaries register Gómez's irritation at Martí being greeted as President, when the Assembly had still not met, or even been convoked. Martí was still merely the Delegate of the Cuban Revolutionary Party – a position from which he intended to resign at the future Assembly in Camagüey – and (appointed by Gómez) a Major-General of the expeditionary forces. Gómez's objection to Martí being hailed prematurely as President of the free territories, interestingly enough in view of Martí's own beliefs in the 1880s that Gómez was hijacking the revolutionary movement as his own personal property, show a fear that the office – as had occurred in the Americas generally – would corrupt the man that held it. According to Martí's *Diaries*, Gómez talked about the need to respect the will of the people, in other words the democratic process. Martí's own position indicated that the military should have charge of the military operations, and the future Assembly hold sway over political planning. But there seems no doubt, in view of Martí's prestige, that eventually he would have reached the top executive post (whatever its name) of the future Republic in Arms.

In fact, Martí did not live to see the Assembly set up, since in a skirmish with Spanish troops at Dos Ríos (Oriente) on 19 May 1895 he rode to the front line in disregard of Gómez's orders and was struck down and killed by three bullets. Lovers of curious coincidence will take note of that date, for on that very day Augusto César Sandino, the great Nicaraguan anti-imperialist fighter, came into the world. Those who believe in metempsychosis or the transmigration of souls, as did Sandino himself, will no doubt see more than chance in the coincidence of two such transcendental events for Latin America. Martí himself had his mystical side, although Sandino's involvement in such beliefs went rather deeper. It does not appear likely, however, that twentieth century historians will pay much attention to such Pythagorean observations, and the present writer merely wishes to register the phenomenon as a closing touch to this chapter.

Notes

1. *El presidio político en Cuba*, Madrid 1871, *Obras Completas*, Havana, Editora Nacional de Cuba, 1963–5, 27 vols., vol. 1, p. 48. The translation into English in this and all subsequent cases, is by P. Turton.
2. *La República española ante la Revolución cubana*, *OC*, 1, pp. 93–4.
3. Letter to Emilio Núñez, 13 October 1880, *OC*, 1, p. 162.
4. Letter to Máximo Gómez, 20 July 1882, *OC*, 1, p. 168.
5. Ibid., pp. 169–70.
6. Notebook corresponding to 1881, *OC*, 21, p. 166.
7. Letter to Antonio Maceo, 20 July 1882, *OC*, 1, p. 172.
8. Ibid., p. 173.
9. Letter to Máximo Gómez, 20 October 1884, *OC*, 1, pp. 177–8.
10. Letter to Enrique Trujillo, 6 July 1885, *OC*, 1, pp. 181–2.
11. Ibid., p. 182.
12. Letter to Ricardo Rodríguez Otero, 16 May 1886, *OC*, 1, p. 194.
13. Ibid., pp. 195–6.
14. Letter to José Dolores Poyo, 29 November 1887, *OC*, 1, p. 212.
15. Letter to Máximo Gómez, 16 December 1887, *OC*, 1, p. 217.
16. Ibid., p. 221.
17. Letter to Manuel Mercado, 19 February 1888, *OC*, 20, p. 124.
18. Letter to Enrique Estrázulas, 15 February 1889, *OC*, 20, p. 203.
19. Letter to the Director of the *New York Evening Post*, 25 March 1889, *OC*, 1, pp. 236–7.

20. Speech in commemoration of 10 October 1868, Hardman Hall, New York, 10 October 1889, *OC*, 4, pp. 243–4.

21. Letter to Gonzalo de Quesada y Aróstegui, 29 October 1889, *OC*, 1, p. 249.

22. Ibid., p. 251.

23. Ibid.

24. Letter to Serafín Bello, 16 November 1889, *OC*, 1, pp. 253–4.

25. Ibid., p. 254.

26. Letter to Juan Bonilla, 8 August 1890, *OC*, 1, p. 261.

27. Speech in commemoration of 10 October 1868, New York, 10 October 1890, *OC*, 4, pp. 247–9.

28. Ibid., p. 251.

29. Ibid., p. 252.

30. Ibid.

31. Ibid., p. 253.

32. 'Darwin ha muerto', in *La Opinión Nacional*, Caracas, July 1882, *OC*, 15, p. 373.

33. Speech in commemoration of 10 October 1868, New York, 10 October 1890, *OC*, 4, p. 253.

34. Ibid., p. 254.

35. Ibid.

36. Ibid., p. 255.

37. Speech known as 'Con todos y para el bien de todos', given in Tampa, 26 November 1891, *OC*, 4, p. 270.

38. Ibid.

39. Ibid.

40. Ibid., p. 271.

41. Ibid.

42. Ibid., p. 273.

43. Ibid., p. 275.

44. Ibid.

45. Ibid., pp. 275–6.

46. Ibid., p. 276.

47. Speech known as 'Los pinos nuevos', Tampa, 27 November 1891, *OC*, 4, p. 286.

48. *OC*, 1, pp. 271–2.

49. Letter to José Dolores Poyo, 5 December 1891, *OC*, 1, p. 275.

50. *OC*, 1, pp. 279–80.

51. Speech made in Hardman Hall, New York, 17 February 1892, *OC*, 4, p. 302.

52. 'Nuestras ideas' in *Patria*, 14 March 1892, *OC*, 1, p. 320.

53. Ibid., p. 321.

54. Ibid., p. 320.

55. 'El Partido Revolucionario a Cuba' in *Patria*, 27 May 1893, *OC*, 2, p. 343.

56. Letter to *El Diario de la Marina*, 10 November 1894, *OC*, 3, p. 360.

57. Letter to the *New York Herald*, 2 May 1895, *OC*, 4, pp. 152–3. See also Jorge Ibarra, *José Martí, dirigente político e ideólogo revolucionario*, Habana, Editorial de Ciencias Sociales, 1980, pp. 245–7.

58. 'La agitación autonomista' in *Patria*, 19 March 1892, *OC*, 1, p. 332.

59. 'El lenguaje reciente de ciertos autonomistas' in *Patria*, 22 September 1894, *OC*, 3, p. 264.

60. 'Las reformas en Cuba' in *Patria*, 8 December 1894, *OC*, 3, p. 426.

61. Letter to Manuel Mercado, 18 May 1895, *OC*, 4, p. 168.

62. See 'El remedio anexionista' in *Patria*, 2 July 1892, *OC*, 2, p. 48.

63. 'El Congreso Internacional de Washington', dated 2 November 1889, published in *La Nación*, Buenos Aires, 19 December 1889, *OC*, 6, p. 48.

64. 'La conferencia monetaria de las repúblicas de América' in *La Revista Illustrada*, New York, May 1891, *OC*, 6, p. 160.

65. 'Carácter' in *Patria*, 30 July 1892, *OC*, 2, pp. 76–7.

66. 'La crisis y el Partido Revolucionario Cubano' in *Patria*, 19 August 1893, *OC*, 2, pp. 367–8.

67. 'A la raíz' in *Patria*, 26 August 1893, *OC*, 2, pp. 378–9.

68. 'Cosas nuevas' in *Patria*, 10 April 1893, *OC*, 3, p. 290.

69. Letter to the *New York Herald*, 2 May 1895, *OC*, 4, pp. 152–6.

70. Ibid., p. 160.

71. Letter to Manuel Mercado, 18 May 1895, *OC*, 4, pp. 167–8.

72. Ibid., p. 168.

73. 'Persona y patria' in *Patria*, 11 April 1893, *Oc*, 2, pp. 278–9.

74. *Montecristi Manifesto*, Montecristi, 25 March 1895, *OC*, 4, p. 94.

75. Ibid., p. 95.

76. Ibid.

77. Ibid.

78. Ibid., p. 99.

79. 'El Partido Revolucionario a Cuba' in *Patria*, 27 May 1893, *OC*, 2, p. 342.

80. 'Las elecciones del 10 de abril' in *Patria*, 16 April 1893, *OC*, 2, p. 296.

81. Ibid., pp. 296–7.

82. 'El Partido Revolucionario a Cuba' in *Patria*, 27 May 1893, *OC*, 2, p. 345.

83. 'La asamblea económica' in *Patria*, 26 March 1892, *OC*, 1, p. 357.

84. 'La confirmación del Partido Revolucionario Cubano' in *Patria*, 23 April 1892, *OC*, 1, p. 413.

85. 'Los Clubs' in *Patria*, 11 June 1892, *OC*, 2, p. 17. It is interesting to contrast Martí's democratic notions with the ideas of the present Polish 'Solidarity' union leader, the Catholic Lech Walesa, trumpeted by the capitalist press as a force for democracy. Walesa, who boasted once of never having read a book, also is reputed to have said that in any herd of goats there is always a leading billy-goat, and that he, Walesa, was the billy-goat of the Polish working class.

86. *OC*, 22, pp. 108–9.

87. Ibarra, op. cit., pp. 218–9.

88. 'Pobres y ricos' in *Patria*, 14 March 1893, *OC*, 2, p. 251.

89. 'Vengo a darte patria!' in *Patria*, 14 March 1893, *OC*, 2, p. 255.

90. 'Cuatro clubs nuevos' in *Patria*, 14 January 1893, *OC*, 2, p. 196. Martí is supposed to have said to Carlos Baliño, one of the future founders (in 1925) of the Cuban Communist Party, 'Revolution? The revolution is not the one we are going to start in the bush, but the one we are going to carry out in the Republic.' In *Mella. Documentos y artículos*, Habana, Editorial de Ciencias Sociales, 1975, p. 269, quoted in the *Anuario del Centro de Estudios Martianos*, Habana, 1980, no. 3, p. 97, by José Cantón Navarro.

91. Letter to José Dolores Poyo, 20 December 1893, *OC*, 2, p. 463.

92. Letter to Alejandro Gómez, 30 December 1893, *OC*, 2, p. 476.

93. 'El obrero cubano' in *Patria*, 2 July 1892, *OC*, 2, p. 52.

94. Ibid., p. 52.

95. 'El Partido Revolucionario a Cuba' in *Patria*, 27 May 1893, *OC*, 2, p. 346.

96. 'El tercer año del Partido Revolucionario Cubano' in *Patria*, 17 April 1894, *OC*, 3, pp. 139–40.

97. Ibid., pp. 141–2.

98. Ibid., p. 139.

99. Ibid., pp. 142–3.

100. Letter to Frederico Henríquez de Carvajal, 25 March 1895, *OC*, 4, p. 111.

2: Martí and Latin America

> I struggled in my homeland and was defeated. It is common knowledge that in the poem of 1810 there is a stanza missing, and I, when its real poets had disappeared, wanted to write it. (Martí, 1881)

The driving passion behind Martí's life was the liberation of Cuba from Spanish colonial rule. This issue was inevitably linked to the wider question of the destiny of Latin America as a whole and, within this question, to the relationship between what Martí called 'our America' and the United States. Martí's thinking on Latin America was to develop considerably over the mature years of his short life, mainly as a response to his own direct experience of Mexico, Guatemala, Venezuela and the United States, in all of which he lived and worked. The last third of Martí's life, previous to his death on a Cuban battlefield at the age of 42, in May 1895, was spent in the 'colossus of the North' at a time when industrial overproduction was forcing that country into increasingly aggressive policies towards its southern neighbours for the purpose of securing new markets. From the mid-1880s onwards (1886–87 are the key years) Martí became increasingly alarmed at this threat to Latin America, and one sees a considerable radicalization in his thinking henceforth.

Yet already at the age of 18, having been deported to Spain, he was extending his diatribes against imperialism to encompass that of the United States. Thus at the same time he was publishing his indictment of Spanish brutality in Cuba (*Political Imprisonment in Cuba*, 1871), he was writing in his (then unpublished) notebooks that the United States could become a new Rome (i.e. the heartless and greedy imperial power which Simón Bolívar, following Montesquieu, saw as the inevitable destiny of large republics). In which case Martí prophesied an equally inevitable decline, mirroring that of imperial Spain, whose domains were then mere tatters of their past. And already, in these notebooks, Martí is postulating the United States/Latin America dichotomy that was to become the cornerstone of his mature thought on the destiny of the Americas:

The North Americans put feeling after practicalilty. – We put practicality after feeling.

And if there is this difference in organization, in living, in being, if they were busy selling while we were weeping, if we replace their cold and calculating heads by our imaginative heads, and their hearts of cotton and ships by such a special, sensitive and new heart that it can only be called a Cuban heart, how do you want us to be governed by the laws that they use for governing themselves?

Let us imitate them. No! – Let us copy them. No! (. . .) Our lives are not like theirs, nor should we be so in so many matters. We feel very strongly about things. Our intelligence is less positive, our customs are purer, so how are we to govern two different peoples with the same laws?

The American laws have given the North a high degree of prosperity, and have also raised it to the highest degree of corruption. They have made money the chief good so as to create prosperity. Cursed be prosperity at such a cost!

And if the general state of enlightenment in the United States appeals to you, in spite of the corruption, and their cold quest for money, may we not aspire to the enlightenment without the corruption?[1]

It is true that here Martí is referring specifically to Cuba, but subsequent writings, as we shall see, make it quite clear that these ideas on Cuba extend to Latin America as a whole.

This idealist dualism is typical of Martí's thought processes, but a similar tendency may be discerned in other Latin American progressives of the era in their attempts to explain the relative poverty and backwardness of their part of the continent in relation to the North. One such intellectual is the Uruguayan José Enrique Rodó, whose *Ariel* (1900) likewise accused the United States of sacrificing spiritual values on the altar of material riches. One feels, on reading Martí and Rodó, that at the back of their minds is the belief that somehow poverty is a proof of inherent virtue, which has refused to countenance 'corruption', at least on the scale demanded by the wealth-creating forces unleashed in the North. However, both Martí and Rodó desired to achieve a comparable standard of living for their part of America and were prepared to accept at least for the time being the formal structures of life in the United States' democracy. There is no question of their opposing 'progress' in this sense. The problem for them becomes therefore (and this they never resolve) how to retain 'virtue' and 'spiritual values' in the teeth of the capitalist whirlwind whose positive results they desire but whose evils they abhor.

Martí does, it is true, in his later writings, attempt some more materialist approach to the North/Latin America dichotomy he perceives, by delving into the history of the Americas and their different colonizers, but he really lacked the ideological tools (and perhaps the time) for getting to the bottom of the problem.

And yet when it is a question of practical politics, Martí comes into his own. Whether in the organization (and indeed the conception) of the democratic Cuban Revolutionary Party, in which he displayed tireless zeal and unbending principle in the face of humiliations, jealousies and suspicion (which he had to endure from certain of his compatriots) or when neutralizing the constant espionage of the Spanish authorities, or in the doggedness he showed in the accident-prone preparations for the final expedition to Cuba (1895) or, most important of all, in his increasingly bitter fight against the rapacity of the United States, Martí can hardly be faulted. Martí's outstanding worth lies more in his qualities as a revolutionary organizer than in his contributions to political theory. In this (as in so many other ways) he appears as the true political forefather of Fidel Castro.

What I hope to show in this chapter is the evolution of Martí's thinking on Latin America, which I see as primarily a series of responses to particular situations that affected Martí and his cause. These responses are coloured, in turn, by the peculiar philosophical prism through which he viewed the world. Very little attention has been paid to this question, which has to be understood when interpreting Martí, quotations from whom have been selected to serve the most varied causes. Martí's whole opus (and therefore the sense of what he is saying) should of necessity be considered in this light, otherwise Martí's thinking may be taken as more eclectic than it really was. The fact is that he was greatly influenced by a form of neo-Kantian idealist thought prevalent among liberal intellectuals in Spain when Martí was a university student there in the early 1870s. This was the Spanish adaptation of the ideas of the German Karl Krause: Krausism or 'harmonic rationalism'. (See the appendix.)

Mexico

By the time Martí arrived in Mexico, where he was to live for two years (1875–76), he was quite convinced that only the inhabitants of the American continent had sufficient knowledge of and sympathy for the New World to produce viable institutions for the latter. Europe, especially Spain, had little to offer. Martí had experienced in an extreme form the full force of Spanish despotism, having at the tender age of seventeen done forced labour in the Havana quarries of San Lázaro, for a very minor offence. Subsequently, during his exile in the metropolis (1871–74), he had acquired first-hand knowledge of Spain itself, which he saw to be archaic, ramshackle, corrupt and turbulent. Even the relatively enlightened first Spanish Republic of 1873, which he broadly supported, refused to relinquish its Cuban colony.

It was with relief and great optimism, therefore, that Martí, on finishing his university studies in Spain and after the restoration of the monarchy there, settled in Mexico, which he saw as a political example for the rest of Latin America. Mexico had a parliamentary democratic system in which the government was in the hands of the Liberal Party led by President Sebastián Lerdo de Tejada, heir to the mantle of the great Benito Juárez, the leader of the Mexican Reform movement and conqueror of the French occupation forces of the 1860s. Lerdo was continuing the progressive, anti-feudal and anti-clerical policies of Juárez enshrined in the restored 1857 Constitution, and Martí described him as a 'lofty democratic intelligence' watching over the 'democracy in action' embodied in the debates of the Mexican parliament, on which Martí reported as a journalist. Even when Lerdo was forced to suspend the Constitution (temporarily, and because of the threat of a military coup), Martí approved of the measure, stating that democracy in Mexico was basically sound and that from time to time such measures were required to enable it to overcome its teething troubles.

The very reason for Martí's eventual departure from Mexico, where he felt very much at home and had influential friends, was a successful military coup, that of Porfirio Díaz in November 1876. Díaz set himself up as a dictator behind a parody of the previous parliamentary Liberal regime for more than thirty years (outliving Martí), and Martí, who had worked for the *Revista Universal*, the prestigious newspaper of the Lerdo government, felt obliged to leave. His later experiences in Guatemala and Venezuela, with similar disguised dictatorships headed by presidents of Liberal affiliation but military origin, were to bring to bloom in Martí's mind the seeds of bitterness first sown in Mexico against the Latin American military *caudillo*. Martí's break in 1884 with Máximo Gómez came mainly because of Martí's conviction that Gómez had similar designs on Cuba.

However, before the Díaz coup, Martí gained valuable experience in Mexico on the problems facing a democratic regime in Latin America. The main areas of his political interest in Mexico centred around the workings and maintenance of democracy in the face of the unruly habits of a politically (and generally) uneducated population, the economy of an underdeveloped Latin American nation, and the evil influence of the Catholic church.

In Martí's Mexican writings re-emerges the old Latin America/ United States polarity. Although Washington, Bolívar and Hidalgo were all Americans, says Martí, the nature of the areas they liberated was very dissimilar. He sees Latin America as characterized by turbulence, passion and vehemence, and a greater heterogeneity than that of the United States. It has inherited negative socio-political habits through the lack of 'culture' of the mother race (i.e. the Indians) and the autocratic practices of the 'western race' (or people of Spanish descent), which displays 'mortal habits of lordliness and laziness'. He finds Mexican (white) upper-class youth unpleasant, frivolous and 'literary' (Martí's word for impractical), whilst the young people of the lower classes have been forced into servility. There is tremendous potential intelligence in Mexico, but the work habit has yet to be inculcated and a system found to make the nation advance materially and politically.

On the other hand, there is no danger of Mexico dying 'the terrible death that oblivion to feeling prepares for other countries [the United States?]: gold will not weigh so heavily on us as to suffocate our heart-beats under its load.'[2] In a later article Martí ventures a new opposition: 'If Europe could be considered as the brain, our America would be the heart. Others will think more, but none will feel as deeply as we.'[3]

Broadly speaking, the future is bright for Latin America: 'The new continent has not yet had time to become corrupt';[4] 'The peoples that inhabit our continent, the peoples in whom the intelligent weaknesses of the Latin races have intermingled with the brilliant vitality of the American [Indian] race, think in a more enlightened way, and feel with greater love'.[5] A true Romantic, Martí believed that intelligence divorced from feeling was valueless, and even pernicious.

The Indians, though sometimes repugnant because of servility and ignorance, really only require education and opportunity to make an important contribution to society: 'From those copper faces a new light will pour forth. Education will reveal them to themselves, and the special knowledge they possess will be applicable by all.'[6] Behind this statement about self-relevation lies the idea that all men are (somehow) equal in essence, and therefore equally 'redeemable' (a favourite Martían concept inherited from Christianity through Kant and Krause).

It was in Mexico that Martí started to formulate his ideas on economic matters. He wanted to see in Mexico general industrial development, disliking the old colonial hangover of great reliance on mining, because wealth derived from this source was 'unsure and shaky' (competition from abroad was already driving down the price of Mexican silver). In any case, the profits from mining only benefitted a tiny minority, and mining did not create industrious habits.

Martí's economic solution for Mexico is basic reliance on agriculture, which, although disorganized and inefficient, nevertheless had great potential due to natural advantages. The following extensive quotation has been chosen because it also serves to illustrate the kind of logic usual in Martí, in which a general principle is first stated, and then a process of modification of this principle takes place, necessarily so if it is to apply to the real world.

> The only constant source of wealth for a country lies in balancing its agricultural production with its consumption. (. . .) Even if industry is slothful, the land will produce enough. Even if trade through the ports falls off, the land will continue to bear its fruits. This is the certain harmony. This is sensible foresight, because it is founded on an unshakeable balance (. . .). Economics lays down freedom of movement as its principle; but each country creates its own special Economics. This science is only the sum total of solutions to different conflicts between labour and wealth. It has no immortal laws. Its laws must be, and are, reformable in essence. Capital and labour have a special history in each country. Certain disturbances between

the two are peculiar to each country, and have their own exclusive features, differing from those that arise from different causes in foreign lands. The historical processes of one country require solutions appropriate to that country. Our life must be regulated by our own laws. The Mexican economist must not tie himself to a rule which may even be doubted in its own country of origin. Here a life is being created. Let an economic system also be created.[7]

In a later article, he amplifies these ideas, saying:

Servile imitation leads one astray in Economics, as in literature and politics. A principle must be sound in Mexico because it was successfully applied in France. This is sometimes stated, without there being a realization that it leads to an eloquent question. Is Mexico's financial system the same as that of France? Are the same things produced? Are the two countries in the same industrial conditions?

In the application of an economic principle one should work on the basis of the differential existing between these two countries.

It is the same with the United States, England and Germany.[8]

What is interesting here is not Martí's economic nationalism in itself but the way it is part and parcel of his general *a priori* neo-Kantian (Krausist) conception of the universe as a conjunction of particularities, even discordances, all equally valuable and which together make up the general harmony or 'balance' (two more key concepts in his thinking). Martí thinks as a premise that natural entities must be allowed their own growth. This is the basis of his liberalism, and also of his anti-imperialism, since for him nations are just as much natural entities as individual human beings. (At times one has the impression he thinks they are more so.) It leads him, likewise, to have no truck whatsoever with racism, unlike most of his intellectual contemporaries, including Latin Americans such as Domingo Faustino Sarmiento and Euclides da Cunha. Unfortunately (because it deprives him of a valuable intellectual tool), it also sets him against the concept of class struggle, as we can see in his strictures on Marx.

Fitting these ideas into the context of the real world and the hurly-burly of politics often proved a distressing ordeal for Martí, and this is reflected in the frequent bitter references to the world of men in his later writings. On the other hand, this philosophy of harmony, balance and eventual universal brotherhood explains Martí's great enthusiasm for North American intellectuals such as Emerson and Whitman (although he may have overlooked the latter's Yankeeism), since American Transcendentalism, like Krausism, had its roots in German idealism. Thoreau, on the other hand, was admired but also found 'austere' and too much of a hermit by a man engaged in gathering together Cubans of all classes and races for the purpose of knitting them together into a nation. The problem with Martí's world-view was its essential (neo-Platonic) dualism. Or, to express the dilemma in Kantian terms, the difficulty in reconciling the world of *phenomena* with the 'real' sphere of *noumena*. Martí's later utterances show an anguished longing to be out of the sub-lunar territory of strife and into the bosom of ultimate harmony.

To return to Mexico, Martí reveals himself, at this stage of his life, to be a true political liberal in his ideas about the relationship of the individual to government. He believes, and he continued to believe, as his articles on Herbert Spencer in 1884 were to prove, that government intervention in society should be kept to a minimum. About Mexico he remarks:

> Government guides and sets society on the right path; but it neither creates anything nor awakens drowsy aptitudes. It mediates in conflicts between existing elements. But for it to do so, something has to exist first. It lays down rules, but for this to happen, it is necessary that there be something to be directed and regulated. It contains and manages forces, but it cannot make them emerge from a wayward and lazy people.[9]

Or, as a corollary, 'One is not born to enjoy the products of others. One has the obligation to create one's own'.[10] These Spencerian musings, however, never led Martí to accept what he saw as Spencer's heartless disregard for the sufferings of the needy.

One of the most pressing problems in Mexico was, for Martí, the lack of its citizens' individual initiative. They expected too much from the government. Martí here seems to see the good society as a nation of hardworking property owners where there are no great extremes of wealth and poverty. Wealth corrupted (usually), whilst poverty degraded man. Better was a more balanced distribution of income.

Another feature of Martí's nineteenth-century Hispanic liberalism was his anti-clericalism. Like many progressive Spanish-speaking people of the time, he joined a Masonic lodge (in Spain), called, appropriately enough *La Armonía*. He had nothing against religious beliefs or even organized religion, as long as there was no interference in politics and only the private individual conscience was concerned. Religious beliefs were seen by the Krausists (and Martí) as connatural with humanity, but dogma merely corresponded to certain stages along man's road toward the univeral religion of man. In Mexico (as in Spain), and despite the restoration of the anti-clerical Constitution of 1857 together with the public disgrace which the Mexican Catholic Church had brought upon itself for siding with the forces of Napoleon III in the French occupation, the Church was strong and extremely intolerant. Its influence was even felt on the Liberal Mexican state.

Martí attacked the hypocrisy of Catholics who had deliberately avoided condemning certain atrocities committed by pro-clerical bandits, who had set fire to the town of Apatzingan 'for the greater glory and honour of the most humble cause of God', in Martí's sarcastic words.[11] He also took issue with a state governor who was seen publicly to set up a

Catholic chapel and attend public Catholic religious ceremonies in his official capacity as a functionary of the Mexican state, thus flaunting the Constitution of 1857, that 'temperate, moderate and just code' which laid down the rule that, as Martí puts it, 'the state may not have religious principles, because it may not impose on the consciences of its members'. As a private individual, the governor might believe in any creed of his choice, but 'because of the domination and desire of the Catholic doctrine to absorb everything', he had been led to violate his public responsibilities.[12]

Whilst in Mexico Martí reviewed a book by an Argentinian writer, Luis Varela, entitled *Practical Democracy*. His comments reveal a set of basic (optimistic) beliefs about the future of Latin America, and he makes several points that were to be amplified some fifteen years later in the great article called 'Our America' likewise written for a Mexican newspaper (*El Partido Liberal*, in its number of 30 January 1891), and which is Martí's definitive statement on the question. Latin America, writes Martí in March 1876, is emerging from 'defeat' and 'martyrdom' into an understanding of itself:

> And that is the law of things: in the formation of peoples, war is the beginning, tyranny is the continuation, revolution is the seedbed, and peace the consolidation. It is never perfect, but gradually moves towards perfection. (. . .) America, that fierce giant (. . .) is gradually tearing off her garments, is freeing herself from those residues that can never fuse together, is shaking off the moral oppression that different dominations have left on her, is redeeming herself from her confusion and from servility to imported doctrines, and is living a life of her own, and at times hesitantly, then firmly, always in the face of attack, hindrance and envy, is finding her path towards herself, is creating original institutions for herself, is reforming and accommodating foreign ones, is subordinating her heart to her brain, and, counting her wounds, is calculating (. . .) the way of exercising liberty. (. . .)
>
> The American democrat, although one in spirit, must be different from the European democrat. Beauty is one, but multiple are the ways of bringing it into being. Freedom is one, but different are the ways of consolidating it. (. . .) Because we are men, we carry into life the principle of freedom; and because we are intelligent, we have the duty to bring it about. A person is liberal, because he is a man; but it is necessary to study, to create much in the art of application, in order to be an American liberal. (. . .) People have given much thought to the inconveniences in the formation of an American system, to its absolute necessity, to the special character of our lands which demands of us special forms. The uncut stone becomes a gem after hard blows: thus a people comes to a prosperous life after the buffetings of revolution.[13]

Again one notices the Platonic dualism of Martí's thinking. The ideal exists everywhere in potential, but the ways of bringing it into the visible world (or of uncovering this essence by a process of redemption) vary according to the avatars of time and space. The problem here is, in the process of adapting the ideal to the world, that one may be led into pragmatism, the very opposite of the Platonic starting-point, and throw the baby out with the bathwater.

Be that as it may, Martí was forced to witness the Porfirio Díaz coup d'état which put an end, some seven months later, to Mexico's promising democracy. Martí ascribed this coup to the selfishness of an ambitious political faction, seeing the issue, typically, in rather moralistic terms. He was forced to leave Mexico, because, he writes, one man had raised himself up over 'the great multiple will of all men', adding 'my ungovernable will sees itself governed by one haughty will; my most free spirit feels all rights to free movement constrained; the blood of my soul ceases to flow, obstructed in its course by the complacent smile of a fortunate and victorious man on horseback'.[14]

Guatemala

After a short stay semi-incognito in Havana, under the name Julián Pérez, in fact his second Christian name and his mother's maiden name, Martí made his way to Guatemala armed with letters of introduction to the President himself, Justo Rufino Barrios, from the family of Martí's closest friend Fermín Valdés Domínguez. He was to live in Guatemala from March 1877 until July 1878, leaving in disgust at the despotic methods of its Liberal President, likewise another disguised dictator.

On arrival, however, Martí's hopes were high. He was granted a prestigious teaching post at the Escuela Normal Central in Guatemala City, and soon became known in university and political circles. He appeared full of optimism about the country, and praised its government for its seemingly progressive nature. Much was being done, for example, to reform the education system, the legal code was being overhauled, and the nation was being developed economically. Moreover President Barrios had actually recognized the insurgent Cuban Government in Arms (in 1875).

In April 1877 Martí wrote to the Guatemalan Foreign Minister Joaquín Macal: 'I arrive in Guatemala and I find her robust and prosperous', adding that from principle he would not interfere in the internal politics of the nation. 'There is a great universal political system, and that is mine, and I shall work for it: that of the new doctrines'.[15] He meant the principles of radical Liberalism.

Macal had sent Martí a copy of the new Legal Code, and Martí, a lawyer himself, found it in harmony with the times:

> In this illustrious age every man has his own creed. And, when monarchy is extinguished, a whole universe of monarchs comes into being. A day which is far off, but certain. (. . .) In free peoples, laws must be clear. In peoples that are master of themselves, laws must emanate from the people.

Guatemala, since 1821, has not produced anything so great as this. At last Independence has found its structure. At last the new spirit has been made flesh in the Law. At last the people are what they wanted to be. At last we are Americans in America, the Republic is living in a republican way, and after fifty years of sweeping away ruins, over these are being laid the foundations of an energetic and glorious nationality.[16]

However, in a letter to his Mexican friend Manuel Mercado, only eight days later, one detects a note of concern at the backwardness of Guatemala:

I come full of love to this land and these people; and if I do not brim over with my love for them, it is because I do not want them to think me servile and flattering. These are my climes and my peoples. If there are not many developed minds, I have come to stimulate them, not to put them to shame or to wound them. I do not like to hear strangers say (. . .) that our sick America is lacking in the ardent intelligences that it has in plenty. – Here, as in Mexico, everybody has talent; Spanish is well spoken; people live honest lives (. . .) by and large people love what is new (. . .). It is not that Guatemala is small, or has a sparse population: rather it is that it is a people that has not bestirred itself much (. . .) it has no literary circles, nor is it used to the higher things of life, – although it has enthusiasm and desire for all these, – it has no newspapers (. . .) the Arts have no temple, or priests or believers. Everything has been swallowed up by dogma.[17]

Martí had plans for bringing out a 'Guatemalan Review', to introduce Guatemala to the world and also open up the nation to 'useful inventions, energetic books, pleasing publications, industrial machinery', all that which 'the Old World, and the northern part of the New, are giving birth to'. He also speaks, in his prospectus for the magazine, which was never to see the light of day, rather wistfully of the advanced societies, 'where the activity of so many men, the eloquence of so many learned people, [and] the vivacity of so many works are bubbling over', 'all that startling machinery which in North America saves so much labour and gives wings to toil, a marvel of precision and speed'. Guatemala also needed useful immigrants:

Our bowels are made of gold; our arms must be made of iron. Let people know that we are worth something, let those who know this come. Let intelligent labour apply itself to the docile and rich earth (. . .) a land which is fertile and impatient, rich in intelligences, beauty and products (. . .) this totality of incorrect and volatile conceptions in American brains, brains of heroes and madmen, of children and giants all at once. America must be everywhere, it must not be merely a miserly hope of making profits, but a loving reply to the laborious request of men of all races and countries.[18]

As in the case of Mexico, Martí thought that the basis for economic progress in Guatemala should be agriculture, and for the same reasons.

As time went on, Martí's optimism became more and more shaken. Only six months after his arrival in Guatemala, he was writing to Manuel Mercado of 'the absolute lack of greatness, energy and liberties, which, by sullying the character of others, displeases and offends my own'.[19] A month or so later (in November 1877) there was an attempt on President Barrios' life, and although Martí, along with his colleagues and students at the Escuela Normal signed a letter of support for Barrios, at the same time he was complaining bitterly in private about the repression unleashed by the latter following the attempt. 'Certain attacks are only plotted against those who have done something to deserve them', he informed Mercado, adding, most significantly in view of his Mexican disappointments and future clashes with the military ethos: 'You and I have already decided that power in Republics should only be in the hands of civilians. Sabres cut people. – Frock coats can hardly make whips out of their short tails'.[20]

By April 1878 Martí was warning Mercado against saying too much in his letters about the Guatemalan situation. He had become increasingly disgusted at the petty squabbles and xenophobia prevalent in both political and academic circles there. He himself had been attacked by both Liberals and Conservatives. An enlightened man, he wrote, cannot live under tyrants. 'My voice, my principles, my honesty, and my conviction (. . .) that a person can live in a country, teaching and thinking, without sullying his soul and perverting his character by paying ignoble court to a lumpish boor, were all causing offence', he remarked acidly.[21]

The last straw had been when the Cuban head of the Escuela Normal, José María Izaguirre, who was friendly to Martí, was summarily dismissed by the 'lumpish boor' himself: President Barrios. Martí resigned his own post in protest, that same April. Three months later, just before leaving Guatemala, Martí poured out his soul to Mercado with a vengeance:

Imagine what the French call an *égout* [sewer]: you will then have an idea of the men and things that are in charge here. The ones that have the same beliefs as the government (. . .) are lackeys; the ones that would like to bite the hand that deals them blows, more than kiss it, lick it. Any common truth is an act of daring; any elementary democratic institution is demagogical propaganda. (. . .) This place has been turned, with even greater speed since November, into a large country estate, where everything jumps to the whip of a capricious overseer.[22]

Martí's departure meant he had to give up his plans for educating the Indians, which consisted of bringing out what he conceived as the innate features of the race: artistry, patience, gentleness and originality, and fusing these characteristics with the few positive elements bequeathed to Guatemala in its Spanish psychological heritage: energy, pride, courage and stubbornness, in order to overcome the result of three centuries of colonial 'darkness' and 'poison', with the aid of modern European and North American ideas and technology.

Martí is a curious mixture of philosophical idealism and its declared enemy in the nineteenth century, positivism. Although calling constantly for thorough empirical investigations of society, in the style of the positivists Comte and Spencer (very influential in Latin America in the second half of the nineteenth century), Martí nevertheless could not stomach their crudely reactionary ideas on race. But he coincides with them in ascribing innate characteristics to the various racial types. We also see this in his North American writings. He does not see 'inferior' and 'superior' races, as do the positivists and social-Darwinists, only different ones. The *patria* or homeland (which every human being needed to fulfil himself) would be that place where major differences (of all kinds, social and economic as well as racial) would be overcome by a kind of alchemy whose catalyst was love. The problem was that in societies where this principle was not applied (through the despotism of rulers, as in Guatemala, or the selfishness of particular social groups), Martí found himself ill at ease, and eventually left.

For Martí the Spanish heritage in the Americas was basically corrupting, although (see above) it did have some positive features. He believed that the history of the area had been brutally interrupted by the Conquest, and that Spain was responsible in the main for its petty divisions and general backwardness. Before Spanish America could 'recover' its freedom it had to solve the problem of disunity. This idea was not new, since it predated Independence, yet it seems to have been so for Martí, since he remarked: 'For the first time I feel the need to tie up all the peoples of America inside one separate enclosure'.[23] Here, apparently, only Spanish America is meant, though this is not clear. At least at this juncture what he was to see as the *irrevocable* contradiction of nature and interests between the North and Spanish America had not yet come to fruition in his mind, although, as we have seen, the seeds of this feeling had already been planted there.

Before his definitive departure from Guatemala, Martí had married. In December 1877 he espoused a Cuban woman of prosperous family, Carmen Zayas Bazán, in Mexico City. A son, José Francisco, was born, in November the following year, two months after Martí's return to Cuba. However, the marriage was unhappy because Carmen objected to her husband's fervent political interests, and the couple eventually separated. Martí was again deported to Spain (in September 1879), this time for his conspiratorial anti-Spanish activities, which he rather unwisely combined with vociferous public declarations in the same vein. After two months in Spain and a brief sojourn in France he reached New York, on 3 January 1880.

Interlude in the United States

As President of the New York Cuban Revolutionary Committee, Martí was involved with winning support for Calixto García's 1880 expedition to Cuba in the context of the so-called *Guerra Chiquita* or Little War, which failed. Martí's public writings and speeches of this time contain many favourable references to the United States. In a journal called *The Hour* he wrote that in the United States 'everybody looks like his own master. One can breathe freely, freedom being here the foundation, the shield, the essence of life. One can be proud of the species here. Every one works, every one reads'.[24] This article, written in English, was one of several aimed at the North American reader, at a time when Martí was practically destitute. These circumstances naturally influenced the tone of these writings, and moreover, after Spain, the United States was bound to appear in a favourable light. However, one must never forget Martí's previously expressed reservations about the latter nation.

Three weeks after landing in New York, in a speech made to Cuban emigrés in Steck Hall, Martí defended Latin America from its detractors in the United States, sketching a comparative historical analysis of the two Americas:

> And let it be said in passing, from this land where the conquerors arrived on their knees and got up from praying to set their hands to the plough. Let it be said from this land of Puritan origins, in order to excuse the sins of which the peoples of Latin America have been unjustly accused, that the monsters that sully the waters are the ones that must explain their muddied waves, and not the thirsty wretch who drinks from them, because the sins of the slave fall totally and exclusively on the master. It is not the same thing to open up the earth with the tip of the lance as with the tip of the plough.[25]

The guilt for Latin America's problems lies, therefore, with the Spanish wolf, and not with the Latin American lamb, if one is to accept Martí's Aesopian allusion. And yet, from the midst of the lambs had emerged a Simón Bolívar, 'greater than Caesar because he was the Caesar of liberty'.[26]

Later on in that year 1880 there is evidence that Martí had already begun to find his impoverished life in New York depressing, especially after the crushing of the Cuban insurgents. Already Martí was expressing in his articles the old idea that North America lacked sufficient spiritual resources to be the true home of liberty. He also disliked the climate of New York, the rudeness and pushiness of its population, and what he saw as the exaggeratedly emancipated behaviour of the women. It would be some time before Cuba would be ripe for another anti-Spanish war, and so it is not surprising to find Martí moving on, this time to Venezuela.

Venezuela

Early in 1881 (probably January) Martí arrived in Caracas, where his first act on disembarking was to pay homage at the statue of Bolívar. Soon he was writing in the prestigious newspaper *La Opinión Nacional*. On 21 March he made a speech to the Caracas Chamber of Commerce outlining the tasks confronting Latin Americans: the rural areas in their lands had to be developed and populated, and much hard work performed. 'We must give back to the interrupted concert of humanity its American voice, which froze sadly in the throats of Nezahualcoatl and Chilam' (respectively the Mexican poet-emperor of fifteenth-century Texcoco, and a Maya prophet), he declared, 'unfreeze, with the warmth of love, mountains of men', 'stop colossal instances of greed', 'pull up (. . .) corrupt roots', 'arm peaceful armies so that they may parade a single banner from the rippling Rio Bravo, on whose banks the indomitable Apache rides, to the Arauco, whose waters slake the thirst of the undefeated natives'. Latin America must have life breathed into it. Its worth was equal to, or greater than, that of Europe. Latin Americans should also eschew undue admiration of the United States, where Martí had seen 'many solitary souls, and petty personalities dressed up as dignitaries' and heard only 'those slow, cold, abrupt and inflexible tongues'.[27]

Martí's stay in Venezuela was even briefer (half a year) than his Guatemalan sojourn, and terminated for very similar reasons. Again he could not stomach arbitrary and despotic rule. The Venezuelan government was remarkably close, in its ideology and practices (which were likewise in contradiction), to the odious regimes Martí had left behind in Mexico and Guatemala. Power was in the hands of a Liberal president of military origins, Antonio Guzmán Blanco, who was encouraging the bourgeoisie to enrich itself in the name of economic development and progress, whilst trampling on the poorer masses of the population from behind the façade of a bogus parliamentary democracy. All opposition was being ruthlessly crushed, to create the 'order' which this positivist-inspired 'progress' demanded.

Martí was particularly shocked by the yawning disparity between town and countryside. 'In the city, Paris; in the country, Persia',[28] he exclaimed. Venezuela was following the general trend of late nineteenth century Latin America by opening wide its doors to foreign (mainly European) capital. The new élites tended to be city-based and Europe-orientated, culturally as well as economically. In an article on the recently deceased Venezuelan poet Cecilio Acosta, a tireless opponent of Guzmán Blanco, Martí stated pointedly that Acosta had wanted 'to make America prosperous, not feeble; mistress of her own destinies and not tied, like a criminal of bygone times, to the tails of European horses'.[29] In this article, published in the second and last number of a magazine (the *Venezuelan Review*) founded by Martí, the latter's own political beliefs were outlined. He asserted that 'the liberal principle is the only one which can organize modern societies and give them a firm base'.[30] By 'liberal' is meant genuinely democratic, as is evident in Martí's commendation of Cecilio Acosta who

> speaks for man as a whole and attacks those modern Brahmins and grave sorcerers who keep the great knowledge to themselves. He does not want mountains that absorb plains, which are necessary for cultivation; he wants the plains to rise, and the mountains to be moved and levelled. A great man amongst ignoramuses is only of use to himself: 'the means to enlightenment should not be piled up in the clouds, but should descend, like rain, to moisten all the fields.' 'The light which is most useful to a nation is not that which is concentrated, but rather that which is diffused.' He wants rounded Americans: 'the Republic does not consist of chopping down, but of raising up characters to virtue (. . .) it is more consoling to be numbered on the side of electricity and matches, than on that of the donkey, even if it has a good pack-saddle, the flint and the old Spanish helmet.'[31]

A friend of Acosta's had been arrested some days previously, tortured and exiled for having made transparent allusions at Acosta's funeral to the latter's fight against Guzmán Blanco. Martí, however, was not intimidated into pulling his punches, and as a result, three days after the article appeared, had to leave Venezuela in a hurry. He sailed on 28 July 1881, probably after threats to his life, never again to fix his residence in Latin America, until his return to Cuba one month before his death.

Martí's harsh experiences in Mexico, Guatemala and Venezuela radicalized his thinking about the social divisions in the nations of Latin America. His notebooks for 1881 offer further evidence of this. Martí had come to see the monopoly of power by the upper classes as a hindrance to progress. 'In America the revolution is in its initial period. – It must be carried out. The intellectual revolution of the upper class has been made: that is all. And from this has come more bad than good.'[32] However, one has to exercise caution in the interpretation of this statement, since it was made by a man who was to declare, a full eleven years later (July 1892), in his own newspaper, *Patria*, 'Our lips burn with these unnecessary words, "workmen" and "classes".'[33] The fact is that, right up to the end of his life, and despite an increasing sympathy for the working people, Martí remained fundamentally a liberal, albeit a radical one. In the context of castigating those Spanish Americans who bewailed the frequency of 'revolutions' and the 'incapacity' of governments in that part of the continent, Martí jotted down angrily in a notebook for 1894 that 'if each one were to do his duty as a man, then bad governments would have to be better'. 'Stop living like filthy limpets, stuck to the state apparatus',[34] was his exhortation.

The 1881 notebooks develop slightly two themes that acquire increasing importance for Martí: the need for home-grown institutions as opposed to those imported into Latin American countries, and the equally desirable search for unity for those peoples. He takes up the Bolivarian ideal of a 'great confederation of the peoples of Latin America' and suggests a 'tribunal of all countries to resolve the quarrels of each', plus financial aid for any country of the area at war with an alien nation. The seat of this confederation could be Colombia (not Panama, as Bolívar had desired, or Cuba, because Cuba might be annexed). He sees Latin America as a natural family of peoples who, though quarrelling incessantly, are nevertheless bound by unbreakable ties.[35]

The Most Painful Exile.
Martí in the United States (1881–95)

I shall now deal with the development of Martí's ideas on Latin America that took place during his second, protracted residence in the United States. This will involve looking at his changing attitudes to the latter country itself (albeit briefly, since that has been done in another chapter), but especially the aspect of United States-Latin American relations. One has also to take into account the literature he read on Latin America during this period. It will be useful to divide the period up into two phases: 1) up to 1886, and 2) from 1886 to 1895, for the reason that during the first phase, although increasingly perturbed by what he saw of the United States, Martí was still prepared to give it the benefit of the doubt. This is apparent in his article on General Ulysses Grant, published in *La Nación*, Buenos Aires, in September 1885. Subsequently, and sparked off by the Cutting affair of 1886 and the Haymarket Martyrs' events of 1886–87, Martí's attitude towards the United States becomes more and more hostile, culminating in his bitter remarks to Manuel Mercado in a well-known letter written the day before his death.

First Phase: 1881–85
The first major issue which Martí faced in his writings of this period concerning Latin America was the projected trade agreement between Mexico and the United States, which aimed at lowering tariff barriers between the two nations. Martí disapproved of the draft treaty as being too favourable to the United States. According to him, Mexican exports to the North were already able to hold their own on the United States market without tariffs being lowered, whereas the United States, having built up its industries behind high tariff walls against European competition, and now (1883) suffering from excess production and liquidity of capital ('at present given over to feverish and unpleasant stock-exchange operations',[36] he remarks disapprovingly), high prices and unemployment, would be able to alleviate all these problems on gaining access to Mexican markets. Hence the projected treaty. But the Mexican treasury, dependent as it was mainly on customs revenues, would be left bankrupt. Another problem was that Mexico needed North American manufactures.

Martí, although disapproving of the principle of protectionism – as we have seen above in his Mexican writings and from what he said in 1884 and reiterated, referring to the United States:

> the protectionist system, which is created so that the nation may become a manufacturing one and, therefore, rich and powerful, is only subsequently maintained by a group of rich and powerful industrialists at the cost of increasing discontent and penury in the nation[37]

nevertheless is in favour of protecting Mexican markets. Broadly speaking, he seems to be in favour of the 'comparative advantage' system in economics. Countries should, in their economies as in all other matters, be true to their particular natures. Thus Mexico should only develop such national industries as can easily flourish on its soil (because of an abundance of natural resources, etc.), and not try to produce goods which are better and more cheaply made abroad. Mexico, as it happens, has good industrial potential, so this must be developed.

Martí does not approach the issue of what a nation poor in natural resources should do. Perhaps this was because his own country, Cuba, the 'pearl of the Antilles', was a byword for wealth in the nineteenth century. In the twentieth century, as we know, the sugar which created Cuba's wealth is now a commodity of relatively small value. What kind of economic policies would Martí have applied in the Cuba of today? He would most probably have followed the present Cuban government in trying to establish close ties with the 'sister' nations of Latin America, despite fundamental political differences.

The longer Martí remained in the United States and the more he perceived of that nation's movement toward monopoly capitalism, the more fervent became his desire for Latin American unity, as a protection against the North. His innate optimism led him to believe that somehow Latin America would be able to avoid the brutal Northern business mentality, and form a 'great spiritual nation', 'the spectacle never before seen of a family of peoples which advances happily with each member in step in a free continent'. He thought this possible because 'In South and Central America there are no inevitable reasons, as there are in Europe and Asia, for struggles between rival races, to excuse and explain wars and make them systematic, inevitable, and at some moments in time, necessary'.[38]

Martí seems here to see what he calls the 'racial' factor as an important cause of historical and social conflict, at least in Europe and Asia and, it seems by implication, North America. In my opinion, although this is not made specific, Martí appears to believe that in what he was to term 'our *mestizo* America' (South and Central America) there was a propensity for separate races to mix, whereas the opposite was true of Europe and Asia (and North America). He was undeniably shocked by the racism of the United States (of which he had had experience himself), and there is no doubt that this was an important factor in his increasing dislike of that country.

On the other hand, whilst arguing that the nations of Latin America could avoid the cut-throat ethos of United States capitalism (presumably through a greater potentiality for harmony), Martí nevertheless (and in spite of his homilies against 'foreign' institutions and ideologies) approves of measures for 'development' very much akin to those being applied in the North. Argentina, for example, is praised for having pushed back the frontier, populated the countryside and imposed the rule of law. The fact that this was done (as in the United State and often in deliberate imitation of it) using great violence against the local indigenous and gaucho population is overlooked, although Martí, as we shall see, was later to alter his attitude to this kind of 'progress'.

The fact is that at this point in time Martí's liberalism leads him to focus on the demise, in Argentina, of the semi-feudal tyrant Juan Manuel de Rosas, who had butchered his enemies (including liberal intellectuals) for over a quarter of a century. Now, says Martí, the great port of Buenos Aires (Argentina's link with European trade, finance and culture) is prosperous and 'generous'. And the wild Chaco region of the north, equally happily,

> covered with thick forests, with its share of cane, is now seeing the arrival in its opulent regions, of the thickset white men, loaded down with their tools for chopping down tree trunks and opening up the land, who are coming contentedly to set up their peaceful and free homes, using the cool wood of the forest.[39]

Martí agrees with the Argentinian government's policy of encouraging massive Italian immigration. These 'poetical Italian workers' have come, he writes, to labour in the fields and not live from hand to mouth like 'the wretched paupers who, like noxious insects, are what the European people habitually shake out onto America' and who are being expelled in great numbers from the United States. The Italians are heirs, moreover, to a civilization which was 'twice universal', and have 'warmth in their souls'. Immigrants must love their new land, declares Martí, and adds significantly: 'The coming together of two opposing races is sterile'.[40] Presumably Italians were better immigrants for Argentina than, say, Germans or Turks, on 'racial' grounds.

The picture Martí paints here is romantic. He seemed not to be aware of the hostility the Italians faced in Argentina at the time, as is made clear in the great national poem *Martín Fierro* (1872 and 1879), which there is no evidence he had read. If he had done so, he would have painted a more sombre picture of the Argentina of that era.

A year later Martí was praising the advances in banking and other financial arrangements in Argentina, which of course formed part of the paraphernalia of a vigorous capitalist expansion. He also welcomed the founding of new towns, just as if this were happening in Texas or Colorado, he exclaimed enthusiastically.[41]

The year 1884 was a particularly hard one for Martí. He gave up his

Uruguayan consulship in New York because of that country's pro-Spanish stance but also to dedicate more time to the Cuban struggle. However, October saw him break bitterly with Máximo Gómez and Antonio Maceo, the two great military heroes of the Ten Years' War, over what Martí took to be Gómez's dictatorial attitude to the new campaign. Martí was personally slighted by Gómez, and retired for the next two years into the political wilderness, after sending Gómez a letter accusing him of treating the Cuban nation as if it were solely a military camp. In a letter to Manuel Mercado, Martí complained harshly of the egoism of tyrants, meaning specifically Gómez.

In September 1885 Martí published in *La Nación*, of Buenos Aires, a long article on the recently deceased Ulysses Grant, the leading general of the victorious Union side of the American Civil War, and ex-President of the United States. This brilliant Plutarchian piece, alongside 'Our America' (January 1891) the most perfect example of Martí's very original prose, is shot through with ambivalence towards the United States, although Martí is still broadly favourable to that nation. Martí believed that the Civil War was 'created more because of a humanitarian goal than out of arguments about internal politics', and continued in the same eulogistic vein:

> Enormous, improvised, unpolished, original and generous was the war of the North, as was then the people that waged it; and the military chieftain that gave it its natural and naive spirit, and expelled from it the exotic academic spirit, was born, like his people, in poverty and hardship. He gave, like his people, more time and liking to fruitful and direct labour than to feeble and secondary book work; he replaced conventional and imported ideas by the new ideas that Nature, in the virgin countryside and local conditions, suggested to him. And always, like his people, did he attack, with all his mass, firmly and irresistibly like the mountains, the object of his desire.[42]

It is true, Martí goes on to remark, that Grant, 'like his people, and much more than them, corrupted his glory through bad political practices'.[43]

Abraham Lincoln was 'that man whose name is always spoken with reverent praise', and the post-bellum United States 'the greatest people in peacetime and the most generous in war to inhabit the Universe of its time'.[44]

However, it was also a 'country which is in danger (. . .), where the consciousness of its strength and the desire to make good are putting at risk the decency of the nation, the independence of its neighbours and, perhaps, the independence of the human spirit itself'; 'but a great country, despite that, where man shapes and exercises his powers with no other dealings or limits than those natural ones imposed on him by the proximity of other men'. And to finish, perhaps swept away by a final flush of optimism, Martí declared: 'The nation of men has begun, and this man [Grant], in spite of his great mistakes, helped to pave the way for it'.[45]

Second Phase: 1886–95

The Cutting Affair and Other Instances of US Jingoism of the Late 1880s
All Martí scholars worthy of the name see the two years following the article on Grant as the start of a radicalization in his thinking. The only disagreement is concerning the degree of this radicalization. The period 1886–87, indeed, shows a real heightening of Martí's fears about the foreign policies of the United States and its internal socio-political workings (issues that were not unconnected, as has been pointed out). In addition, and especially from the time he began to revise his views on the Chicago Haymarket bombs affair, one notices a considerable growth in sympathy for workers as a social group. These feelings were further deepened by his contact with the Cuban emigré tobacco workers of Florida (which started in late 1891). Since the Haymarket question has been dealt with very fully in another part of this book, I shall examine here the other events of the latter part of the 1880s which shook Martí's confidence in the United States, commencing with the Cutting affair.

Colonel Francis Cutting was an agitator for United States expansion. He had been in favour of the annexation of Mexico before the Civil War and was one of the founders of the American Annexation League, set up in 1878 by American businessmen and politicians to acquire new markets for United States manufacturing and investments, through the take-over of territories adjacent to that country, in particular in Latin America, but also including the whole of Canada.

Cutting had been arrested and put on trial in Mexico for an insulting article published in the United States. The Mexican authorities considered they were within their rights to do this, whilst the US federal government did not, although it was anxious to avoid a clash with Mexico. The problem was that Cutting's incarceration unleashed 'the fury of a brutal and ambitious region', in Martí's words. Mobs of Texans were threatening to make war on Mexico, backed by the state government. In the first article that Martí wrote on this question (for the Mexican newspaper *El Partido Liberal*, and published on 2 August 1886), what really shocked him was that the United States appeared to be ruled by the mob:

> In the United States the government does not rule. The country hands itself over to professsional politicians in matters of slight importance, but assumes power of its own accord, and drags the professional politicians along with it, in all serious matters. So that here one does not have to pay court to a king or a president, but to the mass of the nation, which is the real government and president of the country.[46]

Martí felt horrified by the 'idea of dominion that is a fearsome characteristic of the real American',[47] fuelled by a jingoistic press and supported or opposed by politicians according to the interests they represented. The average American's abysmal ignorance of and scorn for Mexico likewise shook Martí to the core. Naturally he bore in mind that Mexico had already lost half its territory to the rapacity of American frontiersmen.

The second article on Cutting, published in *La Nación* the following 18 September, showed a deepening of Martí's alarm. He wrote of 'the aggressive insolence of the rabble that is roaming around and watching out' from the US bank of the Río Grande. North American bridges 'cross the river like claws sunk into the land of Mexico'; 'its ruthless mob (. . .) regards it as a thing of its own, and is longing to fall upon its cattlefields and mines', and evidences a 'fateful scorn for the dark race'.[48] Martí noted that these sentiments were not confined to Texans:

> this idea of conquest is dear to the popular imagination. The great wealth [of Mexico] is desired. One perceives the iniquitous jubilation of strong animals. Any pretext, therefore, for conflict which arises between these two countries finds the frontier desirous of war; the South is willing to help it; the North is convinced that war must come some day, and it is all the same whether it comes today or tomorrow, and the government, obliged through diplomatic morality to seek peace, is however pushed into war by the appetite for invading the frontier, the warlike spirit of the South, and the tacit consent of the nation.[49]

Eventually the House of Representatives refused to vote for war, wrote Martí, because of the protests from a Republican congressman who accused the (Democratic) government of falsifying the facts of the situation. This served as a pretext for the Republicans to

> prove to the country that it is not only themselves or only Blaine who favour a policy of intimidation and intrusion in the American nations of Spanish caste; and out of party political revenge they censured their opponents for what they themselves would have applauded had they been the instigators.[50]

Thus only a quirk of inter-party rivalry in the United States had saved Mexico from war (plus Cutting's release).

Before the Cutting articles Martí had already noticed the same kind of contempt for Cuba itself. Thus we find him writing in May 1886 to Ricardo Rodríguez Otero:

> never, except hidden away in the depths of some generous souls, was Cuba anything more for the United States than a desirable possession, whose only inconvenience is its population, which they consider to be unruly, lazy and worthy of scorn.[51]

Martí's views on the United States continued to harden as time passed and brought with it fresh evidence of North American rapacity. An article published on 1 January of the following year in *La Nación* on the Festival of the Statue of Liberty contrasts the 'very concept of liberty' held in the United States ('selfish and disingenuous') to that of France ('generous and expansive'). Emblematic of the United States and its idea of liberty was the very influential businessman Chauncey Depew: 'Railways are what he occupies himself with; he counts in millions; he is listened to by emperors; the Vanderbilts are his Maecenases and friends.

Man is of very little importance to him; he is more interested in railways'.[52]

And in a striking phrase contained in a letter of the same month to Manuel Mercado, which remarked on the continual scorn for Mexico expressed in United States' newspapers, a contempt extending to all 'our countries', Martí stated that the time had come 'to go for the armpits of this rhinoceros'.[53]

Six months later, in 'Mexico in the USA', published in *El Partido Liberal* on 23 June, Martí's indignation again boiled over. This time the cause was Charles Dudley Warner, editor of the *Hartford Courant*, who had just published some travel sketches on Mexico, in *Harper's Monthly* (no. LXXV, June–July 1887).

Warner's articles were unashamedly racist, and Martí set about countering his opinions. To the accusation that Mexico was infested with bandits, Martí replied that when rural areas in the United States were primitive and of difficult access, exactly the same phenomenon had appeared. In any case, Mexico had largely eliminated its bandits: only in places where there was no work was robbery a problem. And what about 'the enormous frauds committed in the United States, frauds from which Mexico is almost free'? Did this indeed not reveal 'a more widespread and inexcusable national corruption than the romantic banditry' of a nation of vast open spaces and formerly torn by war?[54]

As to Warner's allegations that the Mexican Indians had not progressed beyond their pre-Colombian stage, Martí pointed to their North American counterparts, crushed by neglect and vice. It was not from *their* midst that a Benito Juárez had emerged. Later on in that year Martí was to translate Helen Hunt Jackson's *Ramona*, a novel with whose pro-Indian views he heartily concurred. Martí expressed his opposition to the shunting of North American Indians into reservations, and believed that they should be carefully integrated into the rest of society on the basis of giving each family enough land for its needs. Like Thoreau, Martí had high hopes for the 'natural' man, believing him to possess psychological resources that 'civilized' society, through its distance from nature, had lost. And like Thoreau, at the end of his life he was mulling over this question, as his *Campaign Diary* entry for 8 April 1895 makes clear.

Warner had characterized the Mexican nation as inferior because it was *mestizo*, following the ideas of intellectuals like Gobineau (*Essay on Human Inequality*, 1884), who also asserted the superiority of the Teutonic or Anglo-Saxon races. Miscegenation was held to combine the worst strains of the parent races whilst eliminating the best. This was also the view of Latin American thinkers such as the Argentinian Domingo Faustino Sarmiento and, slightly later, Euclides da Cunha. Martí will have none of these theories (and is practically alone in taking this position). Thus when Warner blames miscegenation for producing in Mexico City, in Martí's indignant words, 'the fops of the town, with their unsteady legs, brainless young men, the garbage of a degenerate civilization, without manliness or purpose', Martí's reply is angrily defensive of Mexico and critical of the United States:

> This Warner should have his beard pulled, as in the times of the Cid! So strong legs make stout hearts! Civilization in Mexico is not declining, but just beginning!
>
> A handful of glorious men have raised it up over a basket of hydras (. . .).
>
> It was the heroic fight of a few annointed ones against the inert millions, and against privileges capable of protecting themselves by treason.
>
> What civilization did Mexico inherit, when it had its own sufficient vigour to proclaim its freedom? That nation was born from those unsteady legs and a few French books! Mexico has accomplished more in raising itself up to where it is than the United States in keeping itself up, although really declining, to the level it started at! (. . .) Unsteady legs! The Davids of this world have done more than the Goliaths; Bolívar only weighed as much as his sword. Don Miguel Hidalgo perhaps only weighed some hundred and thirty pounds.[55]

Martí's slightly obscure phrase about the relative decline of the United States is clarified in a later piece he wrote for *La Nación* that year. The whole nation, he says, has been swallowed up by New York; the only question now asked is how much money a person has. The United States has declined 'perhaps in essential things, from the marvel that was its starting point'.[56] The 'essential things' are moral standards. As time went on, Martí was to notice more and more examples of financial and political corruption there, and pointed out many cases where the two went hand in hand.

It is noteworthy that in the very month that this last article was published (December 1887) Martí was making overtures to Máximo Gómez to settle their grievances and plan together a new invasion of Cuba. The 1884 plans had come to nothing, and Gómez agreed. Early in the new year Martí told Manuel Mercado of

> the serious news that is already coming to light concerning the dangerous and haughty way in which this country [the US] is proposing to treat our countries (. . .) plans that I see which tend, in private and public, to an unjust advancement of its power amongst the Spanish peoples of America.

He also noted 'the declaration, already almost official, that it is attempting to propose to Spain the purchase of Cuba'. 'And I do not know', he added despairingly, 'if that were to happen, how I would stay alive. (. . .) The onslaught is going to be very strong. And I cannot see the defence against it.'[57]

The onslaught, Martí knew, was because of United States overproduction and need for new markets. Because of protectionist policies, unemployment and strikes were rife, and strife between capital and labour had reached fever pitch, as the Chicago Haymarket bombs emphasized. Martí felt that the United States had created within itself such antagonisms that 'the Republic may end up in the same disasters, hatreds and despotisms as the monarchies',[58] repeating an idea that goes back to his earliest writings.

Martí's Uruguayan friend Enrique Estrázulas received, almost exactly a year after the last letter to Manuel Mercado, a very similar communication. Martí told Estrázulas about the possible purchase of Cuba and 'the policy of conquest of the United States, which is announcing through the mouths of Blaine and Harrison a desire to treat all our countries in a high-handed way, as natural dependencies of that country'.[59] The ultra-expansionist Republican Party had won the Presidential elections, and Benjamin Harrison was now President, with James G. Blaine, whom Martí particularly hated, as his Secretary of State.

On 16 March 1889, the Philadelphia *Manufacturer*, an official organ of the Republican Party, published a demeaning article which enquired if the United States really wanted Cuba. Martí replied on 21 March in a letter sent to the New York *Evening Post* and published on 25 March. He denied vigorously the charge that Cubans (and Latin Americans as a whole) were idle, effeminate, verbose and impractical, as had been affirmed in the *Manufacturer*, and pointed out how the best elements of Cuban society admired the United States, as the greatest nation founded on the principles of liberty and republicanism. The heroes of the United States, such as Washington and Lincoln, were also their heroes. However, the United States was being infected by the diseases of excessive individualism, adoration of wealth and the triumphalism of the victors of the Civil War. There were, in fact, *two* United States (note Martí's persistent dualism): that of Lincoln, whom Cubans revered for having liberated the slaves, and that of Cutting, whom they feared. Martí evidently believed that the latter was predominant.

The very day of his reply to the *Manufacturer*, Martí told Manuel Mercado of his intention to found an English-language newspaper in New York to defend the interests of the peoples of Latin America and prove they were good, industrious and capable.

It was in this mood that, some six months later, Martí reviewed the Argentinian Juan A. Piaggio's *Types and Customs of Buenos Aires* for *El Partido Liberal*. Martí used this article to show how post-Rosas politicians in Argentina such as Sarmiento, Alberdi and Mitre were forging a modern, industrious nation through policies of mass immigration, building railways and popular education, in the manner of the United States but 'under a Latin Presidency'. In Argentina the 'enterprising forces of the world'

> have come together, and fused with those of the country, but without invading it or disfiguring it, or taking away from the arrogant soul of the pampas the feeling and novelty with which it embellishes a suddenly industrialized civilization, and holds in check the greed and selfishness that wealth creates, to the detriment of the fatherland.[60]

Martí, in his desire to praise Argentina, appears to overlook the ruthlessness with which the post-Rosas governments attacked the gaucho and Indian cultures in the name of 'civilization'. He seems unaware, likewise, of the racism which was the psychological underpinning for these policies (Sarmiento, for example, considered the 'Caucasian races' as superior, and justified in wiping out the Indian; moreover, he attributed the 'inferiority' of Latin America to miscegenation, which did not occur in the United States). Martí's own philosophy was diametrically anti-racist, and yet he and Sarmiento evinced a mutual admiration which could only have been based on a large measure of ignorance of each other's ideas.

Martí noted the 'frenzied' industrialization of Argentina and declared that Buenos Aires had become 'the tiny rival of the strong Yankee'. His feelings on this subject were obviously ambivalent: on the one hand Argentina had proved it could vie with the United States, and on the other there is a hint that it was falling into the same errors. He regretted there were no lunatic asylums or poorhouses in Buenos Aires. However, he ended on a note of optimism: the Argentinian fatherland had become 'one more fatherland for the workers of the world'.[61]

The Washington International Congress

The Panamerican Congress which began in Philadelphia on 2 October 1889 and reassembled in Washington the following 19 November to continue its deliberations until 19 April of the new year was an event that Martí followed with alarm. The aims of the Congress were to lay down the bases of a Panamerican system in: trade, banking, communications, public health, currency, arbitration between nations, standards of weights and measures and common codes of law.[62] Martí had always been opposed to a gathering of this nature because he knew it would only serve to further the interests of the United States in Latin America. It was the United States that had called the Congress, which was to be held, more-over, on its own soil, which would give it advantages in decision-making processes and set a dangerous precedent. The only positive aspect of the Congress, thought Martí, might be the chance of winning recognition for Cuban independence.

In the first of the five articles Martí penned on the Congress, dated 28 September (before the inauguration) and later appearing in *La Nación*, he mentioned the tour of US industrial cities planned for the Latin American delegates as an appetizer for their trade interests and to per-suade them to buy from the United States and nobody else, even though the goods bought might be dearer and not always better than those of their competitors. Shipping agents were to accompany the delegates because American shipping interests hoped to establish regular lines to Latin America. A Panamerican trading company had already been set up in Washington.

Latin American reactions varied, wrote Martí. Some countries were uneasy about the Congress or even hostile to it, whereas others, unfortunately, welcomed it because they foolishly saw the United States as a 'candy giant, with one arm of Wendell Phillips [the anti-slavery campaigner] and the other of Lincoln, which is going to give wealth and freedom to peoples who do not know how to win them for themselves'.[63] In Martí's mind was the fear that the United States might back a Cuban patriotic war against Spain as an alternative to the outright purchase of Cuba. Once this happened, it would be impossible to remove the United States. It was now, evidently, that the idea of a purely Cuban war against Spain, as the absolute minimum for warding off the United States, started to burgeon for him.

Like that of Latin America, the United States camp at the Congress was divided:

> whilst some are preparing to dazzle the delegates, to divide them, to intrigue against them, to seize the most succulent morsel with their thieving eagle's beak, others are preparing to be worthy of the trade they desire, by having honest dealings and respecting the freedom of others.[64]

The intriguers were repeating the tactics of the Spanish *conquistador* Alvarado (who like them had light hair), when he manipulated the traditional animosity between the Quiché and Tzotzil Indians in the conquest of the Mayas.

Martí's second article pointed out that the power behind the scene of the Congress was the US Secretary of State James G. Blaine, who was using it to curry favour with businessmen in order to win their support for his own Presidential candidacy in future elections. Blaine had originally planned for a similar Congress in 1881, and invitations had already gone out when President Garfield was assassinated. However, the new President Arthur revoked the invitations, and Blaine was left high and dry. He had now intrigued his way into presiding over the present event.

The third article, written on 2 November and published in two instalments (19 and 20 December) by *La Nación*, has a tone of real urgency. The United States, 'glutted with unsaleable products, and determined to extend its dominions in America', was inviting 'weaker American nations, with free and useful trade ties to the peoples of Europe (. . .) to forge a league against Europe'. Spanish America, if this happened, would become a puppet of the United States. The time had come 'to declare its second independence'.[65] The interests of the two halves of America were antagonistic. This was proven by

> the eternal and declared policy of predominance by a thrustful and ambitious neighbour, which has never wanted to encourage them [the nations of Latin America], nor has turned to them save for the purpose of preventing their expansion, as in Panama; or seizing their territory, as in Mexico, Nicaragua, Santo Domingo, Haiti and Cuba; or cutting off through intimidation their dealings with the rest of the universe, as in Colombia; or obliging them, as now, to buy what it cannot sell, and form a confederation which it will dominate.[66]

Characteristic of the United States was 'the cohabitation of eminent virtues and rapacious gifts' (note once more the philosophical dualism, reflecting Martí's view of the world as a battlefield between good and evil). Its idea of liberty was always circumscribed by its own selfish interests. Martí is now beginning to see the links between the puritanism of the founding fathers and the later rush towards monopoly capitalism. The United States was never the land of harmony and brotherhood that all countries (especially those of America) should aspire to be. It could never be, therefore, a *patria*.

> From the merchant Dutchman, from the selfish German, and from the domineering Englishman was kneaded, with the yeast of local government dominated by the seigneurial classes, the people which did not see it as a crime to leave a mass of men, on the pretext of the ignorance in which they themselves kept them, enslaved under the very people that resisted slavery for themselves.[67]

A point made implicitly here is the moral superiority – as Martí might have termed it – of the Spanish American liberators who, inspired in part by the North American Revolution of 1776 and its principles of freedom and democracy, nevertheless were truer to these principles than the Washingtons, Jeffersons and Hamiltons themselves, in that they did not leave the infamous institution of slavery intact. Martí, as a late nineteenth century *Cuban* patriot, necessarily saw the survival of slavery after North American independence as a more glaring anomaly than many would see it, since the freedom of his own nation was inextricably bound up with abolition. With slavery intact, Cuba would not, even though politically independent, be a real *nation* (or *patria*), but a disguised colony. Nationality, for Martí, meant nationality for all. Slavery had in fact by this time been completely abolished in Cuba by the Spaniards, but this was only thanks to the insurgents of 1868–78, who had started the process in the liberated areas.

The United States had never helped the emergent nations of Latin America in their struggles for independence. It had actually preferred to back Spanish rule in Cuba, from the 1820s onwards, in order to have the country for itself when Spain (as would happen inevitably) was forced out. Texas and other large Mexican territories had been annexed, and even in the midst of the American Civil War a plan was mooted for peace between the belligerents in order to expel the French from what was left of Mexico and complete its annexation.

Martí runs through a whole inventory of American statesmen, from Jefferson to Blaine, citing their views on the desirability and inevitability of United States domination of Latin America. He concludes that the United States is 'a people rooted in rapacity which has grown up with the hope and certainty of possessing the continent', a nation 'jealous of Europe', 'desirous of being an imperial power', and one whose economy was based on 'the wrong kind of production, which it believes necessary to maintain and increase'.[68] It had to be stopped in its tracks.

Behind the Congress were also the big US shipping companies, desirous of government subsidies for their planned routes to the South. They had already contributed to party political funds with that end in view. And then there were the over-productive manufacturing concerns in search of markets. Stockbreeders and mining interests, on the other hand, were being assured that their interests would not be harmed by cheap imports. Most United States capitalists, especially those linked to the Republican Party, were protectionists, and wanted outlets for their products, but disliked the idea of concessions to imports from Latin America. The whole problem could of course be resolved by simply annexing desirable territories. Hence the expansionist fervour of industrialists and the politicians associated with them or who wanted their votes.

As far as Latin America was concerned, the major problem connected with the trade agreements desired by US industrial interests, was that the former's markets would be swamped by North American manufactures and economic development severely stunted, in return for a few grudging concessions to Latin American goods on the US market.

Probably more than any other event in the United States, the Panamerican Congress opened Martí's eyes to the concrete working of imperialism, and showed him, especially, the link between big business and foreign policy. He now believed that Latin America should struggle to keep its links with the rest of the world and not allow itself to become the backyard of the United States, which itself was rent with divisions and had enormous problems. It had become a 'disdainful juggernaut' that was 'starting to see liberty as its own privilege (. . .) and to invoke it for the purpose of depriving other peoples of it'.[69]

The most harmful proposal put to the Congress, in Martí's view, was that for an arbitration tribunal which would decide issues in dispute between American nations. The United States would inevitably dominate this tribunal and play the role of Big Brother for Latin American nations, some of whom would be bribed or dazzled into supporting its interests. The idea for a Panamerican customs union, likewise, was bad, since most Latin American countries derived most of their revenues from customs duties. They would do better to trade with one another. Railways links would also be disastrous, a new Pizarro. Doubtless Martí remembered Lerdo de Tejada's dictum: 'between Mexico and the United States [there should be] a desert'.

Although the Democrats had often supported imperialist ventures (starting with Jefferson's Louisiana Purchase and ending in their support for US interference in Haiti in 1889), it was the Republican Party, traditionally the party of big business, that was the main expansionist force in the United States, and therefore the party most likely to benefit from the Panamerican Congress, according to Martí. (Martí, in fact, had generally nothing but praise for the previous US (Democratic) President,

Grover Cleveland, and his policies). Yet because of Republican adherence to protectionism, there would be no Latin American collaboration on the trade question, and matters would remain as before. The whole Congress, really, was only a manoeuvre by Blaine to further his own ambitions, as certain US quality newspapers such as the *New York Times*, *Herald*, etc., mooted. Or perhaps it was also a subsidy-hunt (for US shipping lines). The article ended with an idea, subsequently developed, that the true independence of Latin America held the key to the world balance of power, since it would check United States aggrandizement.

As a corollary to this notion, Martí put forth the idea, in a letter to his friend Serafín Bello, that the annexation of Cuba would be the prelude to the annexation of the whole of Latin America, as that of Texas had been to the seizure of other Mexican territories in the 1848 war.[70]

The fourth article on the Congress (dated 11 December and published on 24 January the following year) warned Martí's Argentinian readers of a specific threat to Haiti and Nicaragua, citing an 'odious' article in the New York *Sun* that wondered which direction US expansion should take, whether north, south or to the Antilles. The frequency with which schemes for purchasing Cuba were being aired in the press was also noted. Midway through the Congress Martí intervened from the sidelines, by making a speech at a cultural event organized by the Spanish American Literary Society for the Latin American delegates in Washington on 19 December 1889. The printed version of this speech bears the title *Mother America*.

Martí introduced himself, in order to explain his own reasons for being in the United States, as one of those Cubans who had gone there 'to write (. . .) the last stanza of the poem of 1810',[71] that is, to complete the Independence struggles of the first quarter of the century. The phrase quoted is an echo of his words to the Caracas Chamber of Commerce in 1881, shortly after he arrived in Venezuela. The purpose of the oration in Washington was to instil into the delegates a pride in Latin America and a faith in its separate destiny, if these were not already felt. In a typically apostolic outburst, Martí declared that the America of Benito Juárez was greater than the United States 'because it is ours and because it has been more unfortunate'. The comparison that follows, between the two Americas, is couched in metaphor and looks forward to Martí's most brilliant piece of writing, 'Our America', of a year or so later.

The United States was born out of a desire for freedom, but this freedom had become cankered by selfishness:

> The people that afterwards was to refuse help to others, accepted help itself [from France]. The freedom that triumphed was like the people itself, haughty and sectarian, with lace cuffs and velvet hangings, more concerned with its own local circumstances than with those of humanity, a freedom which hung, selfishly and unjustly, over the shoulders of a slave race, which before a century had passed shook off the litter it was carrying on to the

ground; and then emerged, axe in hand, the woodcutter with the pious eyes, from amongst the clamour and dust raised by the chains that fell from a million free men. Amongst the broken foundations in the tremendous convulsion strode victory, greedy and arrogant. The factors that made up the nation reappeared, accentuated by war; and beside the corpse of the gentleman, lying dead on top of his slaves, the pilgrim struggled for predominance in the republic, and in the universe, the pilgrim who had not accepted any master over himself or servant underneath, or any other conquests than those made by the seed in the earth and love in the hearts of men. Came the cunning and rapacious adventurer, accustomed to acquiring possessions and driving on through the forest, with no other law than his own wish or other limit than that made by his arm, a solitary and fearsome companion to the leopard and the eagle.[72]

The pious woodcutter is of course Abraham Lincoln, the North American most esteemed by Latin Americans and whose symbolic presence was invoked by the Chilean poet Pablo Neruda in his magnificent *Canto General* as the most genuine spirit of the North American people, at a time when the Cold War was the United States policy towards the socialist countries emergent from the defeat of European fascism. Neruda's portrait of Lincoln uses Martí's very words.

In general, the first immigrants to North America possessed admirable qualities. There were blots like slavery and slave-traders, witch-hunters and the odd colonial governor opposed to education, but Martí admired the bulk of that population:

people who studied, (. . .) lettered, mystical Swedes, fervent Germans, free-speaking Huguenots, proud Scots, thrifty Batavians; and they brought their ploughs, seeds, looms, harps, psalms, books. They lived in houses built by their own hands, masters and servants of themselves (. . .). The schools were of the kind where one is taught by rote and whipped; but to get to them through the snow was the best schooling.[73]

The origins of Spanish America were strikingly different: 'North America was born of the plough, and Spanish America of the hunting dog'.[74] The Spaniards who conquered America were rough, fanatical unemployed soldiers, fresh from their victories over the Moors and who, 'clad in their iron breastplates and armed with their blunderbusses, threw themselves on Indians protected only by cotton wadding'.[75] These elements were led by hungry mobs of impoverished noblemen, non-commissioned officers, lean university graduates and clerics, who sacked Indian palaces and grabbed land in the name of the king, betraying courtesies and the hospitality sometimes offered them by the native aristocracy. They cleverly divided the local population and, over the ruins of gutted temples, placed the red standard of the Inquisition. The Indians were crushed, humiliated and enserfed; the Spaniards fought constant wars amongst themselves, out of jealousy and greed for privileges. All the fanatical rigmarole of Spanish society was brought over, along with the attendant scholastic abstractions that passed for learning in Spanish schools and universities.

And yet, from the start there had been rebellions and 'from under the cape of Torquemada emerged, bloody and sword in hand, the redeemed continent'.[76] Bolívar had many forerunners, and when the time came to expel the Spaniards, the continent rose up as one man, alone, without outside help (unlike the North Americans, who had been aided by the French).

> And all this poison changed to sap. Never, from so much opposition and misery, was a more precocious, more generous and more steadfast people born. We were a cesspit, and we are beginning to be a crucible. We laid down foundations over hydras. We have knocked down Alvarado's pikes with our railways. In the public squares where heretics were burned we have built libraries. We have as many schools as before we had Inquisition spies. What we have not done is because we have not had time to do it, because we were busy eliminating from our blood the impurities bequeathed to us by our forefathers. Of the missions, religious and immoral, there only remain peeling walls, where the owl peeps out and the lizard takes his melancholy walk. From amongst the races frozen in time and the ruins of the monasteries and nunneries and the horses of the barbarians the new American opened up a path, and is inviting the youth of the world to pitch its tent in his field. The handful of apostles has triumphed.[77]

Despite such unpromising beginnings Latin America had finally cast off its chains, and the difficulties inherited from the past would in turn be overcome:

> What do the struggles between the city with its university learning and the feudal countryside matter? What matters the scorn, filled with wars, of the lackey marquis for the half-breed workman? What matters the duel, sombre and tenacious, between Antonio de Nariño and Saint Ignatius of Loyola? All is being overcome by our capable and indefatigable America, which is planting its banner higher and higher (. . .) for humanitarian and generous liberty, not that of locality, race or sect.[78]

'Our America of today, with Bolívar on one arm and Herbert Spencer on the other', where 'all races' are welcome, and whose destiny is to 'even out, in freedom and peace, without wolfish greed or strictures from petty sextons, the appetites and hatreds of the world',[79] must resolve its local squabbles and unite, as Nature intended, to forge its own wealth and future. Its turbulence was in fact necessary, for only after such struggles could its true human nature emerge. Self-confidence and self-reliance would do the rest.

Whilst Martí was delivering this homily, James G. Blaine was engaged in trying to foist on the Panamerican Congress his arbitration scheme, in which a special court would be set up in Washington to deal with

> all questions of diplomatic privileges, territorial limits, indemnification, rights of navigation, interpretation and implementation of treaties, and all other disputes of whatever nature, except only such matters as, in the exclusive judgement of any one of the nations involved, should invoke its independence,

in Philip Foner's words.[80] Blaine, as Martí knew, had already meddled in the internal affairs of Latin America, when in 1881, as Secretary of State, he had backed the Landreau claim to guano territories ceded by Peru to Chile in the wake of the former nation's defeat in the War of the Pacific (1879–83). Landreau was a businessman who claimed, on doubtful grounds, to be an American citizen, and Blaine had used the occasion to set a precedent of US arbitration in disputes between Latin American states. Chile, as a result, almost declared war on the United States.

Blaine's new scheme for arbitration, with its obvious implications of United States hegemony over the entire continent, was in fact fiercely opposed, and a counter-proposal by the Argentinian delegate to the Congress (Roque Sáenz Peña) put forward in its stead. Finally, a pact was signed on 9 April 1890, differing substantially from Blaine's original plan. But even this won the support of only seven of the seventeen Republics represented. Sáenz Peña was also responsible for foiling the idea of a Panamerican customs union.

Martí's fifth article on the Congress (dated 18 April and published in *La Nación* on 31 May) called attention to the statements of Senator Ingalls, temporary leader of the US Upper House and possible future President, who had declared that soon all the American continent would belong to the United States. Martí praised Sáenz Peña for having blocked Blaine's schemes to make the United States a continental Big Brother. What finally emerged was a defeat for the United States.

> Instead of the guardianship of the continent demanded by Senator Fry, the power behind convocation of the Conference, who asked for a perpetual tutor for the hot-headed peoples of the South, the Conference approved a plan drawn up by the Southern peoples against any guardianship or tutelage.[81]

The last piece written by Martí on the Congress (published 15 June) makes the gleeful point that a previously fragmented Latin America had emerged united from it, whereas the United States (one single country, after all, not twenty) had broken up into different factions through the jockeying for power of its politicians. The lesson was clear: the United States respected strength and unity in its opponents. Its most intractable adversary, the Argentinian delegation, was in fact the one to receive most marks of respect in the post-conference festivities.

By the time that Martí returned to the problems of Argentina, he had shifted his viewpoint towards a more critical appraisal of the 'progress' its politicians were forcing down the throats of its inhabitants, obviously because by now he had seen too much of it in the United States. Reviewing *La Pampa*, by the Frenchman Alfred Abelot, in an article published on 20 May 1890, Martí now evinced a greater admiration than before for the primitive and heroic life of the pampas which was disappearing under the onslaught of the railway, the surveyor and the ruthlessly positivistic ideology of nineteenth century 'civilizers'. 'Why read Homer in Greek, when he is wandering alive with his guitar over his shoulder through the American desert?' he asked.[82] He mentioned two classics of the literature of the pampas, Echeverría's *La cautiva* and Sarmiento's *Facundo* (but ignored, significantly, the former's anti-Indian stance and the latter's main thesis: the need for taming the in some ways admirable society of the wilderness). Martí had not read José Hernandez' *Martín Fierro*, the impassioned reply to *Facundo*.

Martí objected to Abelot's belief in the racial inferiority of gaucho society. Of course that society was primitive, retorted Martí, and had of necessity to disappear eventually as man acquired mastery over his environment, but to speak of racial inferiority was nonsense.

> Where he [Abelot] could and should have seen the heroic feats of society in its initial stages, the primitive fight between man and beast, the assiduous sadness and violent pleasures of nomadic life, the submission of unprotected lance-wielding horsemen to the cautious, Herculean captain, the quarrel between vigorous tribes close to Nature and the literary city with all its rules and regulations, and the sudden and happy victory of culture, beautiful and useful, over bedazzled barbarity, he sees the persistence of old characteristics, and deviations and selections, and atavism. He is carrying his theory about with him, and that is like wearing a blindfold.[83]

If the Indian and the gaucho still seemed cruel and bloodthirsty, Abelot ascribed this to their psychological proximity to the wild animal. Martí replied that these traits were due to their environment. Moreover it was logical for the Indian to answer the invasions of his lands and government persecution with the bloody justice of his ancestors. Likewise the gaucho's bloodthirstiness could be attributed to his being used to the slaughter of cattle. So-called civilized societies, however, also had their slaughterhouses. The passion for gambling noticeable in primitive man, again, is not exclusive to him, for 'gambling is only the violent and uneducated form assumed by hope, and holds sway in civilizations where men wear frills on their shirts and organize themselves to applaud or boo in the theatre'; it is not, as Abelot would have it, a form of regression and a manifestation of the barbarism always lurking below the surface in man.[84]

Martí's point is that *all men* have a dual nature:

The attraction of the abyss, the vertigo of the sea and the mountains, the consistent tendency of man to enter into the absolute, to leave his own being and disperse himself, is judged by him [Abelot], because he is blinded by scholastic rules, to be a return to the celebration of primeval chaos. If one sees the world as a series of stages, each one of which is identical, whatever may be the time in which this stage manifests itself, taking into account modifications caused by locality and environment, one will have a major and infallible philosophy for understanding each social phenomenon, and one will enjoy witnessing it, and not be sad at its passing-away, like some French pedagogue regretting the demise of the rustic carnivals of old-time Buenos Aires, when ladies and gentlemen engaged in violent water battles. One must only be sorry at the sight of changes which have not occurred from the inner workings of the country itself, because this inner life is what gives nourishment and persists. Such extraneous influences in the long run deprive peoples of their own personality, that which has been born from within itself and is their very salt and leavening. Why seek in local particularities what is naturally common to all peoples starting out on their life? The Argentinian gaucho has his wakes, like the peasant of the Canary Islands and the lower-class Irishman. In the pampas they dress up the body of the departed in his best clothes, as if for a celebration, and in Colombia they put gold shoes on his feet, because the road to Heaven is strewn with thorns, and his mother does not want, oh, she does not want her son's feet 'to be prickled'! The huntsman of the pampas pummels his meat before cooking it, just like the North American Indian. Lawless is the life of the gaucho from Choel-Choel, and the Yankee cowboy lives the same lawless life. Once he 'gets a skinful' of gin in the local store, the gaucho emerges, to challenge any man to stick his foot outside, and the Colorado miner makes the city dude dance by shooting at his feet, just as the gaucho does to the 'dandy', once whisky has maddened his blood. The outlaw gaucho becomes proud of the number of men he has killed; the plains cowboy of Upata, far-away in Venezuela, used to tell the schoolmaster: 'Mister Teacher, I like stabbing them in the back, just to hear the "push" of the knife going in.' The person who knows anything about wandering and unruly Arabs knows about gauchos. And the tower of desert forts, is it not the tower of African tribes? Man is one, and order and entity are the healthy and irrefutable laws of Nature.[85]

The main target of Martí's attack here is racism. All 'races' have the same potentialities, and differ only because of environment, which has a considerable influence on development. There are no 'inferior' or 'superior' peoples (and neither did miscegenation lead to inferiority). One must give Martí full credit for standing practically alone among the intellectuals of his day in having no truck with the half-baked theories of Social Darwinism.

'Our America'

Had one to select a single piece of writing emblematic of Martí at his best, this would be the article 'Our America', published in *El Partido Liberal* (Mexico) on 30 January 1891. It is a literary *tour de force* of dazzling metaphorical prose summing up Martí's views, at this late stage in his life, on both the history and the future possibilities of Latin America. It also allows the reader a deep insight into the fundamental premises of Martí's view of life in general. For this reason it is worthy of extensive quotation. Moreover it shows how the essential Martí, rather than a theorist on society and politics, is more a poet, who thought in images rather than abstractions.

He starts by appealing to the nations of 'our America' to forget their petty 'village' squabbles and wake up to the dangers coming from the 'giant with the seven-league boots' (the United States). Serious thinking has to be done, and this is even more important than the will to resist the threat (which Martí knows to be present). 'Trenches of ideas are of more worth than trenches of stone'; 'No ship's prow can cut through a cloud of ideas. An energetic idea, held up in all its flaming glory before the world, can stop, like the mystic banner of the Last Judgement, a whole squadron of armoured men'. The peoples of Latin America have to get to know one another, and themselves, because they will have to unite and fight. Now is the time for 'taking stock and marching together (. . .) in a tight block, like the silver in the roots of the Andes'.[86]

Those Latin Americans who dream of Europe and the United States, and of merely importing ideas born in those very different regions, because they are ashamed of being Latin Americans, are traitors. Latin America, for all its turbulent history and past and present misfortunes, has a brighter future than North America; it has already succeeded in overcoming greater obstacles.

Ambitious politicians may despair of Latin America because of its relative poverty and a supposed incapacity for progress, but in fact the fault is theirs:

> This incapacity is not in the country which is in the process of being born, which is demanding structures suitable to itself and practical greatness, but rather in those persons who want to govern original peoples, whose make-up is strange and violent, by laws inherited from four centuries of free practice in the United States, from nineteen centuries of monarchy in France. By a decree made by Hamilton one cannot stop the onrush of the Venezuelan cowboy's colt. By a sentence of Sieyès one cannot cause to flow once more the clotted blood of the Indian race. One must look to reality, when it is a question of government, in order to govern well. And the good ruler in America is not the one who knows how the German or the Frenchman is ruled, but he who knows of what elements his country is made up, and how he can guide them along a common path, in order to arrive, through methods and institutions born of the country itself, at that desired state where each man knows himself and acts from his own individuality,

and all enjoy the abundance that Nature laid out for all in the community that they fertilize with their labour and defend with their lives. The government must be born of the country itself. The spirit of government must be that of the country itself. The kind of government must be in keeping with the particular make-up of the country. Government is only the balancing out of the natural elements in a country. Because of this the imported book has been defeated in America by the man who is close to Nature. These natural men have defeated the artificial men of letters. The native mixed-breed has defeated the white American of foreign habits. It is not a question of a battle between civilization and barbarism, but between false learning and Nature.[87]

Here we really see Martí taking up cudgels with his admired Sarmiento, although he does not name him. Sarmiento's famous classic of Argentinian socio-historical analysis, *Facundo* (1845) was subtitled *Civilization and Barbarism*, and saw post-independence Argentina as a battlefield between two societies. On the one hand there was 'civilization', by which Sarmiento meant liberal capitalism, bourgeois democracy upheld by a strong central authority emanating from Buenos Aires and the cities of the interior, which he saw as oases in a desert of rural ignorance and savagery. Progress was to be achieved through the importation of foreign ideas, methods, capital and people (the native race, the mixed-bloods and the Spaniards being inferior), plus a generalized educational system. When Sarmiento wrote *Facundo*, he was in exile in Chile, and the other type of society prevailed in Argentina ('barbarism'). The country was ruled by the Buenos Aires dictator Juan Manuel de Rosas (a cattle-breeder whose realm of terror Sarmiento viewed as an archaic, semi-feudal throw-back to the colony). Rosas had formed an alliance with other cattle-barons such as himself, and their rule was enforced by gaucho armies. The town had been invaded by the countryside, the 'cultured', white city bourgeoisie was being terrorized by a half-breed and negro plebs. Or, as Sarmiento's ideological and literary predecessor Esteban Echeverría expressed it in his eponymous allegorical tale, Argentina was really just one vast slaughterhouse.

After the fall of Rosas, in 1852, the 'civilizers', including Sarmiento himself (President from 1868 to 1874) had their turn, and their methods turned out to be almost as 'barbaric' and cruel as those of Rosas. The national poem of Argentina, *Martín Fierro*, written by one of Sarmiento's political adversaries, José Hernández, is a moving portrayal of the suffering wreaked on the countryside by Sarmiento's government.

Martí now comes out squarely against the civilization/barbarism dichotomy. (Sarmiento himself was later to speak bitterly of the 'Kalmucks' of the cities whom he himself had helped to establish.) No doubt Martí's increasing alarm at the evolution of the United States, of which Sarmiento especially, among the Argentinian 'civilizers', was an impassioned admirer, played its part in the slight shift in Martí's thinking.

In any case, Martí had always believed deeply, as we have seen, in the integrity of a person's individuality (his 'entity') and conciliation (not imposition) as a method of forging society. The key concept here is 'balance'. Society should be thoroughly investigated, before its direction was to be decided, and its heterogeneous elements somehow harmonized. This is why Martí, right up till his death, disliked concepts such as the class struggle, racial difference, or even the too rapid acquisition of wealth. Essential and apparently predetermined harmonies were upset by these imbalances. One might ask, therefore, why such a conciliatory man was always in favour of war against the Spaniards. Martí would have replied that Cuba was an oppressed 'entity', and so war, though cruel, was just. Nothing could be farther from Martí's way of thinking than that of a man (Sarmiento) who in 1863 could write to the Argentinian President Mitre telling him not to spare gaucho blood because it was a necessary fertilizer for the nation and the only human attribute of the gaucho. To his racism Sarmiento also added the feeling that Argentina was a 'secondary' country. All of this was anathema to Martí, as can be seen in 'Our America'.

> The natural man is good, and respects and rewards superior intelligence, as long as the latter does not use its sway over him to harm him or offend him by ignoring him, which is what the natural man does not forgive, being desirous of winning back through force the respect of the person who wounds his pride or harms his interests. It is because they knew how to use these natural elements that had been scorned that the tyrants of America have risen to power, and have fallen once they betrayed them. The republics have purged through tyrannies their incapacity for getting acquainted with the real elements that make up their countries, by deriving from them the type of government and governing with them. A ruler, in a new people, must be a creator. (. . .) To know one's country, and to rule it according to this knowledge, is the only way of freeing it from tyrannies. The European university has to give way to the American university. The history of America, from the Incas down to the present day, has to be taught in all its details, although that of the Greek archons be not taught. Our Greece is preferable to the Greece that is not ours. It is more necessary to us. National politicians must replace foreign politicians. Let the world be grafted on to our republics. And let the defeated pedant hold his tongue; for there is no fatherland in which man may take more pride than our suffering American republics.[88]

Moreover the reality of 'our *mestizo* America' is its heterogeneity. Even its independence struggles took different forms in different places. The real problems came after the defeat of the Spaniards, the main one being how to find lasting democratic institutions to fit these new, complex and very contradictory nations with no tradition of democratic practice. Eventually the old seigneurial Spanish habits re-emerged in different guises. The 'cultured', i.e. educated, cities tried to ride roughshod over the rural areas and their ways, when the latter had played a major role in the defeat of colonialism.

The new political chiefs who drew their ideas from (foreign) books did not realize that they should rule their nations 'in accordance with the soul of the land' and 'not against it or without it'.[89] Martí ignores the question of antagonistic material interests in the new 'patria', and believes that a politics of conciliation will be enough to consolidate it. Once 'the reason of all in matters concerning all'[90] held sway, the 'patria' was safe. The real problem was not even that of structures, he affirms, but of *spirit*. Martí does not see governments in terms of class interests, but rather as having or lacking good will towards their citizens. The tiger of despotism, driven away by the flash from patriot guns, returns stealthily to its old haunts, to sink its teeth into the unaware, because governments have not known how to stamp it out as a breed, having themselves narrow, despotic interests. This tiger is the main problem in Latin America (dictatorships being common there), but eventually its kind will become extinct.

> The colony continued to live on in the republic; and our America is gradually rescuing itself from its past mistakes – the haughtiness of the capital cities, the blind triumph of the despised peasantry, the excessive importation of foreign ideas and formulae, the iniquitous and impolitic disdain for the native race – through the superior virtue, fertilized by necessary bloodshed, of the republic in its battle with the colony. The tiger lurks behind every tree and around every corner. It will die, eventually, waving its paws in the air and with flames coming from its eyes.[91]

The striking image of the tiger of despotism most certainly comes from Martí's reading of Sarmiento's *Facundo*, which purports to be partly the biography of the notorious 'tiger of the plains' of Argentina, Facundo Quiroga. Facundo was eventually slain, and Martí expresses his confidence in the demise of American despotism in general. He quotes the optimistic words of even Bernardino Rivadavia, first President of the Argentine Republic and thorough-going Europeanizer, subsequently overthrown by Rosas and his allies in the countryside. Rivadavia is correct in saying that these countries will be saved, because, in Martí's words,

> with the genius of moderation which seems to be holding sway, through the serene harmony of Nature, in the continent of light, and through the influence of critical reading material that has superseded in Europe books containing tentative or utopian theories which the previous generation soaked itself in, the real man, in these real times, is being born in America.[92]

In other words, reason plus moderation is bound to win out. Echoes of Krausism's 'harmonic rationalism'!

There follows an extraordinary piece of poetic prose, which is worth quoting extensively because it reveals the essential Martí:

> We were a sight to behold, with an athlete's chest, a fop's hands and a child's forehead. We were a mask, with English breeches, a Parisian waistcoat, North American over-jacket and a Spanish bullfighter's hat. The Indian, in

his silence, roamed around us, and went off into the mountains, to the summit of the mountains, to baptize his children. The Negro, watched with vigilance, sang in the night the music of his heart, alone and unknown, amongst the waves and the wild beasts. The peasant, the creative man, turned, blinded by indignation, against the scornful city, against his own creature. We were épaulettes and professorial gowns, in countries that came into the world wearing Spanish rope-soled slippers and an Indian headband. The stroke of genius would have been to unite, with heartfelt charity and the boldness of the founding fathers, the Indian headband and the gown; to get the Indian moving again; to make room for the capable black man; to fit freedom to the bodies of those who rose up and won a victory in its name. The colonial judge, and the general, the university graduate and the ecclesiastic living off a stipend all disappeared. Angelic youth, as if caught in the tentacles of an octopus, lifted up its cloud-crowned head to the heavens, only for it to fall again in sterile glory. The uneducated people, close to nature, with the vigour of instinct, swept away, blinded with triumph, the golden batons. Neither the European book nor the Yankee book held the key to the enigma of Spanish America. Hate was tried, and the countries went further downhill with each passing year. Tired of useless hate, of the resistance put up by the book to the lance, by reason to the church candlestick, by the city to the countryside, by the impossible empire of the divided urban castes over the uneducated nation, close to Nature, tempestuous or inert, people started to try love, as if unknowingly. The nations stood up, and greeted one another. 'What are we like?', they asked one another; and they started to tell one another what they were like. When a problem appears in Cojímar [a small Cuban town], they do not go to Dantzig for the solution. The frock-coats are still French, but the thought is beginning to be American. The young people of America are rolling up their sleeves, sinking their hands in the dough and making it rise with the leaven of their sweat. They realize that there is too much imitation, and that salvation lies in creation. Creation is the password of this generation. The wine may be made from bananas, and come out bitter, but it is our own wine. They realize that the governmental structures of a country have to be in keeping with its natural elements; that absolute ideas, in order to avoid failure through a mistake in their form, must be applied relatively; that liberty, in order to be workable, must be sincere and complete; that if the republic does not open its arms to all and go forward with all, the republic will die. The tiger inside will get through the crack, as will the tiger outside. A general holds back the cavalry on the march to allow the infantry to keep up. Or if he leaves the infantry behind, the enemy surrounds the cavalry. Politics is a matter of strategy. Nations must live by self-criticism, because criticism is health; but this has to be done with one single breast and one single mind. Stoop to the level of the unfortunate and pick them up in your arms! With fire in our hearts, let us thaw out clotted America! Make the natural blood of the country flow bubbling and tumbling through its veins! Standing upright, with the merry eyes of workers, the new Americans are greeting one another, from country to country! Native statesmen are coming to the fore from the direct study of Nature. They are reading in order to apply their reading, not merely to copy. Economists are studying a problem in its origins. Orators are beginning to restrain themselves. Dramatists are bringing native characters on to the stage. Academics are discussing workable topics. Poetry is cutting off its long Romantic locks, and hanging up its scarlet waistcoat on the glorious trees. Prose, sparkling and sifted, is loaded with ideas. Rulers, in Indian republics, are learning Indian.[93]

This generous piece of Romantic prose, whilst admirable in its way (and not only for its stylistic originality), nevertheless underestimates the difficulties faced by the nations of Latin America. Martí's repeated basic recipe of love and understanding, coupled with an empiricist self-reliance plus hard work, is not enough to resolve major problems like class and race. And the application of 'general' principles in a 'relative' way is likewise fraught with dangers, because at a certain point in the process of relativization a qualitative change must take place in the 'principle' itself. Martí was too influenced by empiricism (in combination, curiously, with an apostolic moralism) to be a dialectical thinker. He relies too much on exhortation. He shared with Marx the nineteenth century optimism which saw man as ascending inevitably to ever-higher planes, yet whereas Marx ascribed this process to the dialectical workings out of economic contradictions through the class struggle, Martí, in his Krausist way, believes its motive force to be reason, aided by a sort of constant moral illumination. Never a socialist, Martí nonetheless believed in the advent of a civilization illuminated by a 'religion of humanity', where all were brothers. This is why his strictures on Marxists were only half-hearted. It is significant that he uses the same phrase to characterize both Marx and Carlos Baliño (a member of Martí's own Cuban Revolutionary Party and future founder, in 1925, of the Cuban Communist Party). They both 'went too fast'.

The problems that Latin America had still to overcome, but from which those nations were gradually emerging, were stagnation, love of luxury and a hatred of some states for others. These problems had to be solved, because otherwise, the United States, an 'enterprising and thrusting' nation, whose 'origins, methods and interests' were in contradiction to those of Latin America, of which it was ignorant and disdainful, would pounce.[94] To stop this, unity is primordial, and the assertion of a separate identity. If this was achieved, the United States might respond to 'the purest elements in its blood' and refrain from conquest, direct or indirect. The eyes of the world were on the Southern continent, and it had to maintain a certain 'decorum' (a key concept for Martí). The dualistic nature of Martí's thought processes is also evidenced in the following passage taken from the same paragraph: 'One must have faith in the best in man and mistrust the worst in him. One has to give an opportunity for the best to emerge and prevail over the worst. If not, the worst prevails'.[95]

'Our America' ends with Martí's most important statement on race, which, again, is better transcribed than paraphrased:

> There is no such thing as racial hatred because there are no such things as races. Puny thinkers, thinkers who never leave the lamps of their studies, string together and try to infuse life into races only found in books, races which the fairminded traveller and the amiable observer seek vainly in the justice of Nature where, in victorious love and turbulent appetite, the universal identity of man stands out. The soul emerges, equal and eternal, from bodies diverse in form and colour. It is a sin against humanity to encourage and propagate racial opposition and hatred. But in the process whereby peoples are formed and condensed, in the neighbourhood of other diverse peoples, peculiar and active characters, with ideas and habits of expansion and acquisition, vanity and avarice, which could, from a latent stage of national problems, turn, during a period of internal disorder or sudden crystallization of the character of the nation, into a serious threat to the neighbouring lands, isolated and weak, which the nation declares to be perishable and inferior entities. Thinking implies service. And one must not presume, out of petty dislike, that the fairheaded nation of the continent is congenitally and necessarily evil, just because it does not speak our language or look upon the home as we do, or because it is unlike us in its political faults, which are different from our own. Or because it has little esteem for the quarrelsome and dark-skinned peoples, or no charitable feelings, from the heights of its still shaky eminence, towards those who, less favoured by History, are striding heroically along the republican road. Neither must the patent facts of the problem be hidden. The problem can be solved, and give lasting peace, through being studied now and if the soul of the continent is tacitly united, as is required with urgency.[96]

The main thrust of Martí's message to Latin Americans in 'Our America' may be resumed as follows: No peoples or races are congenitally inferior. If some appear, at a particular historical moment, to be less advanced or capable than others, this is an accident of evolution or a passing illusion, since all possess the same latent capacities. Latin Americans should realize this and not kow-tow to the predatory forces to the north. They must forget their quarrels and unite to resist United States expansionism. Only then could they win the respect of the latter nation.

The International Monetary Conference

'Our America' was published in Mexico during the International Monetary Conference held in Washington between 7 January and 3 April 1891. This Conference was the consequence of a recommendation by the previous Panamerican Congress, and represented an opportunity for Secretary of State Blaine to claw back some of the points he had lost in that Congress. Blaine proposed that all the republics of America adopt a common silver currency for trade between them. The United States was the largest

producer of silver in the world at that time, but the aim was also to stop
Europe trading with Latin America (silver being unacceptable to its
European trading partners). As in the case of the Panamerican Congress,
Blaine largely failed to achieve his goals, and this was now even more due
to the efforts of Martí, who represented the interests of Uruguay at the
Conference and in fact drew up the official report of the Latin American
republics to the Conference.

Martí wrote a chronicle of the Conference for the New York Spanish
language *Revista Illustrada* (May 1891). In this he laid bare the real
reasons for the attempt to impose a common silver currency in the
Americas and in passing, as usual, gave his readers an insight into the
more general workings of his mind:

> One must not look principally at the outside appearance of things, but
> rather at their spirit. What is real is the important thing, not what appears on
> the surface. In politics what is real is that which is not visible. Politics is the
> art of combining, for increasing prosperity inside a country, the diverse or
> opposed factors of a country, and of saving the country from the open
> enmity or greedy friendship of other countries. [97]

Note the neo-Kantian dualism (appearance and reality) and the
emphasis on the nation-state as the basic political entity, to whose
interests those of all particular groups within this state should be subordinated. In many ways Martí was a nineteenth century nationalist of the
Romantic era (which in America carried over into the second fifty years),
a Cuban Mazzini. The nascent nation-state is seen as a kind of family,
where the *paterfamilias* (the liberator or leading politician) has to forge
unity at all cost in order to throw off the bonds of servitude. Thus
problems of class and race are seen by Martí as secondary to the drive for
independence. In this sense he was the most suitable leader for the Cuban
struggle against Spanish colonialism.

As for the United States, Cubans and Latin Americans in general
should take heed of the antagonism of interests between the two halves of
the continent, and beware:

> If two nations have no interests in common, they cannot come together. If
> they do come together, they clash. The smaller peoples, who are still in the
> upheavals of their gestation, cannot unite without danger with those who
> are seeking a remedy to the excess production of a tightly knit and aggressive
> population, and a conduit for their turbulent hordes, in a union with smaller
> peoples. The political acts of real republics are the result of the combination
> of the elements of national character, economic needs, party political needs
> and the needs of leading politicians. [98]

Martí then sets out an idea which is close to the Marxist concept of
hegemony, saying: 'A people grows and acts on other peoples according
to the elements which make it up. The action of one country, in a union of
countries, will be in accordance with the elements which predominate in

it, and cannot be different from them'.[99] It is hard to see how this notion can be squared with Martí's concept of politics as a process of bringing about equilibrium. Another difficulty arises if one tries to reconcile the following passage with the previously stated hopes that somehow 'decorum' will prevail in the United States:

> If a plain, a grassy fragrant plain, opens out before a hungry horse, the horse will throw itself on the grass and bury itself up to its neck, and furiously bite anybody who disturbs it.
>
> Two condors, or two lambs, may get together without as much danger as a condor and a lamb. The young condors themselves, taken up with the fiery games and boastful battles of their infancy, would not defend well, or arrive on time and together to defend the prey which the adult condor had snatched away from them.[100]

Whilst Martí believes that the diverse elements contained in one nation may be brought together, he sees this same diversity as prohibitive in international relations:

> For life in common, there must be common ideas and habits. It is not enough for the goal in life to be the same for those who are to live together; the way of life must be the same. If not, there will be fighting, and mutual scorn and hatred, just as much because of differences of manner as of goals. The countries that do not have common methods, even if their aims are identical, cannot unite to realize their aims by the same methods.[101]

Behind these passages are Martí's feelings – abundantly expressed in his writings – of revulsion for the brutal, money-grubbing selfishness he saw as the prime mover of society in the United States, whose population lacked the courtesy and warmth he found among Latin Americans. His *Campaign Diaries* likewise bear testimony to this, and from the opposite angle. His joy at being in the countryside of Santo Domingo, Haiti and Cuba, and receiving the heartfelt hospitality of the local people, shines through these journals most movingly.

In his report on the Monetary Conference, Martí declared that the United States had gone wrong from the start. Even the 'most human and virile element' of 'rebel colonists, second sons of noble families or puritan bourgeoisie' was 'always selfish and bent on conquest'. It 'destroyed the native element, encouraged and lived off the enslavement of another race and defeated or acquired by robbery the neighbouring countries'.[102] This propensity to greed and conquest was accentuated by constant immigration from Europe of peoples used to political and religious despotism and whose only desire was to exercise over others the tyranny they had suffered in their homelands. Martí does not see that the capitalist development of North American society required precisely these daemonic forces.

Whilst he had little good to say for Spain's role in America, his underlying assumption is always that Latin America would avoid the evils of North American society precisely because of the presence of social values like the concepts of honour, dignity, decorum and the like (dear to Martí's own heart) bequeathed by Spain, a society that had still not emerged psychologically from feudalism. These values were conspicuously absent in the United States, whose development was vitiated, in Martí's eyes, by this fact. One has the impression that Martí wanted the same kind of economic and political progress as in the United States, but tempered somehow by a certain pre-capitalist Hispanic courtliness.

But the picture Martí drew of the United States was hardly that of a nation susceptible to the gentle winds of humane reform:

> They believe in necessity, in the right of barbarians, as the only right: 'this will be ours because we need it'. They believe in the unquestionable superiority of 'the Anglo-Saxon race over the Latin race'. They believe in the inferiority of the black race, which they enslaved in the past and now insult, and of the Indian race, which they are exterminating. They believe that the peoples of Spanish America are formed, in the main, of Indians and blacks. As long as the United States does not improve its knowledge of Spanish America and does not have more respect for it – as by the constant explanation given urgently, variously and wisely of our constitutive elements and resources, it could eventually respect it – may the United States invite Spanish America to a union which is sincere and useful for Spanish America? Is political and economic union with the United States suitable for Spanish America?[103]

Then Martí formulates his famous dictum on the necessary relation between politics and economics, to which he had been led by his experiences of North American expansionism:

> Economic union means political union. The country which buys is the one that commands. The country which sells, obeys. One must balance trade out, in order to ensure freedom. The people that wishes to die sells to a single people, and the one that wishes to be saved, sells to more than one.[104]

This statement has to be read in the context of United States aims in the Monetary Conference, i.e. to prise Latin America away from its European trading partners. Martí continues:

> The first thing which a people does in order to dominate another, is to separate it from other peoples. A people desirous of freedom must be free in business. It should spread out its business interests among countries of equal strength. If it has to prefer one of these, let it be the one that has least need of it, the one which has least scorn for it. Neither unions of America against Europe, nor with Europe against one people in America. The geographical circumstance of living together in America does not oblige anybody, except in the mind of some candidate or some high-school lad, to acquiesce in political union. (. . .) Union with the world as a whole, and not just one part of it; not with any part of it against another part. If the family of republics in America has any task to perform, it is not that of trailing behind any one of them against future republics.[105]

The 'candidate' is obviously Blaine, and 'future republics' means Cuba, which Martí viewed as a test case for the avoidance of the United States dominance over its southern neighbours. History has proven Martí right in this last point, although the 1959 revolution of Fidel Castro, and not Martí's own liberation struggle of the 1890s was the real beginning for 'rolling back' the United States in the countries of America.

As far as the silver currency question went, Martí pointed out that on the one hand the United States could produce silver in excess and through legislation establish an artificial price for it. This harmed the silver of other countries, including some in Latin America. On the other hand, the US House of Representative itself failed to decide on the free coining of silver (the Conference had actually been held up while it deliberated), most US politicians being in fact against the Conference, which they correctly saw as a manoeuvre of Blaine towards the US Presidency. Moreover European hostility to silver was also taken into account as a deterrent.

Blaine's plans were frustrated, due in a large measure to Martí's lobbying the other delegates to the Conference and his report made on behalf of the Latin American nations present. This report, presented to the Conference on 30 March 1891, suggested in lieu of the US proposals the convocation of a world monetary conference in Paris.

The Final Stages: the Cuban Revolutionary Party and the 1895 Insurrection
In April 1892 Martí founded the Cuban Revolutionary Party, to prepare democratically the final anti-Spanish campaign and establish at the same time the basis for a future democratic Cuban nation. By this time he had given up all major activities (such as his consular posts and columns in Latin American newspapers) not directly linked to preparations for the insurrection. His writings, too, centre on Cuban problems, as his newly founded newspaper *Patria* and his letters show. These writings have already been analysed in another chapter, but insofar as Martí's thinking on Cuba was inextricably bound up with his ideas on Latin America as a whole it will be necessary to give a brief overview of his declarations concerning the latter for the period 1892–95.

Martí's main worries now were that Cuba should stave off the United States and avoid the mistakes of the first Spanish American republics. At the onset of these last years of his life he took no theoretical step forward. In 1892 he still believed in the dichotomy of a 'spiritual' Latin America and a 'material' United States. He spoke, for instance, to the Spanish American Literary Society of New York in a meeting held there in honour of Venezuela of 'our disinterested America',[106] which had to be cherished, fought for and publicized. And in another speech to that Society made probably in that same year (only an undated draft survives), he affirmed: 'we have up to now been so prodigal in our scorn for material wealth or in subordinating it to affairs of the spirit that we were falling behind the world'.[107]

Once again we see how Martí is trapped between a neo-Kantian idealism and a positivistic empiricism, between, in fact, succeeding nineteenth-century ideologies, as was Krausism itself, whose 'harmonic rationalism' was an attempt to combine the two and seems to provide Martí with the basic premises of his own approach to the world. On one hand there is a belief in abstract categories like goodness, beauty, truth, justice, etc., and the value of intuition as a method of cognition, wedded to a perception of the universe as ultimately harmonious. On the other hand there is an acceptance of 'progress', empirical analysis and rationalism itself. In Martí's mind live two very distinct ideologies: one, quasi-religious and rather static, based on love; the other, accepting science, evolution and struggle. This incongruity is illustrated well in his attitude to Darwin: general praise for the man and his achievements, yet tempered with a criticism that regrets Darwin's not having traced the evolution of the spirit. Of course, for Martí Darwin's monism was the problem.

Martí would like to preserve the 'spiritual' values he ascribed to Latin America and saw as so greatly lacking in the United States, and yet have the former partake of the material progress of the latter. He seems to desire a society halfway between a too greedy capitalism and what he called sarcastically the 'tottering university of the clouds'.[108]

Martí's younger contemporary, the Uruguayan intellectual José Enrique Rodó, perpetuated the idea of a 'spiritual' Latin America battling with a 'material' United States, and drew the analogy with the Ariel/Caliban opposition in Shakespeare's *Tempest*, an image that has remained in the minds of many Latin Americans. This kind of thinking was scotched by the first major Marxist thinker of Latin America, José Carlos Mariátegui, writing in 1928, nearly three decades after Rodó's *Ariel*.

> Against capitalist, plutocratic, imperialist North America it is only possible to set effectively a Latin or Iberian America which is socialist. The era of free competition, in the capitalist economy, is finished in all fields and in all aspects. We are in the era of the monopolies, that is, the empires. The countries of Latin America are arriving too late to compete on a capitalist basis. The first places have already been definitively assigned. The destiny of these countries, within the capitalist order, is that of mere colonies. The opposition of language, race, spirit, is not decisive. It is ridiculous to speak still of the contrast between a Saxon America which is materialistic and a Latin America which is idealistic, between a blond Rome and a pale Greece. All these are clichés which have been irremediably discredited. Rodó's myth no longer has – and has never had – any useful or fundamental effect on people's minds.[109]

This is well said, and yet it would be ludicrous to criticize Martí or Rodó for the idealist cast of their thinking. One must take into account that Mariátegui enjoyed the advantage of living after Lenin and the 1917 Revolution, in times when the nature of imperialism had been much more clearly elucidated.

The fact is, however, that Martí's revolutionary zeal forced him into a political *praxis* which was in advance of any other such in the Latin America of his day and, indeed, at times outstripped the basic ideological premises that had formed his view of the world. In Cuba he is now defined as a 'revolutionary democrat', by analogy with the progressive lower-class Russian intellectuals of the mid-nineteenth century such as Belinski, Chernishevski and Dobroliubov who, along with the aristocrat Herzen, were the forerunners of the men of 1905 and 1917, as Martí is the precursor of Fidel Castro. In the last years of his life Martí had to establish intimate contact with the Cuban workers' movement in Florida (it became the main base of his support), and naturally grew more sympathetic to the realities of their problems. He fought bitterly against the idea of dictatorship for either the insurrectionary movement or the new nation it would spawn. But he was not a socialist of any hue, much less a Marxist. He was what he was, in his place, time and peculiar psychology, and to project him into the future as Cubans of varying political beliefs have tried to do, in order to justify their own positions, is a task fraught with difficulties.

As Martí increasingly involved himself with the practicalities of the Cuban struggle, in the context of the threat from the United States, his analysis of Latin America and its problems, whilst not entirely avoiding the traps set by his fundamental philosophical idealism, shows him delving deeper and deeper into concrete issues and material realities. One may resume his main arguments on the question (laid out in *Patria* for the benefit of Cuban and Puerto Rican patriots) in these last three years as follows.

The main cause of the backwardness of Latin America vis-à-vis the United States was the legacy of Spanish colonialism. The Spaniards had exercised a tyrannical, divisive and corrupt rule over an area already very heterogeneous in its geographical, racial and cultural configurations. Those who argued the racial superiority of the North Americans (as, indeed, did some Latin American thinkers of the time) were mistaken. The true reason for the 'comparatively slow and painful progress of the Spanish American nations'[110] was to be found in their internal contradictions, exacerbated by the Spaniards. These contradictions were what led to the Wars of Independence, the main source of bitterness being Spain's monopoly on trade. The ideas of the Enlightenment were not an important cause of the anti-Spanish revolts, and indeed may well have served to perpetuate the backwardness of Latin America, insomuch as they were applied too mechanically. Martí criticizes Bolívar himself for being too fond of 'theoretical and artificial structures which did not fit reality'.[111] The outcome of the Revolutions of Independence was a group of nations bitterly divided amongst and between themselves, 'feudal or theoretical republics', whose main ills consisted of:

> The concentration of a merely bookish culture in the capital cities; the erroneous attraction, felt in the republics, for the lordly customs of the

colony; the creation of rival *caudillos* due to the suspicious and imperfect relations between distant regions; the rudimentary conditions of the only industry, whether this was in agriculture or stockbreeding; and the abandonment of and scorn for the fertile Indian race in disputes over belief or locality.[112]

This is a far cry from such concepts as 'our disinterested America', and shows Martí on the road to a more materialist view of history, however unwillingly he might have been pushed in that direction. The last passage quoted comes from the *Montecristi Manifesto* of 25 March 1895, penned by Martí and Máximo Gómez as the official theoretical justification for the war in Cuba, and as such must be taken very seriously.

Martí believed that Cuba would avoid the errors of the first Spanish American republics, for various reasons. Valuable political lessons had been learned between the 1820s and 1890s. Cuba lacked the 'indolent patrician caste, the false or theocratic constitutions and the ignorant and inaccessible countryside'[113] which had delayed progress in its sister nations. Moreover, as the *Montecristi Manifesto* proclaimed:

Cuba returns to war with a democratic and educated people, one that jealously knows and guards its rights and those of others; or a people which is much more educated, even in its humblest elements, than the cowboy or Indian masses with which, to the voices of the great heroes of emancipation, the silent colonies of America turned from roving herds into nations.[114]

There was not the same yawning gulf between the educated elites and ignorant masses that had made for instability in the new republics of the 1820s. Cuba, in short, was more homogeneous and politically mature, and, given correct political leadership, could become a modern, rich and progressive nation. Martí's ideas on the nature of this political guidance (basically the skilful and selfless balancing out of the diverse factors which constituted a nation) are put in an article of April 1894 in *Patria*:

Every public party must tailor itself to its people, and politics is, or should be, only the art of guiding, with one's own sacrifice, the diverse or contrary factors of a country so that, without unduly favouring the impatience of some or being guilty of denying the need for order in societies – which is only ensured when the rule of law prevails – the various elements that have an equal right to be represented and enjoy happiness should live together without clashing, and with the freedom to strive towards or resist certain goals. A people is not the will of one single man, however pure it may be, nor the childish insistence on realizing in a collection of human beings the naive ideal of a celestial spirit, the blind graduate of the tottering university of the clouds. Of hatred and love, and more hatred than love, are peoples made; it is only that love, like the sun it is, consumes and melts everything; and what greed and privilege continually accumulate over whole centuries is knocked down by one blow, alongside its natural train of oppressed souls, from the indignation of one pious soul. With these two forces: expansive love and

repressive hatred – whose public forms are interest and privilege – nationalities are built. Compassion for the unfortunate, for the ignorant and
dispossessed, cannot go so far as to put itself at the head of their errors or
encourage them. (. . .) A people is the composition of many wills, vile or
pure, frank or twisted, blocked by timidity or precipitated by ignorance.
(. . .) it is necessary to bring out virtues from deep down, without falling
into the error of ignoring them because they come in humble attire, or
denying them because they are accompanied by wealth and culture.[115]

What Martí envisages here is a multiclass society where antagonisms are resolved by enlightened rulers standing morally above the
population, whose excesses they check and whose potentialities they
awaken.

The concept of balance is central to Martí's way of thinking. Polari-
ties were in general to be avoided, or somehow brought together. In the
internal politics of a nation, this is the task of the patriotic politician, as we
have seen. But Martí extends this concept to the international politics of
the Americas, and to those of the whole world (insofar as the former will
affect the latter). The war against Spain is necessary, for Martí, in order
to halt the encroachments of the United States, 'before the disproportionate development of the most powerful nation in America turns into a
theatre of universal greed the lands which may still be the garden of their
inhabitants and, as it were, the fulcrum of the world'.[116] It is for this
reason that the responsibilities of Cuba and Puerto Rico are even greater
than those of the first republics of Spanish America struggling against
Spain. The Antilles, in their situation at the point of equilibrium of the
continent,

would be, if enslaved, a mere bridgehead in the war of an imperial republic
against the jealous and superior world which is already preparing to deny it
power, – a mere fort of the American Rome; and if free – and worthy of
being so because they rest on equitative and hardworking freedom – they
would be in the continent the guarantee of balance, that of independence
for Spanish America which is still being threatened, and that of honour for
the great northern republic (. . .). An error in Cuba is an error in America,
is an error in modern humanity.[117]

Of course, the 1895 war, in which Martí was killed very early on, did
not result in the check to North American power in the continent that
Martí had desired. The United States intervened in 1898 and did not leave
until it had ensured that the notorious Platt Amendment was written into
the Cuban constitution, giving the United States bases, coaling stations
and the excuse for intervening practically at will in Cuba. Although later
abrogated, the Amendment was instrumental in ensuring the informal
colonization of Cuba to the United States, until 1959, when the revolution
of Fidel Castro gave the check. But in principle, Martí was right in seeing
Cuba as the fulcrum of the Americas, and the fact that a combination of

preconceived ideas and strategic realities themselves was what led to Martí's correct prognosis should not lead anybody to deny the clarity of his vision in this matter. What he did not envisage, however, were the economic problems any free Cuba would face, because of the basic scarcity of its resources vis-à-vis those of an industrialized world. Sugar may have been enough in the nineteenth century for guaranteeing a certain prosperity, but this is certainly not the case now. The myth of Cuba as a horn of plenty has its origins in Columbus' first vision of the island, but has no relevance five hundred years later.

The word 'honour' used by Martí in the last passage quoted is a measure of the extent to which an idealist frame of reference still remained in his mind. Did he really believe that the United States would give weight to such concepts as 'honour'? Or were his last written words more truly indicative of his feelings about that country? Martí told Manuel Mercado, in an oft-quoted letter dated 18 May 1895, only one day before being killed by Spanish bullets, of his (Martí's) 'duty (. . .) to prevent in time, by the independence of Cuba, the United States from reaching out over the Antilles and falling, with that additional force, on our lands in America'. He added vehemently:

> All that I have done up to now, and shall do, is to that end (. . .) with our blood we are blocking (. . .) the annexation of the peoples of America to the turbulent and brutal North that despises them (. . .). I lived in the monster, and know its innards, and my sling is that of David.[118]

Notes

1. *OC*, 21, pp. 15–16.
2. In *La Revista Universal*, Mexico City, 29 July 1875, *OC*, 6, pp. 284–5.
3. Ibid., 15 January 1876, *OC*, 6, p. 423.
4. Ibid., 29 June 1875, *OC*, 6, p. 248.
5. Ibid., 11 May 1875, *OC*, 6, p. 200.
6. Ibid., 26 October 1875, *OC*, 6, pp. 352–3.
7. Ibid., 14 August 1875, *OC*, 6, pp. 311–12.
8. Ibid., 23 September 1875, *OC*, 6, p. 335.
9. Ibid., 14 August 1875, *OC*, 6, p. 310.
10. Ibid., 14 July 1875, *OC*, 6, p. 270.
11. Ibid., 2 June 1875, *OC*, 6, p. 219.
12. Ibid., 7 August 1875, *OC*, 6, p. 297.
13. Ibid., 7 March 1876, *OC*, 7, pp. 348–9.
14. In *El Federalista*, Mexico City, 16 December 1876, *OC*, 6, p. 362. Cf. Kant, quoted by Bertrand Russell in *The History of Western Philosophy*, London, 1984: 'There can be nothing more dreadful than that the actions of a man should be subject to the will of another.' p. 678.
15. Letter to Joaquín Macal, 11 April 1877, *OC*, 7, pp. 97–8.
16. *Los códigos nuevos*, *OC*, 7, pp. 99–102.

17. Letter to Manuel Mercado, 19 April 1877, *OC*, 20, pp. 27–9.

18. Unpublished prospectus for the *Revista Guatemalteca*, *OC*, 7, pp. 104–6.

19. Letter to Manuel Mercado, 21 September 1877, *OC*, 20, p. 32.

20. Ibid., 10 November 1877, *OC*, 20, p. 37.

21. Ibid., 20 April 1878, *OC*, 20, p. 48.

22. Ibid., 6 July 1878, *OC*, 20, pp. 51–2.

23. *Guatemala* (pamphlet), December 1877, *OC*, 7, p. 118.

24. 'Impressions of America (1)' in *The Hour*, New York, 10 July 1880, *OC*, 19, p. 103.

25. Speech to Cuban emigrés, Steck Hall, New York, 24 January 1880, *OC*, 4, pp. 202–3.

26. Ibid., p. 202.

27. Speech to the Caracas Chamber of Commerce, 21 March 1881, *OC*, 7, pp. 285 & 288.

28. See Jean Lamore, 'José Martí frente a los caudillismos de la época liberal (Guatemala y Venezuela) in *Anuario del Centro des Estudios Martianos*, Habana 1980, no. 3, p. 144. The quote comes from Lamore.

29. 'Cecilio Acosta' in *La Revista Venezolana*, Caracas, 15 July 1881, *OC*, 8, p. 158. Guzmán Blanco was the model for Joseph Conrad's ferocious old tyrant, Guzmán Bento, in *Nostromo*.

30. Ibid., p. 158.

31. Ibid., p. 158.

32. *OC*, 21, p. 178.

33. 'El obrero cubano' in *Patria*, 2 July 1892, *OC*, 2, p. 52.

34. *OC*, , 21, pp. 385–6.

35. *OC*, 21, p. 160.

36. 'El tratado comercial entre los Estados Unidos y México' in *La América*, New York, March 1883, *OC*, 7, p. 20. In fact the treaty was never signed.

37. 'México, Los Estados Unidos y el sistema prohibitivo' in *La América*, February 1884, *OC*, 7, p. 30.

38. 'Agrupamiento de los pueblos de América', etc. in *La América*, October 1883, *OC*, 7, p. 325.

39. 'Buenos Aires', etc., in *La América*, June 1883, *OC*, 7, p. 323.

40. Ibid., pp. 323–4.

41. 'Juárez' in *La América*, May 1884, *OC*, 7, pp. 327–8.

42. 'El General Grant' in *La Nación*, Buenos Aires, dated 12 August 1885, published 27 September 1885, *OC*, 13, p. 104.

43. Ibid., p. 105.

44. Ibid., pp. 106 & 108.

45. Ibid., pp. 109 & 115.

46. Letter to *El Partido Liberal*, Mexico City, published 2 August 1886, *OC*, 7, p. 37.

47. Ibid., p. 38.

48. 'México y los Estados Unidos' in *La Nación*, dated 9 August 1886, published 18 September 1886, *OC*, 7, p. 46.

49. Ibid., p. 47.

50. Ibid., p. 48.

51. Letter to Ricardo Otero, 16 May 1886, *OC*, 1, p. 195.

52. 'La fiesta de la estatua de la libertad' in *La Nación*, published 1 January 1887, *OC*, 11, pp. 102 & 114.

53. Letter to Manuel Mercado, January 1887, OC, 20, p. 103.

54. 'México en los Estados Unidos' in *El Partido Liberal*, 23 June 1887, *OC*, 7, p. 55.

55. Ibid., p. 57. Our retranslation of Martí's Spanish translation of Warner's words.

56. 'La República Argentina en los Estados Unidos' in *La Nación*, dated 22 October 1887, published 4 December 1887, *OC*, 7, p. 330.

57. Letter to Manuel Mercado, 19 February 1888, *OC*, 20, p. 124.

58. 'La Repúblic Argentina en el exterior' in *La Nación*, dated 3 May 1888, published 22 June 1888, *OC*, 7, p. 341.

59. Letter to Enrique Estrázulas, 15 February 1889, *OC*, 20, p. 203.

60. 'Tipos y costumbres bonaerenses, de Juan A. Piaggio' in *El Partido Liberal*, published 3 October 1889, *OC*, 7, p. 358.

61. Ibid., pp. 360 & 363.

62. See Philip S. Foner, ed., *Inside the Monster, Writings on the United States and American Imperialism by José Martí*, New York, Monthly Review Press, 1975, pp. 352–3, note.

63. 'El Congreso de Washington (1)' in *La Nación*, dated 28 September 1889, published 8 November 1889, *OC*, 6, p. 35.

64. Ibid., p. 35.

65. 'El Congreso de Washington (3)' in *La Nación*, dated 2 November 1889, published 19 December 1889, *OC*, 6, p. 46.

66. Ibid., pp. 46–7.

67. Ibid., p. 47.

68. Ibid., p. 48.

69. Ibid., pp. 53–4.

70. Letter to Serafín Bello, 16 November 1889, *OC*, 1, p. 255.

71. 'Madre América', speech made to the Spanish American Literary Society, 19 December 1889, *OC*, 6, p. 134.

72. Ibid., pp. 135–6.

73. Ibid., p. 135.

74. Ibid., p. 136.

75. Ibid.

76. Ibid., p. 137.

77. Ibid., p. 138.

78. Ibid., pp. 138–9. The Colombian Antonio Nariño was the first Latin American to publicize the doctrine of the Rights of Man in Latin America.

79. Ibid., p. 139.

80. Foner, op. cit., p. 353, note.

81. 'El Congreso de Washington (4)' in *La Nación*, dated 18 April 1890, published 31 May 1890, *OC*, 6, p. 100.

82. 'La pampa' in *El Sudamericano*, Buenos Aires, published 20 May 1890, *OC*, 7, p. 368.

83. Ibid., p. 370.

84. Ibid.

85. Ibid., pp. 370–1.

86. 'Nuestra América' in *El Partido Liberal*, published 30 January 1891, *OC*, 6, p. 15.

87. Ibid., pp. 16–17.

88. Ibid., pp. 17–18.

89. Ibid., p. 19.
90. Ibid.
91. Ibid.
92. Ibid., pp. 19–20.
93. Ibid., pp. 20–21.
94. Ibid., p. 21.
95. Ibid., p. 22. See Martí's strictures on Darwin's monism.
96. Ibid., pp. 22–3.
97. 'La conferencia monetaria de las repúblicas de América' in *La Revista Illustrada*, New York, May 1891, *OC*, 6, p. 158.
98. Ibid., p. 158.
99. Ibid., p. 159.
100. Ibid.
101. Ibid.
102. Ibid., pp. 159–60.
103. Ibid., p. 160.
104. Ibid.
105. Ibid.
106. Speech made to the Spanish American Literary Society in honour of Venezuela, 1892, *OC*, 7, p. 291.
107. Speech on Santiago Pérez Triana, made to the Spanish American Literary Society, no date, *OC*, 7, p. 426.
108. 'El tercer año del Partido Revolucionario Cubano' in *Patria*, 17 April 1894, *OC*, 3, p. 139.
109. José Carlos Mariátegui, 'Aniversario y balance' in *Amauta*, Lima, año 111, no. 17, September 1928, reproduced in *La organización del proletariado*, Lima, Ediciones Bandera Roja, 1967, pp. 193–4.
110. 'La sociedad hispanoamericana bajo la dominación española. Libro nuevo del sr. Vicente G. Quesada, ministro argentino en España' in *Patria*, 14 February 1893, *OC*, 7, p. 390.
111. Speech made in honour of Simón Bolívar to the Spanish American Literary Society, 28 October 1893, published in *Patria*, 4 November 1893, *OC*, 8, p. 246.
112. *Manifiesto de Montecristi*, 25 March 1895, *OC*, 4, p. 95.
113. 'El Partido Revolucionario a Cuba' in *Patria*, 24 May 1893, *OC*, 2, p. 345.
114. *Manifiesto de Montecristi*, p. 95.
115. 'El tercer año del Partido Revolucionario Cubano', pp. 139–40.
116. Ibid., p. 139.
117. Ibid., p. 143.
118. Letter to Manuel Mercado, 18 May 1895, *OC*, 4, pp. 167–8.

3: Martí and the Great Crisis of Labour in the United States

Some Introductory Comments

The years 1886–87 saw the ferocious class struggle between capital and labour in a nation given over to a frenzied process of industrialization reach a high point in the Chicago Haymarket affair. The latter events caused a shift in Martí's views on social questions and also on the nature of the United States itself. The Haymarket clashes between police and workers, with deaths on both sides, and the subsequent trial and execution of a group of anarchists, provided Martí with a new and bitterer insight into the workings of the giant northern republic, so that by the time he died in Cuba in the final anti-Spanish war he had labelled the United States a monstrous Goliath and cast himself in the role of its David.

This chapter will concentrate on the Haymarket affair, since it was decisive for Martí's change of attitude insofar as it made him more aware than he had been of the antagonistic nature of the relationship between capital and labour under the beginnings of monopoly capitalism. It was this apparently unbridgeable chasm that so disillusioned Martí the harmonizer and conciliator, and pushed him even further down the road leading away from the concept of the United States as in any way a model for his own country. As previous chapters have indicated, there were other circumstances in those key years that increased Martí's intuitive dislike of the United States and set the seal on his determination to eschew its basic values. Specific reference must be made to these in the present chapter, also, but what will not be attempted is a detailed analysis of Martí's whole stay in the United States and of his reactions to each and every facet of what he saw there. The reason for this turns on a question of correct emphasis. This book is concerned with giving a balanced picture of what is basically important in Martí: the development of his thinking on political, social, and to a lesser extent more abstractly philosophical matters. Martí was first and foremost a struggler for his country's independence, and then an upholder of the sovereignty of Latin America as a whole. To each of these two paramount categories that of Martí as a chronicler of the United States must be subordinated, although the three are inextricably linked. It is true that one-fifth of Martí's writings (five out of the twenty-five volumes first published by the government of socialist Cuba in 1963–65) deal with matters relating to the United States, and that Martí did spend as much as a third of his entire life (and two-thirds of his mature life) there. But however long was his residence in the North (as Cubans call their vast neighbour), this was only a preparatory stage for Martí's Cuban concerns.

The United States and the 'Gilded Age'

A few words must be given, however, to the North American background into which Martí inserted himself, however temporarily, in the early 1880s. Martí lived through part of what Mark Twain, its increasingly embittered satirist (of whom Martí was very fond), termed the 'Gilded Age' of the United States. This was an era, following the defeat of the South in the Civil War, of tremendous capitalist expansion, which had been initially set in motion by the needs of the war itself. When the North won, industrialism became the primary fact of the United States economy, and a frenzied business mentality swept the length and breadth of the nation, culminating in the beginnings of the monopoly capitalist system.

Hordes of (mainly European) immigrants poured in, new lands were opened up in abundance, railways and mining expanded along with the rest of the economy. The political processes of these post-bellum years were dominated, although not totally so, by the victorious Republican Party, the party of Lincoln but also now the party of big business, standing for high tariffs against foreign imports so as to build up the industrial base of the nation, high taxes to swell the Treasury coffers, subsidies to business and transport, and expansionism in general. The Democratic Party was associated with non-industrial business, and agrarian and labour interests, although there was considerable overlapping between the two parties in many questions and interests. Generally, however, and unlike the Republicans, the Democrats pursued a non-expansive foreign policy and were for the lowering of tariffs and taxes so as to cheapen the cost of living. Insofar as Martí felt it necessary to voice his support, he gave it to the Democrats, and especially to Grover Cleveland and his wing of the party. However, as mentioned, it was the Republicans who called the tune in those times. To quote a modern historian:

> 'The world after 1865', wrote Henry Adams, 'became a banker's world' of millionaires. The American continent offered more natural resources than any country, except Russia, and for the man of ability and energy, the rewards for exploiting them were so huge as to stagger the imagination. Carnegie's annual income exceeded twelve and a half million dollars; his total fortune reached 1,000 million; the cheque that he received for the sale of his share of United States Steel totalled more than the entire value of the United States in Washington's day. Rockefeller amassed slightly more than

fifteen hundred million. The Guggenheim interests took 2,000 million from the Montana copper ranges. Vanderbilt II inherited a hundred million dollars and added ninety million to it in six years. Morgan's fortune equalled Carnegie's, while those of Gould, Harriman, Stanford, and Huntington (railroads), Stewart (real estate and stores), Swift and Armour (meat-packing), and Duke (tobacco) were not far behind. In 1890 an economist calculated that about 125,000 men controlled at least half the national wealth.

The most significant and far-reaching development in American business during the late nineteenth century, and the greatest factor in the amassing of huge personal fortunes, was the development of monopoly. Business men soon found, in the intense competition of business life, that the best way to treat a dangerous competitor was to combine with him. By combining instead of competing, businesses could cut production costs, control prices, fix profits, and suppress rivalry.[1]

By 1887, the most sophisticated manner of pooling resources had been found: this was the trust,

a device by which the stockholders of competing or related firms agreed to deposit controlling portions of their stocks with a board of trustees in return for trust certificates. The Sherman Anti-Trust Act of 1890, despite the vigour of its language, was difficult to enforce and easily beaten in the courts. The trust reached its highest development in Rockefeller's Standard Oil Company, which eventually controlled four-fifths of the national output, while the combined Morgan and Rockefeller interests held control of 341 major firms. By 1904 there were 319 trusts capitalized at 7,000 million dollars or more.[2]

Enormous profits were made, enormous frauds perpetrated and equally enormous bankruptcies declared. The nation was almost wholly in the grip of the robber barons and captains of industry. Its ethos, stemming originally from the independent yet frugal pioneering spirit, had been transmuted into a horrifying caricature. 'Emersonian self-reliance was never meant to produce captains of industry, but it helped to justify them'.[3] This was the paradox that was so to bedevil Martí (a great admirer of Emerson) until he was forced to dig into its roots (by examining with a more critical eye the earliest history of the United States, hitherto admired rather unquestioningly as an example of the liberal spirit). But this examination was to come later, and even then Martí never really came to grips with the problem of finding a way to reconcile the spirit of individual enterprise with the recognition of moral obligations towards the needy.

In the 'Gilded Age', which has still not come to an end in the United States,

The wealthy men of the period did not consider themselves to be bad men or 'robber barons'. They believed that if individuals of exceptional ability were encouraged to develop the national economic resources the whole of society would benefit, even though a few did enrich themselves enormously in the process – otherwise, where was the incentive? They assumed that it was the function of government to aid and protect business, to guarantee an industrial prosperity that inevitably percolated down to all the people and to some degree enriched them all. Great wealth was a divine gift, a mark that God had chosen the recipient as a steward for His worldly goods, to be used for the benefit of less capable men – an echo of the Calvinist justification of wealth a century earlier. 'Great private fortunes', remarked Senator Ingalls of Kansas, 'are inseparable from high civilizations. All the great enterprises that exalt and embellish existence and ameliorate the conditions of human life, come from the conception of money in the hands of the few'.[4]

The intellectual underpinning for this mentality was provided by the theories of Herbert Spencer, who arrived in the United States in 1882. Spencer had attempted to adapt what he thought were Darwin's ideas to human society, and the product of his efforts came to be known as Social Darwinism. His thesis was that the struggle for existence was natural and good, and that social or political action directed against the free play of human forces was unnatural and harmful. Many agreed with the Yale sociologist William Graham Sumner, who declared from his lofty vantage point that the millionaire was 'the first flowering of a competitive society'.[5]

But, of course, not everybody in the United States acquiesced in the law of the human jungle. Many Christians and those people who had inherited the Transcendentalist ideas of the previous age, let alone the socialists, were horrified at the kind of place North America was becoming. The idea that the United States should be all about a rush for money and the weakest to the wall shocked, for instance, even such an aristocratic figure as Henry Adams (or shocked him precisely because of the fineness of feeling and fastidiousness of his own soul), leading him to speak out against the blatant selling of democracy in the market-place known as bossism. Wealth divorced from responsibility was viewed by many as a great danger. In 1871 the preacher Henry Ward Beecher declared: 'We are today in more danger from overgrown pecuniary interests – from organized money – than we ever were from slavery'.[6] Ambrose Bierce remarked acidly in 1881: 'The frosty truth of the situation is that we are a nation of benighted and boasting vulgarians, in whom the moral sense is as dead as Queen Anne at her deadest'.[7]

It was thus not only on his own impressions that Martí was to formulate, a few years further on, his theory of the *two* United States, and side, obviously, with that of Lincoln and the New England intellectuals so wittily (and unfairly) satirized in Henry James' *The Bostonians*. Nobody who was so great an admirer of Ralph Waldo Emerson could do otherwise. It did not need a foreigner and outrageous aesthete such as Oscar Wilde to denounce the swinish direction that the country was taking. Wilde, at one of whose lectures Martí was present when the former made his controversial and enormously successful tour of the United States, remarked in 1882 that American man was 'entirely given to business'. 'For him Art has no marvel, and Beauty no meaning, and the Past no message.' 'America is a land of unmatched vitality and vulgarity, a people who care not at all about values other than their own, and who, when they make up their minds, love you and hate you with a passionate zeal.'[8] On another occasion Wilde stated his opinion that the United States had passed directly from barbarism to decadence without pause for civilization. Martí's mixed feelings about Wilde which peep through his account of the lecture he attended may be attributed at least in part to the fact that, at the time (1882) Martí still entertained rather positive feelings for the United States, whereas Wilde appeared to be playing the decadent.

Thus North American society fell into the clutches of the businessman, who exercised influence over government through the system of delivering votes to political parties in return for favourable legislation. Congressmen and senators, Martí came to see, were in the pockets of big business. Tammany Hall was a by-word, and the Republicans naturally had their own version of those practices which outstripped that of their rivals.

The Republican Party, with its policies of high tariffs against foreign competition, subsidies for railways and shipping lines, hard money, a stable currency and easy credit, dominated American politics from the Civil War until 1912, during which time the Democrats only held the Presidency twice. Congress too, although to a lesser extent, tended to be a Republican fief. In other words, an expanding industrial capitalism held sway, tending towards monopoly. A crisis of overproduction soon made itself felt (in the mid-1880s), when goods produced under the protectionist system became too dear and started to lack markets. Businesses collapsed, masses of workers were put out of jobs, and increasingly aggressive policies towards the neighbours of the United States were pursued, mainly for the purpose of securing markets. Martí witnessed the build-up of this crisis, the social turmoil unleashed and the high-handed treatment of Latin American nations and Canada. He lived through the culmination of the labour unrest in the Haymarket affair. As the crisis unfolded, his views on the nation naturally hardened, and it is this process that will now be examined.

Martí's Views on the United States before the Haymarket Affair

Prior to the fateful years 1886–87 and the Haymarket affair, Martí was still willing to give the benefit of the doubt to the United States. His articles on Ulysses Grant, ex-hero of the Civil War and less admirable President, whilst exposing Grant's failures as a peacetime politician who allowed himself and his close circle to be corrupted, still concluded that Grant – an emblem of the nation as a whole – was a great man. There continued to be a way forward in North American life, according to Martí in mid- and late 1885 (when he published his pieces on Grant in *La Nación*). As has been noted, even prior to his arrival in the United States Martí believed that the country was too given over to money-grubbing and placed material prosperity higher than any other value. This opinion became reinforced when he went to live there. Nonetheless, during the early 1880s Martí felt thrilled at the great possibilities of the United States. He thought that in this particular battlefield between the forces of good and evil, the former would carry the day. After the Haymarket executions, however, he concluded that evil had gained the upper hand.

Evil for Martí with respect to this question was greed, selfishness and brutal disregard for the sufferings of others. At first he believed, in true liberal style, that it was inevitable that the health of the nation should rest on the creation of riches. He had seen too much poverty in Cuba, Spain, Latin America and the United States itself, where in New York alone (Martí's place of residence), 200,000 people lived in the squalor of filthy tenements. The trouble was that as time went on Martí saw wealth increasing, often stupendously, but poverty increasing as well. The new Rome (or as he later termed it, the new Carthage) was becoming split into the two irreconcilable camps of the rich and the needy. The austere and admirable spirit of the Mayflower, which still infused the New England Transcendentalists of the previous age, was fast being choked by the demon of lucre. The values held by Martí's North American heroes, Lincoln, Henry Ward Beecher, Peter Cooper, and above all Emerson, on whom he wrote most movingly and in a spirit of total identification, these were the foundations he wished to see for the United States. But this was not to be, and Martí finally turned away from the United States, outraged and bitterly disappointed. In the year of his death in Cuba, nonetheless, Martí still showed a degree of ambivalence about that nation, which was always something of a paradox for him. In private he was calling it a 'monster', whilst in a letter to the *New York Herald* he suggested that its 'honour' could still be saved. But whether he really expected the expansionist juggernaut of monopoly capitalism to retain notions of honour is a moot point.

In the early 1880s Martí saw the United States as childish yet powerful, marvellous yet at the same time repulsive. Its corruption became more and more evident to him, but he noticed with hope its honest elements. He knew there were people who wanted to purge the Jeffersonian temple of its filth. The efforts of these noble individuals, however, were being fast overwhelmed by the worst instincts of man, his animal greed, aggression and selfishness. History, for Martí, as for the Krausists and the Transcendentalists, was the ascension from beast to man. Man still contained much of the animal, but in higher man the passions were held in check by reason. Indignation, for instance, according to Martí, led in some to fanaticism, in others to self-sacrifice, according to the amount of spirituality possessed. Thus he could describe the deplorable Guiteau, the assassin of President Garfield, as a human insect, a vixen and a wolf, following the Emersonian dictum that each quality of humankind is represented in an individual animal species. Martí quite soon noted that since the Civil War two US Presidents had been assassinated and two arraigned for corruption. The United States, it seemed to him, was fast creating the human jackal as its most representative type.

One of its defects was that it was too 'masculine', i.e. calculating, heartless and aggressive. It was good that women should have the vote, be educated and have a profession. Yet some women had overstepped the mark, and were being drawn into a masculine orbit. The suffragettes, with all their intelligence, seemed at times like men. Martí believed in woman's innate femininity: she should behave as the nature of the sex demanded, and be warm, soft and selfless. The best of these outgoing women in the United States were comrades; in Latin America, they were 'flowers' still, and Martí felt more at home with this woman. He also extended the masculine-feminine dichotomy to serve as an emblem of the two halves of the Americas: the North was avaricious, the South faithful; the material prevailed in the former, the spiritual in the latter; a person was a lone individual in the United States, but was comforted by sociability in the South. Martí's tendency to draw dualistic divisions led him also to remark that the United States gave one an impression of quantity, whereas Latin America offered quality.

It has already been pointed out that Martí perceived quite clearly, and lamented, the great division in the United States between capital and labour. His position in these early years of his residence in the United States was that capitalism was getting out of control, and that the greed, corruption and adventurism it engendered were fast weakening the moral fibre of the nation. Sooner or later it would provoke a violent backlash from its victims, and this was also to be deplored. He saw the trusts, the machine politics where votes were traded for jobs, sinecures and other favours, he knew the country was falling into the clutches of big business, which controlled the newspapers and elections. He hated fraudulent speculation, although having nothing against institutions like stock markets. He also knew the cause of the crisis of the 1880s: the high tariff barriers behind which US business developed free from healthy competition. This brought dear goods, which the workers and others could not afford, and which the very producers could not sell abroad. As a consequence, there were strikes against lay-offs and low pay, with the attendant violence. Two armies, indeed, were ranged against each other, and it did not need Marx to tell Martí who they were. If something were not done, capital and labour would soon be locked in a struggle to the death, which he deplored. By the end of the century, he thought, in his more optimistic moments, a peaceful solution would be found. He did not specify which. But he always disliked social revolution, seeing it as the last resort with respect to the internal problems of a nation. In some way a new distribution of profits had to be made, and perhaps the key was the lowering of the tariff barriers and the entrance into the country of foreign goods in competition to cheapen the cost of living for the lower classes.

For a time he espoused Henry George's schemes for the single tax system, which called for the nationalization of land and the renting out of that land to all those who wanted it. These people would be the only ones to pay taxes, and thus life would be made cheaper. Moreover, the city would be alleviated of its masses of slum dwellers, such an eyesore in the land of the free. This scheme possessed the advantage, in Martí's view, of putting people back in contact with Nature. Following the Krausists, he always believed life in the big city to be harmful for the human spirit, which needed the proximity of Nature. Politically, Martí supported Henry George in the latter's attempts to realize his programme via the United Labour Party. Prior to this, however, he favoured Grover Cleveland, the Democrat who was twice to hold presidential office and who stood against Republican big business, high tariffs and aggressive foreign policy objectives. Martí also admired Cleveland's conciliatory policy towards the defeated United States South, as against the triumphalism shown by the heirs of Lincoln's party, if not his politics. When, later on, Martí visited the South, he felt rather at home. Its courtly values must have reminded him of Latin America, as must its climate also. Once slavery was no more, there could be no reason for viewing it with enmity.

Although Martí perceived that big business and monopoly were turning the United States into a human jungle, he was not against capitalism *per se*. He believed that a certain amount of competition was necessary for the human spirit. Life, after all, was a struggle everywhere in Nature. But struggle without compassion for the weak was wrong. In any case, capitalism in the United States did not seem to be playing by its own rules. The immense swindles perpetrated and the unholy alliances forged between politicians and big business proved this for Martí. He even declared that in the United States elections had become merely a kind of inspectorate by the rich and powerful of their own interests. He saw the greatness of the nation, but hated the moral pygmies it was producing. The problem was really that Martí had no *system* to put in the place of monopoly capitalism. He thought socialism, at its best, premature, and at its worst guilty of the cardinal sin of setting man against man in class warfare. This is the hub of his objections to Marxism, not that there exists any evidence of his having acquired any deep knowledge of that system. And yet, as time went on, he felt an increasing sense of brotherhood with working people. The common people everywhere, he stated, were good, whereas the rich had generally been corrupted by their wealth. It was possible to make an honest fortune, though never quickly. In 1884 he was still of the opinion that the nation, as he put it, was destined for salvation. A year later he saw it being corrupted by love of lucre, yet still a nation of fifty million crowned heads.

As far as his attitude to the working class went, Martí had always had bias towards the poor, in a rather evangelical way. He was appalled at the poverty of many workers in the United States, and contrasted their low wages with the advantages enjoyed by the capitalists, such as easy credit, political favours, and so on. But he disliked the very idea of the class struggle, although seeing it as a fact. This is why he gave his support to the Knights of Labour, the trade union organization founded in 1869 by Terence W. Powderly, which was against violent methods in its struggles on the behalf of workers. Its very name, he noticed with pleasure, had a courtly and gentlemanly air: every worker as a (potential) knight. It has been suggested that Martí allowed himself to be unduly influenced by the anarchist Johann Most's claims to be the true voice of Marxism in the United States, and thus received a distorted view of Marxism as the ideology of the pathologically violent. Be this as it may, he was horrified by the hordes of often violent European immigrant workers who poured into the United States, full of hatred for the boss class, having felt the full force of European tyranny. He had a special dislike for anarchists, and within this category, German anarchists. This is understandable in a man for whom the concept of the *patria* or fatherland was politically paramount, in a rather early nineteenth century European way. And violence, which the anarchists were preaching in the 1880s, was for Martí, as we have seen, always the last resort in the settling of human affairs. It tended to be the prerogative of the lower, more animal type of human being, in his eyes.

This led him to comment unfavourably, for example, on Fenian violence in Europe, such as the Phoenix Park killings. He declared that to the Fenian leader O'Donovan Rossa he preferred Parnell. Although specifically condemning racism in other, later areas of his writings (such as his articles for *Patria*, aimed at a Cuban audience), Martí seemed prone to sketching a rather hasty human typology based on race. The Irish, for example, tended to be corrupt, full of hate, lazy and aggressive, although Martí admitted the existence of another, better type which was racially different. Again, there were too many violent Teutons in the United States, though the majority of Germans generally appeared peaceful and respectable. The Russian immigrants he on one occasion characterized as 'angels of iniquity', probably thinking of the Bakuninists. Martí even went so far as to state that 'the dark eye is happy; the blue eye is sad'.[9]

It worried Martí that the United States had become a 'pandemonium of races', a mass of peoples at loggerheads. This was no basis for the *patria* he conceived as necessary for every human being to lead a decent life. There was always some madness, he remarked once, in living in a foreign land, and in the United States the floodgates had been opened wide for hordes of different types of immigrants who generally had no love for their new country of residence. This seemed horrific to Martí. At first the fault seemed to lie with the immigrant, who poured into the nation in flight from European tyranny with hatred in his heart for any master and determined to put into effect utopian ideas of revolution in a land where there was no need for revolution. Another type was the unsuccessful entrepreneur. Those who did manage to better themselves, Martí knew, tended, on the other hand, to become integrated. Martí believed that a nation should be based on a communion of spirits, and this required its citizens to have sunk long roots there, generally speaking. Thus his major political premise was likely to be invalidated in the United States. No wonder that nation came to appear a seething cauldron of hatreds, and no wonder Martí eventually turned his back on that country. Likewise, his lack of sympathy with European immigrants may be understood with reference to his initial premise. And of course Martí had not arrived in the United States to settle there and carve out a new life for himself, like the immigrants, but rather to bide his time in a conveniently neighbouring country until a new Cuban campaign could be got off the ground.

It is in this context, also, that his ideas about Karl Marx must be considered. At the time he made his famous speech on Marx, in the year of the latter's death (1883), Martí still believed in the United States in the sense that, with all its faults, a prosperous and decent life for all could be made there, under the prevailing socio-economic system. In short, he still shared the American Dream. Hence, it was inapt to think of socialism. It is worthwhile quoting extensively from this piece, as dishonest writers of many different political persuasions have hacked it about so as to distort its message.

> Karl Marx is dead. As he sided with the weak, he deserves to be honoured. But he who points out wrong, and burns with generous longing to remedy it, is not [necessarily] doing good. It is, rather, the person who indicates a gentle remedy for the wrong. The task of setting men against men is frightening. The forced bestialization of some men for the profit of others arouses one's indignation. But it is necessary to find an outlet for indignation, in such a way as to stop the beast appearing, so that it does not run amok and sow terror. Look round this room: over it presides, in a frame of green leaves, the portrait of that ardent reformer, who brought together men of diverse peoples, and was a tireless and forceful organizer of them. The International was his work: men from all nations come to pay him homage. (. . .)
>
> Karl Marx studied the ways of setting the world on new foundations, and awoke those who were asleep, and taught them to pull down the broken supports [of society]. But he went too fast, and a little unclearly, and he did not see that children who have not developed in a natural and laborious way do not come to fruition, whether they are born of a people in history, or of a woman in the home. Here are present good friends of Karl Marx, who was not only the titanic force behind the anger of European workers, but who saw deep into the reason for human miseries, and into men's destinies, and who was a man eaten up by the pressing desire to do good. He saw in everything what he himself bore in his own person: rebelliousness, a striving upwards, struggle.[10]

Martí here is stating, within the general framework of praise for Marx's feelings towards the needy, his own preference for evolution as against revolution, and a dislike of violence and class struggle. It seems obvious that he had never perused even the Communist Manifesto, otherwise he would have noticed what Marx says there about the working class being in some sense the historical creation of the bourgeoisie, which also creates the conditions for the revolution of the former, over a long span of time. For Marx, evolution is not opposed to revolution; it merely precedes it.

To prove somehow that Martí stood closer to Marx than he in fact did, dishonest propagandists of the left omit the criticisms contained in Martí's article, whilst retaining his praise of Marx. On the other hand, the full quotation is often trotted out by their unscrupulous counterparts on the right, in an attempt to prove that Martí was irredeemably anti-Marxist. This argument is also wrong, because Martí became more radical vis-à-vis the cause of the working class, as the present chapter shows, and came to believe that if violent revolution happened in the United States it would be the fault of the rich. He seemed in the end not to see how violence could be avoided if the workers were to obtain a radical, and necessary, improvement in their conditions. To say that Karl Marx went 'too fast' is of course not at all to condemn him out of hand, but rather to admit that although his methods were wrong, his goals were not. It is interesting that Martí uses exactly the same words to characterize the actions of Carlos Baliño, the Cuban Marxist who was a member of Martí's own Cuban Revolutionary Party in the 1890s, and later on (in 1925) a founder-member of the Cuban Communist Party. The problem for Martí was that *in spite of himself* he discovered the workings of monopoly capitalism, and towards the end of his life was even forced to attempt some more materialist scrutiny of history than he had hitherto entertained. His political *praxis* drove him towards this, especially his contact with the Cuban tobacco workers of Florida, who formed the basis of his Cuban Revolutionary Party. One must not exaggerate this shift, however, for even at the very end of his life Martí was still largely a prisoner of his early idealist (neo-Kantian) view of the world.

To return to the North American scene, prior to the Haymarket affair: Martí at that time favoured the pragmatic politics of the native North American worker, who was usually opposed to violence. The Knights of Labour, as we have said, with their ideas for cooperatives and peaceful negotiation, seemed to him to be the appropriate trade union organization for workers in the United States. The fact that they were not socialists also predisposed Martí to them. Socialism was not necessary, he stated on one occasion, because there were no hierarchies to be over-thrown. This of course came into contradiction with his increasing awareness of the domination of big business and monopoly. There was a worker-capitalist problem, even a grave one. But by the end of the century it would be resolved, hopefully in a peaceful way. This of course meant understanding and good will on both sides, and Martí still believed this possible.

One has to see these views in the more general context of his ideas about the world as a collection of differences which, when seen as a whole, balance out. The politician should help this balance be realized, as should the trade unionist and the capitalist. Martí knew from his experience that this was not happening, but still believed it could be achieved. How? It seems, by the gradual enlightenment of the individual consciousness that is a mark of progress. If politics was still 'villainy', it would become the 'priesthood' it ought to be, led, one supposes, by the force of the Moral Imperative. The future could still be conquered by kid gloves, especially in a country where every citizen had the vote. Martí had to modify this view when he saw how votes were bought and sold. But he still believed that there was no worse country for exercising violence than that where the rule of law held sway, as it apparently did in the United States. Thus he reacted with horror to the Haymarket bomb of 4 May 1886 that killed and wounded several policemen. But, as he admitted subsequently, when in fuller possession of the facts of the issue, that bomb was in a sense *necessary*, since only the outrage provoked by it (an outrage that the press gleefully fanned) could jolt people (such as himself) who were not directly engaged in the struggles out of their optimism regarding the United States, and prompt them to take a much closer look at the 'innards' of that nation.

The Haymarket Affair

Early on in 1886 Martí called the attention of his readers in *La Nación* to the increasing social turmoil and polarization between capital and labour in the United States. An article in January remarked, as a reflection of his unease: 'In man, the trader should be cultivated, yes; but so should the priest'. Also that 'A people is not a conjunction of cogs; nor a mad horse-race; but a step higher taken by real men acting in concert'.[11] He saw the exploitation of workers with alarm, and castigated the capitalists for this. In late March he was writing: 'It is the eternal battle! All the gluttons of today (. . .) against the disinterested and fervent spirits whose only salary is their pleasure in doing good, which is a delicious payment'.[12] He went on to praise 'the most noble order of the Knights of Labour':

> This is the tremendous growth of an association of workers in all kinds of jobs, who have come together (. . .) to arbitrate in questions of differences between the capitalists and the workers, lead and maintain strikes, make laws in accordance with a just distribution of the products of labour, and suspend on one given day the entire labour of the nation, for as long as there is one single abuse to be set right, one employee dismissed wrongfully, one hateful wage which is not enough to buy bread; one example of persecution of workers who are defending their rights or those of their class.[13]

However, the workers themselves were not entirely blameless:

There are unjust strikes. It is not enough to be unfortunate to be right. The justice of a cause is often sullied by the ignorance and the excess shown in the manner of pleading it. It is true that one cannot demand of a person brought up to do bull's work that he should turn into an angel; and the workman, uneducated in mental niceties and not disposed, because of what he suffers and sees, to angelic sweetness, when he does have to speak or act, speaks his mind like a workman; if he is a tramdriver, in his driver's gloves; if a cobbler, with his awl in his hand; if a blacksmith, holding his hammer.

That is the vice that harms almost all the workers' disputes: the thinking person excuses them, and logically it is right to do so; but in social action it is dangerous, and the rulers have to repress them; that is the cause of the glorious failures of thinking men in government.[14]

This was written on the occasion of a tramdrivers' strike, which the men in fact won. Although Martí's sympathies went basically with them, he felt worried about the repercussions of the growing strength of the workers, commenting, at the end of the same article:

It was felt that the recognition of their power, given to them by their organization, could precipitate their demands in the areas of discontent, and acquire such proportions as to stop, or cause an upheaval in the life of the nation.[15]

At the time of writing there were a full 60,000 workers on strike, and considerable violence broke out, to Martí's dismay.

However, a month later he informed his readers that these conflicts were really part of the death agony of a moribund century. In the next there would be 'a new state of affairs in which labour is remunerated at a price sufficient to maintain a household without wretched poverty and provide shelter for old age, without that dependence on avarice or strange whims in which they [the workers] now live'.[16] Such were the hopes of the workers, and Martí fully concurred.

The problem was that in the United States, because of its colossal size and the suddenness of the crisis, the issue had become magnified. It was certainly not helped by the fact that many of these workers were immigrants who had no love for the United States, but rather only concerned themselves with their own interests. What he saw was a 'march of Irishmen, of Scotsmen, of Germans, of Swedes, of people that eat meat and drink beer, and have colossal backs and hands'.[17] A rather small (five and a half feet), fastidious and courtly man himself, and one whose main source of nourishment in New York, according to accounts, was tonic wine, Martí evidently felt overwhelmed by the sheer size and power of these northern Europeans; it was tempting to see them as a voracious and animal mob. But they certainly had a case: the capitalist crisis, he repeated, had its roots in overproduction and the resulting unemployment. The workers were now refusing to listen to arguments for them to lessen their demands because they saw and quite rightly resented the tremendous dividends accruing to the bosses through their combinations, trusts and frauds, whilst they themselves lived in penury. They were determined to face the capitalists head on.

The capitalists had been too greedy, and now they faced a slaves' revolt, in which the slaves themselves had decided that they were to be the masters:

> since the working people have had to suffer so much from the lordly conduct of those who employ them, they feel like becoming despots themselves, and are not content with getting together as brothers with those who have made them suffer, but rather, breaking the constraints of reason, they want to put themselves over their heads, they want to subject them to the terms that would prevent the employers from enjoying the same dignity and human liberty that the employees claim for themselves. That is where their weakness lies, in their injustice: and for the time being, there lies their defeat.[18]

With regard to the Missouri railroad strike, Martí castigated the trade unionists, who had been 'whipped up, set alight, fustigated by a steely-tongued fanatic, a Scot who has visions of fat-bellied, stinking vampires, and warlocks with wings the size of locomotives in the capitalists'. On the other hand, the leaders of the Knights of Labour, 'who allow justice to shine forth through prudence', received his warm acclamation. The kind of hatred whipped up by the Scots extremist was evil in principle. 'Everybody who does not have regard for the rights of others as well as for his own, deserves to lose his own'. The Missouri railroad strike reflected the character of its fanatical leader. 'It was badly thought out, with little judgement; proclaimed without sufficient visible reason; maintained against the will of the leaders of the order of the Knights of Labour, and against their methods; sullied by attacks, arson, acts of violence and deaths'.[19]

The laudable aims of the Knights of Labour consisted of trying to prevent strikes where possible and using conciliatory tactics. They believed, along with their Cuban supporter, that 'only in education resides definitive strength (. . .). Instead of strikes, argument; instead of threats, expoundings, examination and arbitration'.[20] However, other, more extreme elements were infiltrating the Knights of Labour, and even demanding workers' control, which Martí denounced as absurd, since the workers, he said, constituted only one factor of production. He even went so far as to applaud wealthy strike-breakers who drove trams, and a baker-woman who refused to be intimidated by strikers' demands to black scab labour, and accepted money and orders from the rich. For Martí, workers' demands such as the imposition of their own representatives as foremen in factories would leave the owners destitute of rights.

The situation had become so serious that Martí believed only the Knights of Labour could prevent a bloody insurrection, because the owners showed just the same intransigence as the workers. In the last article Martí wrote for *La Nación* before the Haymarket bomb, he summed up the situation as follows:

> It is true that the workers have their demagogues, and very vile they are and very worthy of hanging; but the upper classes also have their demagogues, and it is a mystery for nobody, from the times of Grant, that the moneyed people, the Church and the army, are more preoccupied with accumulating means of attack against the poor who are rising in the world than with lopping off the heads of their anger by applying an honest remedy to their lawful grievances.[21]

On 4 May 1886, during a demonstration in Haymarket Square, Chicago, seven policemen were killed by a bomb thrown from amidst a crowd of workers. Many more were wounded. The demonstration had arisen from a strike at the McCormick Harvester works, but was also for an eight-hour day. The Knights of Labour had called the strike, but more violent elements were also present. Martí, in his first chronicle on the incident, drew a lurid picture of labour unrest, and he called his readers' attention to the hateful bomb factories set up by the anarchists, adding

> all the East is strewn with lodges of German socialists, who go there to drink their beer, and to bring together their angers in the company of their women and their children, who bear in their earth-coloured faces and skinny hands the marks of passion and the hour of hate in which they have been engendered (. . .) there are not only Germans, but American patriarchs, men of good faith and prophetic speech, old men grown grey in the beliefs and propaganda of an epoch that was more just, apostles in the style of John Brown, that starry madman.
>
> In other places, what has been brought over from Europe, violent and criminal, predominates in the workers' movement, and stains it and makes it ugly.[22]

The latter reference is to beer-swilling Teutonic Cyclopses whom he had noticed before. He had seen the 'unhappy and desperate' lives of the working people, and wondered whether the moderates (meaning usually native Americans), relying peacefully on the democratic process, would win out over the apostles of violence, those who

> with the impetus of rage accumulated over centuries, in the despotic lands of Europe, have come over here from there with a workshop of hatred in their breasts and wish to achieve social reorganization by crime, by arson, by robbery, by fraud, by murder, by 'scorn for all morality, law and order'.[23]

Triumphant America was being invaded by the bloody filth of that toothless old queen, Europe.

He praised the Methodist Church ('Blessed be the hand that reaches down to the poor') and Henry George ('the most healthy and innocent reformer who today is studying the labour problem').[24] George, with his single tax system, aimed at getting the surplus population out of the cities and onto the land, which appealed to Martí's belief in the human need for contact with Nature inherited in part from Krausism and Emerson. Marx and Engels pointed out, on the other hand, that George's ideas really aimed at rescuing the capitalist system. This was quite true, and Martí still believed at this time that it was worth saving. He condemned 'those who are sullying the victorious march of the human spirit with unnecessary acts of violence in a country where hour by hour, from all tribunals, men can say what they want and congregate to do so'.[25] He continued, even more ingenuously: 'So the labouring majority cannot convince the wealthy minority of the need for a change? Then it has not the capacity to govern with justice, and he who lacks the capacity to convince should not govern.'[26] 'The government of men is the highest mission of mankind, and should only be entrusted to him that loves men and understands their nature.'[27] Quite so, but here Martí seems to be moving in a universe where the Moral Imperative reigns supreme, and not in the one we know.

Practically the whole nation, he declared (and he included himself here), agreed that the workers had a right to a better share of what industry produced, and that the present wage system had to be replaced. He did not say by what. The whole nation had to be reconstructed on a fresh basis so as to allow the 'harmonious and improving development of all its elements'. Again, he did not indicate how. He admitted that despite the 'full exercise of human liberty', the social system of the United States encouraged 'hatred, a growing disequilibrium, a war amongst the inhabitants of a free, generous and rich country'. This was in the nature of a paradox for him, and he felt it would only be unravelled by time:

> One feels in the air without fear, and almost with affection, the arrival of the era of the worker; but public opinion, the government, the press, the clergy, what! labour itself, are rising up against the hordes of fanatics that, instead of using their power to remake the laws, are strengthening and justifying the present laws with the horror that their crimes inspire.[28]

One notes that though 'the arrival of the era of the worker' was regarded by Martí as desirable and perhaps inevitable, it still inspired in him a degree of unease. The above passage continues:

> Both artisans and bankers; both the grand master of the Knights of Labour and the capitalists of the famous New York Union League club; both the isolated guilds of American workers and the newspapers of the stock-exchange magnates, are relinquishing to public anger and the law those people who with their stupid hatred (. . .) are holding back the reform of the industrial constitution, which entails that of man himself, through the just alarm caused in public opinion, without which victory is impossible.
>
> Neither the police, nor the judges, nor the grand jury, which is opinion in general, pardon those who have made bloody the streets of Chicago, or those who imitate them.[29]

Everybody is reacting to the bombthrowers as to a dog with rabies, and this is only natural.

The second part of Martí's first article on the Haymarket affair, published in *La Nación* six days later (2 July), made the point that those arrested were not American workmen at all, but rather the kind of embittered European immigrants he had already warned against.

In Germany, one realizes quite well, the anger of centuries, deprived of safety-valves, is exploding. There the worker does not have the free vote, a free press, or any shield to protect him. The worker there does not elect, as he elects here, the deputy, the senator, the judge, the President. There he has no laws to guide himself by, and jumps over those that block his path. There violence is justified, because justice is not allowed. (. . .)

These rough workers from Germany, sharpened by spirits of hatred, or by those of their own caste in whom pain culminates in words or actions, are avenging whole centuries, in their cloudy understandings, when they toss a lighted bomb at the guardians of the law, who are a symbol for them in their own land of the bitternesses in which they live. Thus every just spirit has compassion for the wayward acts of those sad people who come into life with anxious hands and feverish judgement! But in no honest soul does justice sink to the level of crime![30]

There is a lesson here for other countries that are receiving European immigration (Martí is probably thinking here mainly of Argentina); there has to be a careful selection principle which includes, among other things, consideration of the particular nationality of the immigrant.

One knows with certainty. It is Germans, Poles, Swedes, Norwegians, that make up the great mass in which these preachings of arson and killings have taken root. (. . .) That is the element here of the worker problem which is to be feared: that Germany and Poland, that Norway and Sweden, all that scum of Europe, have poured out over the entire country, and it is not known whether the workers of the country will be more powerful than these. Those Germans, those Poles, those Hungarians, brought up in wretched poverty and thirsting to shake it off, with no other heaven above their heads than the heel of a riding-boot, did not bring, on coming to this land, in the pockets of their white overcoats, in their caps, in their pipes, in their leather boots and their old overcoats, that habit of and faith in liberty, that august feeling of mastery, that confidence born of being a maker of laws that pervades and strengthens the citizen of republics: they brought the hatred of the serf, the appetite for other people's fortunes, the fury of rebellion that periodically is unleashed in oppressed peoples, the wild longing to exercise once and for all the authority of men, which ate away at their spirit, in the search for release, in their lands ruled by despotic governments.[32]

Evidently Martí felt particularly alien from Northern Europeans, with whom he had minimal contact up to his arrival in the United States.

As for the idea that oppression and despotism automatically create their own mirror image in their victims, was not Martí himself a proof to the contrary? One is reminded here of Joseph Conrad's fears of Russian revolutionaries. Conrad and Martí show several similarities, principally their stoical faith in an individual ethos ever endangered by the lower passions of the many. Martí continues:

> What was engendered there, is procreating here. For that reason it will perhaps never come to fruition, because it has no roots here!
>
> Those workers, mainly Germans, brought over with them that fair-headed stubbornness, those square heads, those hairy and tangled beards that are never aired and in which ideas stick. They brought over their anarchists, who want no laws, and do not know what they want, and only preach arson and death for everything that lives and stands, with such disordered means and confusion of ends that they cannot enjoy that consideration and respect which must be given to any kind of doctrine born of good faith and aiming to serve man best. Those Germans brought over Most, Schwab, Spies – Spies, like Guiteau, a shrunken man, a malformed man, in whom the clay had not been properly baked so that from amongst the wild animals of Nature should emerge, endowed with all the light of reason, a real man; – Most, with a tongue as outsized as his beard, fat, puffy, with the look of a bloodthirsty lover, an orator who in days past spoke in New York to his audience with a rifle in his hand, shouting at his hearers to do the same as himself, and to drag all the capitalists from their lairs, and blow up their houses and their wealth with the bombs that he in his books teaches how to make and use; Schwab, a sinister and sickly person, with hair and beard waving about, and frightening eyes behind large spectacles, boney and avid.[33]

Martí's pictures of these anarchists resemble nothing so much as the *cuadros de costumbres* so dear to the nineteenth-century Spanish and Spanish American Romantic taste: colourful sketches of exotic peoples and places to fire the dulled imagination. There is more to come:

> twelve thousand men rush where he [Spies] goes, take out banners and guns from their hiding-places, put in their lapels like a bloody flower a red ribbon, storm shops, break up the beerhalls of the enemy, fight battles to the death with corps of policemen, and throw at their ranks a dynamite bomb which, on exploding with an infernal din, leaves sixty men prostrate on the ground. They want the working day to be reduced to eight hours, and they are within their rights to want this, and it is just; but it is not their right to prevent those who offer themselves in their places from working. It is not their right to stone the factory owners who shut their workshops, because they cannot continue to produce in this time of low prices, in conditions that would require greater production costs. It is not their right to pursue with that bestial hatred that mobs have those unfortunates who offered themselves on one day to fill the places of some strikers.[34]

This type of riot has occurred in several places in the United States, and has been put down quite rightly, according to Martí. It is in Chicago, however, where the situation is direst:

Only in Chicago, where Spies and Schwab are writing, where in public squares orators incite people to arson and to take up arms, where the anarchists drill daily with weapons in their backyards and tunnels, where a mulatto woman marches at the head of the processions waving a red flag like one possessed, where in the sun and the electric light two anarchist banners float day and night from Spies' windows, whilst in books and secret workshops his followers learn to use sinister substances and manufacture bombs. Only in Chicago, which for nine days has been a battlefield, at each hour is a battle to the death being waged, between the depleted ranks of the police and the frenzied mob, a battle in which revolver barrels fire at one another mouth to mouth, in which the women from their windows help their husbands who are fighting by throwing bricks, benches, stones and bottles, where twelve heroic policemen stand up, with no other coat of mail than their blue shirts with their gilt buttons, to twenty thousand workers who have mutinied and who shoot at them from point-blank range from windows and waggons, from their ambushes, who rush upon them and surround them, who get in amidst their accurate fire, who, on seeing reinforcement squads arrive in their patrol cars, flee in terror through the nearby streets, twenty thousand of them before the twelve![35]

Martí tells of the deaths of both police and workers, the storming of a chemist's shop by the mob, who douse themselves with perfume and drink up any liquid resembling wine. A beerhall is broken into, and more usual beverages are consumed. Three policemen are killed by a bomb. 'And on the night of the bomb that killed them, not a single one retreated, or fled death'.[36]

There is no question, therefore, that Martí still stood basically on the side of law and order. He concluded the article by asserting that the nation wanted to see a peaceful solution to these problems, and noted with satisfaction how 'the air of liberty has an energy-giving power which kills off the serpents'.[37]

Martí's confidence in the capacity of the United States to pull through its labour crisis had still not been shattered by the time of his second article on the Haymarket troubles, written three weeks later (3 June, published in *La Nación* on 15 July). He used this article to reassert, with qualifications of course, his general faith in the future of the nation.

From this people of the North there is much to be feared, and much that appears to be virtue is not, and many outward forms of greatness exist that are hollow inside, like sculptures of sugar-candy. But it is a thing worthy of great admiration how each man here owes to himself the magnificent concept of liberty and decency in which all people maintain themselves and join together, and it produces spectacles of virile and gigantic indulgence, or of peaceful and radical turnabouts, that in nothing give way to the epic élan and marmorean splendour of the public greatness of Greece.[38]

He declared his enthusiasm for the beginnings of a reconciliation (initiated by the Democratic President Grover Cleveland) between the North and South, and expressed his belief that perhaps the pressing social crisis (two million were unemployed) would be alleviated by a general tariff reduction. Industry was bursting with unsaleable products and trade went at snail's pace. He thus backed a plan put forward by the Democrat Marrison 'to lower tariffs gradually so as to set the nation's industry slowly on the road to cheap, constant and lawful production'.[39] He reasserted his support for the Knights of Labour and their non-violent policies, but deplored the way big corporations were buying up the land, which he saw as 'holy'. As we have seen, the land could serve the function of providing a living for the surplus urban population, and moreover fulfil a basic human need for proximity to the natural world of which man was becoming an increasingly alienated part.

Martí was given a rude shock around this time, however, by the Cutting affair, about which he wrote a long and indignant article for the Honduran newspaper *La República*, dated 12 August. The question has been reviewed in detail in a previous chapter. Suffice to say here that it deepened his feelings regarding essential differences between the peoples of the United States and Latin America. Northern contempt for Mexico, Martí pointed out, extended to the whole of the continent south of the Río Grande, which he considered to be his greater fatherland.

Nevertheless, his next article on the Haymarket affair for *La Nación*, dated 2 September of that year 1886, was just as unsympathetic as before to the arrested anarchists, who had been tried and seven of them condemned to death. He noted that only one of them was a native North American (in fact the brother of a general). The rest had brought their hatred over with them from Germany. He repeated his bitter diatribes against the anarchist propaganda of vilification of the rich. These 'gloomy ideas' had taken root 'in the less rational spirits, those more disposed by nature to destruction',[40] and were responsible for the death-dealing bomb. Elaborating on these Emersonian musings, he asserted:

> all great reforming ideas are condensed in apostles and petrified in crimes, according to whether in their flaming course they fire loving souls or souls bent on destruction. The two forces go through life, both in men's bosoms and in the atmosphere and the earth. Some are pledged to build and raise things up: others are born to knock down and destroy.[41]

Even the 'most advanced of socialists' in the United States, fortunately, were opposed to murder and arson to win rights. Crime was unnecessary in a republic because one could always have recourse to the law. This was why the condemned men got no support, except from some two thousand of their German compatriots. Martí concluded that there was massive evidence as to the guilt of the men sentenced.

On the other hand, Martí's general vision of the United States was acquiring a more pessimistic hue. He now called it a kind of jungle, where all fought all to satisfy their appetites. Nobody helped anybody else. Instead, 'All march on, pushing one another, cursing one another, elbowing and biting their way, trampling over everything, everything, in order to be first.'[42] The successive waves of immigrants merely accentuated this tendency to brutal egoism. Many of them had even left their family behind, and thus were even more rootless in a community where hardship made them cruel and thrusting. Their souls had died through lack of work. The result of this was that the 'puritan' influences in the United States (Martí meant the inheritors of the Transcendentalist tradition), which were trying to steer this thrusting mass 'by means of culture and the religious sentiment' found themselves swamped in a sea of vulgarism. 'The crude spirit of the mass is sweeping away those attempts at refinement, neutralizing or annulling their influence'.[43] 'Neither charity nor the kid glove are a natural product of the United States (. . .) this country of aggression and combat (. . .) made up of men who see life as a field for conquest'.[44] Electoral frauds, votebuying and lies were rife in its political life.

Shortly afterwards, in an article describing the celebrations around the Statue of Liberty and the centenary of North American independence, Martí maintained that the very concept of liberty had become perverted in the United States. It was now a selfish liberty, in contrast to the generous concept of the French, who had aided the United States to win independence. Emblematic of the egotistical *Zeitgeist* of the mid-1880s in the United States was Chauncey Depew, the railroad magnate and speculator. So was the corrupt political scene, where the Republicans, with their greedy policies of high tariffs to aid big business, their expansionism and their disdain for the common man, were particularly to blame. But the Democrats had nothing much to boast about, since they had done nothing since being put in power to clean up the public life of the nation. True, President Cleveland was an honest and courageous man (Martí held him in high regard), but he faced opposition from within his own party, precisely because of this. In general, both parties had discredited themselves.

Another matter that concerned Martí was the power and corruption of the Catholic Church. We have already observed Martí's objections to that Church and its participation in public life regarding Mexico. All churches should keep out of politics, and religion should be purely a matter for the individual conscience, without mediation by an instituted body. Interestingly, it was to the Mexican newspaper *El Partido Liberal* that he sent his two main articles on the persecution by the Church of Father McGlynn, a supporter of Henry George and his United Labor Party.

The first of these pieces, entitled *The Schism of the New York Catholics*, dated in New York on 16 January 1887, also appeared in *La*

Nación. Martí accused the Catholic Church of having become 'the most effective instrument of the keepers of the human lineage', and stated that the Gospel was not to be found in the Church but, as always, amongst the humble. 'The truth is better revealed to the poor and those who suffer.'[45] Martí's views on religion, which we have already touched upon in another chapter, may be summed up in a sentence he wrote in this first article on the McGlynn case for *El Partido Liberal*: 'Ah! Religion, always false as dogma in the light of a lofty intelligence, is eternally true as poetry: what are the dogmas of religion but the infancy of the truths of Nature?'[46]

Because Father McGlynn was encouraging his parishioners in New York to vote for Henry George's party, he was being threatened with excommunication by his superiors. The problem for the Catholic Church was that it backed the Democratic Party, and tried to make sure the faithful delivered up their votes to the latter. In return for this political support, it received the same benefits that any other large corporation with similar links to one of the two major parties could count upon, i.e. favourable legislation to enrich itself. That a church should behave in this way was anathema to Martí's evangelical nature. He thus came out strongly for Father McGlynn, comparing him to Jesus Christ for his love of the poor and lowly. He also compared him, at the same time, to Charles Darwin, which sheds further light on Martí's Krausist 'harmonic rationalism'. Father McGlynn's archbishop had got him turned out of his living, and tried to force him to go to Rome to see the Pope. McGlynn refused even to carry out this order, and the Pope excommunicated him. However, McGlynn had massive support amongst lower-class Catholics (who would include many poverty-stricken Irishmen), and Martí mentioned the figure of ten thousand Catholic schismatics.

Gradually Martí came over more and more to the side of the working classes, in the measure that he became increasingly aware of their problems and the conspiracy of the powerful against them. 'Nobody has the right to sleep easily whilst there is a single unfortunate man',[47] he wrote in mid-March of that year. And whilst still abhorring violence as a means of settling social problems, he now appeared resigned to the inevitability of its use. Of course, he had for a long time already accepted warfare as a necessary strategy for ridding his Cuban homeland of its colonial oppressors. But then, the *patria* was sacrosanct for Martí, to the point that for its salvation he was willing to countenance extremes that he denigrated in other contexts. Thus he was able to write, in May of that year 1887, that 'a people of fanatical patriots, or imperfect ones, is preferable to a people of selfish individuals'.[48]

The article of mid-March quoted above contained, one notices, a shift in Martí's attitude to popular social violence. Justice would arrive in time, whether lawfully or through violence. The upsurge of the workers' movement was proving this, heralding a new, more advanced era in the history of mankind. This 'friendly and just state of society', he now affirmed, would have a prelude which was 'probably violent':

The thinkers, the seers, those who listen to what men are thinking, observe the change and announce it; but the peoples of the world are like the guests at Belshazzar's feast, who do not decide to leave the feast until anger is flaming on the wall.

The worker, who is Atlas here, is getting tired of carrying the world on his back, and seems to be determined to throw it off his shoulders, and seek a way of going through life without so much sweating.

The wealthy, the ones who hope to be so, those who prosper in his shadow, do not bother to attend to these demands as justice requires, but rather are busy bribing those who make the laws, so that public liberties are placed, in bondage, at their feet![49]

The political parties are too given over to their own squabbles and internal manoeuvering to see the threat. The press fears to tell the truth to its masters. Congress tries to pacify the workers whilst in reality serving the interests of the rich. But the time of the masses has not yet come, because in a land of immigrants 'a glass of beer and a fallen woman seem to these young men of nowadays to be the most pleasing freedoms'.[50]

Nevertheless Henry George's United Labor Party received much support, although Martí pointed out that through the practice of vote-buying, Congress was in the pocket of the rich and powerful. Most Congressmen were 'serfs, made to obey by a golden whip'.[51] Pressure was building up mainly, however, because of Congress's refusal to lower tariffs and taxes, and this under a Democratic regime in theory committed to that policy. People were starving because of too much party politics, although Congress, rather than being split between Democrats and Republicans, was in fact divided into free traders and protectionists. A few good things had been done, like Congress's refusal to vote a military pensions law for those not wounded in the Civil War, and to spend large sums on armaments when there was no war. Land was also being given back, after its seizure by large corporations. But where were the huge budget surpluses going?

The nation, Martí informed his readers in *La Nación* and *El Partido Liberal*, in a piece written in New York in April that year, had divided into two: 'on one hand "the masses", as they call themselves, on the other "the classes"; – the "citizens", Republican or Democrat, – the supporters of "Law and Order".'[52]

He called attention to widespread discrimination against blacks, especially in the South where a black man was killed every day for having relations with a white woman, even if these were merely ties of friendship. Martí's position on the possibilities of the black race was that it needed education, but was potentially just as worthy as any other. What faults it showed now could be ascribed to its having been left behind by history and then perverted by slavery.

Martí's political position before his final judgement on the Haymarket affair is clearly shown by his comments on Henry George's party.

He disapproved of that faction that tried to win votes by courting the anarchist vote, and backed the one that, along with George himself, repudiated European socialism and an alliance with European socialists. This latter faction was in a majority, and Martí described it thus:

> respectful and steadfast (. . .) it does not want to confuse its plan for getting rid of all tributes, and apply to the nation's costs the sum to be paid through the sale of land by its occupier, and reserve to the State the administration of and profit from natural monopolies, space, soil, water, – with the socialists' plan, which calls for the land, the instruments of production, the machines, the factories and the products of labour to belong all of them to the people as a whole, and for everything to be shared out among everybody and produced for everybody, under the leadership of the cooperative community, which will distribute the products according to the labour that each one has put into them, and to individual needs.[53]

The next mention of the Haymarket affair comes in September 1887, when, after noting with a certain revulsion the masses of poor Eastern European immigrants who are now entering the United States, 'these misshapen beings, who come speaking barbaric languages from the empty spaces of Turkey. (. . .) these boatloads of gypsies that are arriving here with no other tools than their tents',[54] and seeing in them one of the causes of the opposition to a pardon for the Chicago anarchists, who were close to the day of their execution, Martí now states that it was 'publicly known that the person who threw the bomb is not among them'.[55] He repeated the gist of this statement later on that same month, in his chronicle for *El Partido Liberal*, writing 'there is hardly anybody who believes that among the eight condemned to death is the one that threw the bomb'.[56] He now mentioned the fact that they were not 'uncultured' people, and for the first time described instances of police brutality, some of which had taken place in New York, and which therefore Martí himself might well have witnessed, as he did not witness the same in Chicago, because his chronicles on the Haymarket affair were written from New York and presumably relied on press which was hostile to the workers. Some of this police brutality he attributed to the fact that many of the police were Irishmen who resented their fellow immigrants of German, Russian and Polish origin. By now his attitude towards the European propaganda of violence had acquired a more understanding tone. Not all those who preached this were rabble-rousers. There was even a Russian prince among them (Kropotkin?).

By the time that Martí came to write his fourth large article for *La Nación* on the Haymarket events, it was evident to his readers that his position had shifted considerably in relation to the one he had taken in his previous pieces for that journal. This was for the reasons given above, but also because powerful movements carrying great working-class support had been set in motion to get the condemned men pardoned. In the end, four anarchists from the originally sentenced group were hanged, one committed suicide in his cell, and the rest had their sentences commuted. Martí, always sensitive to any form of human suffering, was appalled at the executions, with their equally barbaric preamble, especially when he had come to believe that proof of the men's guilt was lacking. What had been done, in fact, was a legal murder. The exemplary bravery of the four anarchists in the face of the gallows also touched him.

He now (13 November) mentioned that six workers had been killed by the police *before* the tossing of the bomb in Haymarket Square. Perhaps he had previously not been aware of this fact. The animal imagery he used formerly to describe the anarchists he now transferred to 'the whole republic, which with a kind of wolf-like rage' had fought against any of the prisoners being pardoned. The nation as a whole, and not the anarchists, had become the guilty party:

> The republic, made fearful by the growing power of the lower class, by the sudden accord reached by the working masses, which had only been held up because of the rivalries between its leaders, and by the coming demarcation of the population of the nation into the two classes of privileged and discontented people that cause turmoil in European societies, determined to use, by a tacit agreement similar to complicity, a crime born as much from its own crimes as from the fanaticism of the criminals to strike terror by making an example of them, not into the suffering rabble that will never be able to triumph in a country governed by reason, but into the tremendous classes in the process of being born.[57]

The fact that the four hanged men had to perform their horrible dance of death of course resolved nothing. The poor had no more 'fire in their stoves, bread in their larders, justice in the sharing-out of society's goods, safeguard against the hunger of the able-bodied, light and hope for their hovels' than before. 'This republic, through the excessive cult of wealth, has fallen, unchecked by any traditional shackles, into the inequality, injustice and violence of the monarchies.'[58] What Martí had always feared had come to pass. The United States had followed the pernicious path of Ancient Rome, from Democracy to Despotism.

How to explain this falling-off into corruption? Martí embarked on a deeper and deeper sounding of North American history, which he continued to the end of his days. At this point of time (late 1887) he only went as far back as the immediate post-Civil War period. In later years he was to see the seeds of corruption as having been planted at the very inception of Independence. But for the time being, he saw the cause of the corruption somehow in the Civil War itself. In the ante-bellum era, with abundant land and true 'republican' life (Martí by 'republican' always really means 'democratic'), the revolutionary theories of European workers fell like mere drops of blood into a vast sea.

> But then came the corrupting war, the habit of authority and dominion which is its bitter sequel, the credit that stimulated the creation of colossal

fortunes and disordered immigration, and the idleness of those cashiered off after the war, people who were always willing, so as to maintain their standard of living and because of the fatal liking of the person who has smelt blood, to serve the impure interests which arise from it.[59]

A true *patria*, for Martí, would never have exploded into a civil war. Oddly enough, Martí does not at this juncture mention slavery, one of the issues of the war, although later on in his writings he does indicate the continuing acceptance of that infamous institution by the newly independent nation of 1776 as one of the cankers of that state.

From a peaceful village, worthy of admiration, the republic changed into a hidden monarchy.

The European immigrants denounced with renewed anger the evils that they thought they had left behind in their tyrannical homelands.

The rancour of the workers born in the country itself, when they saw themselves to be the victims of the avarice and inequality of feudal peoples, exploded with more faith in the liberty that they expect to see as triumphant in matters of social justice, as it is triumphant in matters political.[60]

The Haymarket bomb, Martí now stated, had been necessary, in order that the corruption of the system be uncovered, and to bring together American and European workers on the same side to fight the capitalists. The throwing of the bomb was still a horrendous act, but it was understandable in view of the unjust sufferings of the workers and the general state of corruption and injustice. The passions awoken by this appalling situation had to lead to violence. What else could be expected from people degraded by cold, hunger and living in stinking slums? This was why hell was opened up, bomb factories proliferated and incendiary propaganda distributed. All other alleyways had been blocked by the rich, who manipulated forces of the state like the judiciary and the police against the workers' cause. The workers were not at fault, but

They do not understand that they are a mere cog in the machinery of society, and that it is necessary to change, so that the cogs may change, the entire machinery. A boar when pursued does not hear the music of the merry air, or the song of the universe, or the grand movement of the fabric of the cosmos: the wild boar buttresses itself against a dark tree-trunk, sinks its tusk into its pursuer's belly, and rips out his guts.[61]

Society thus had become unbalanced; a new equilibrium had to be found. For this a readjustment was needed, to give the workers a better share of what was produced. Martí, none the less, did not say how this was to be done, and neither was he arguing for workers to take society over, as the quotation makes clear. But his indictment of the operations of the capitalist system in 1887 is very severe.

The worker thinks he has a right to a certain security for the future, to a certain well-being and cleanliness in his home, to be able to feed without worry the children he produces, to a more equitable part in the products of labour of which he is an indispensable factor, to the odd hour in the sun in which to help his wife sow a rose-tree in the yard of his house, to some corner to live in that is not a stinking slum where, as in cities like New York, one cannot enter without feeling sick. And each time the workers asked for this in Chicago, the capitalists got together and punished them by denying them the work which for them is meat, fire and light. They set the police on them, who were always willing to use their truncheons on the heads of shabbily-dressed people. From time to time the police would kill some daring fellow who resisted them with stones, or some child. They reduced them finally to returning to their labour through hunger, sullenly, with their wretchedness inflamed, their sense of decency offended, chewing on vengeance.[62]

In stark contrast to Martí's early articles on the affair, here he evinces considerable repugnance for the police, who now appear as largely responsible, through their brutality, for the anarchists' recourse to the bomb and the gun. He even puts the latter' case, as seen by them, though of course not agreeing with their exalted logic. He gives detailed and not unsympathetic thumbnail sketches of each of the four condemned men, and significantly shows them in their immediate social context. The fact that Martí now offers far more information about them points, probably, to a certain ignorance on his part when he penned the first articles. After all, he had had more than a year to soak up some more sympathetic information about them, since that was the length of the campaign waged by their supporters. He mentions that the American among them, Parsons, had even been proposed as a candidate for the Presidency of the United States. The police, on the other hand, he depicts as a rabble 'drunk on hangman's wine, like all plebeians cloaked in authority',[63] the very antithesis of the knightly defenders of society he had described earlier.

The only full account that Martí gave of the Haymarket events was contained in this fourth article for *La Nación*, and must be taken as superseding everything he had written previously on them. He started by painting a moving portrait of one million workers mobilized in early 1886 for an eight-hour day, over the United States.

Whoever wants to know if what they were asking for was just, let him come here; let him see them return, like beaten oxen, to their filthy dwellings, in the black of night; let him see them come from their far-away slums, the men shivering and the women uncombed and livid, when the sun has still not ceased from its rest![64]

This appears to be an eye-witness account of something that Martí would have seen in New York. Martí went on to relate the Chicago events.

The police had decided to challenge these peaceful demonstrators, who were not stepping outside the bounds of the law, and indeed had seemed to reject the anarchist incitements to violence. When demands for the eight-hour day were presented by workers in the factories in March, the workers were locked out, like dogs with scabies, as Martí put it. The Knights of Labour called a strike, but the McCormick Harvester plant, alone in Chicago, kept going, with blackleg labour. Eight thousand workers advanced on the factory, and one of the anarchists delivered an impassioned speech. The workers attacked the scabs as they finished their shift, the police appeared on the scene and were stoned. A police car arrived, vomiting fire, and six workers were left dead. The anarchists through their press called for the workers to rise up in arms, and a mass demonstration was held in Haymarket Square, of some 50,000 people, with women and children. An inflammatory speech was made by an anarchist, but the kind of thing which regularly appeared quite legally in the anarchist press. Some 180 armed police appeared, and opened fire. A bomb was thrown at them. A pitched battle started, where both policemen and workers were killed and wounded.

The police then embarked on a manhunt for the European extremists, and plucked as many anarchists and their associates as they could from their lairs. Three hundred prisoners were taken in one day alone. All this was fact, but it was not fact that there was a conspiracy on the part of eight anarchists to kill the police. The witnesses, remarked Martí, were the police themselves, plus four anarchists who had been bought, one of them being a confessed perjurer. The actual person who had thrown the bomb was never identified.

One of the anarchists eventually hanged, Parsons, had given himself up voluntarily so as to share the fate of his comrades. His wife Lucy, of mixed blood (was she the same mulatto woman that Martí had previously reported unfavourably on as leading demonstrations?) toured the length and breadth of the United States pleading for her husband and his comrades and painting a heart-rending picture of the conditions in which the workers were living, often in the face of hostile mobs. Nina Van Zandt, 'of distinguished family', married another condemned anarchist, Spies. Martí's romantic soul evidently responded to the courage and selflessness of these people.

Seven received the death sentence, whilst one man, Neebe, was sent to prison, merely, said Martí, for publishing inflammatory propaganda, not in itself an illegal act, since the anarchist newspapers were circulating freely. Martí considered the conspiracy charges (always a dubious form of indictment) as not proven, but whatever the rights and wrongs of the trial, society itself was to blame for the social upheavals and deaths occurring from them, and not the workers themselves.

> Who punishes crimes, even ones that have been proven, and yet does not take into account the circumstances that cause them, the passions that attenuate them, and the motive with which they are committed? Peoples, like doctors, must prefer to foresee the illness, or cure it in its roots, to allowing

it to flourish in all its vigour, and fight the evil which has developed through their own fault, with bloody and desperate means.[65]

Not all the seven were to die, as it turned out, although the Supreme Court, 'in a verdict unworthy of the affair', confirmed the death sentences. The mood of Chicago changed, and clemency was demanded with the same fervour that death was one year before. The trade unions attempted to get the authorities to intercede. But by this time another of Martí's illusions had been smashed: his belief in the 'free press'.

The entire press, from San Francisco to New York, giving a false image of the trial, paints the seven condemned men as dangerous beasts, puts every morning on the breakfast table the image of the policemen who had been blown to pieces by the bomb; describes their deserted homes, their golden-haired children, their desolate widows.[66]

The press tries to get the state governor to order the sentences to be carried out, at a time when the private Pinkerton police (notoriously anti-union) had recently got off scot-free after killing a worker's child with no provocation. Lingg, one of the seven to be hanged, blows himself up in his cell. Fielden and Schwab receive a pardon. But four victims for the gallows remained, and Martí presents a long drawn-out account of their taking leave of their loved ones, and emphasizes the barbaric cruelty of the law.

One man, Engel, sings the song of the Silesian weavers' revolt, which Martí, significantly, reproduces in full. He sketches the moving drama of the four prisoners' last moments, obviously impressed by their bravery and dignity. The shroud put on them by the hangman is even compared by Martí to the shrouds the Christians wore in the catacombs. They are hanged, with the attendant horrors of this form of execution. Afterwards, a huge funeral, from which Martí quotes with approval the oration of the defence counsel, Captain Black.

These are not abominable felons, drunk with disorder, blood and violence, but men who wanted peace, and hearts full of tenderness, loved by all who knew them and saw from close up the power and glory of their lives! Their anarchy was the reign of order without force! Their dream, a new world without wretched poverty and without slavery! Their pain, that of believing that selfishness will never give way peacefully to justice! Oh, cross of Nazareth, which in these corpses has been called gallows![67]

Martí ended his chronicle, significantly, with words taken from the German newspaper, the *Arbeiter Zeitung*: 'We have lost a battle, unfortunate friends, but we shall finally see the world ordered as justice demands. Let us be as wise as serpents, and as inoffensive as doves!'[68]

Martí's faith in the United States had received a mortal blow in the Haymarket events, and later occurrences only served to confirm and deepen his rejection of that nation as a model. One thinks especially of the *Manufacturer* article, the Panamerican Congress, the International Monetary Conference and the 1891 lynchings of Italians in New Orleans. The Haymarket affair also made him more radical in the sense that it turned him towards the working class. Indeed, his own political support within the Cuban Revolutionary Party came from the Cuban tobacco workers of Florida. The republic he envisaged for liberated Cuba would be anything but an imitation of the United States, and the working class would have a special role in that multi-class nation. This does not mean that socialism itself was envisaged for Cuba at that point, and Martí most certainly showed too much optimism if he thought that his radical republic could be set up peacefully in the shadow of the Goliath to the north which, even if it respected Cuba politically, would by the laws of economics be forced to dominate it in another, more fundamental way. The sort of independence envisaged by Martí in fact meant a complete break with the capitalist system, and Martí had not yet realized this. So it is that the true independence of Cuba came with the revolution of Fidel Castro, and the introduction of socialism into the nation. Nevertheless, the seeds of the 1959 revolution are undoubtedly to be found in Martí's heroic and painful struggles at the end of the previous century.

Notes

1. R. B. Nye and J. E. Morpurgo, *A History of the United States*, Harmondsworth, Penguin, 1955, vol. 2, pp. 563–4.

2. Ibid., p. 564.

3. Ibid., p. 566.

4. Ibid.

5. Ibid., p. 567.

6. Ibid., p. 568.

7. Ibid., p. 581.

8. Montgomery Hyde, *Oscar Wilde*, London, Methuen, 1977, p. 102.

9. Letter to *La Nación*, Buenos Aires, dated 27 November 1884, published 11 January 1885, *OC*, 10, p. 127.

10. Letter to *La Nación*, dated 29 March 1883, published 13 & 16 May 1883, *OC*, 9, p. 388.

11. Letter to *La Nación*, dated 16 January 1886, published 18 February 1886, *OC*, 10, p. 376.

12. Letter to *La Nación*, dated 25 March 1886, published 7 May 1886, *OC*, 10, p. 393.

13. Ibid., p. 394.

14. Ibid., p. 396.

15. Ibid., p. 399.

16. Letter to *La Nación*, dated 27 April 1886, published 4 June 1886, *OC*, 10, p. 411.

17. Ibid., p. 412.

18. Ibid., pp. 413–4.

19. Ibid., pp. 414–5.
20. Letter to *La Nación*, dated 27 April 1886, published 6 June 1886, *OC*, 10, p. 418.
21. Letter to *La Nación*, dated 2 May 1886, published 17 June 1886, *OC*, 10, p. 433.
22. Letter to *La Nación*, dated 16 May 1886, published 26 June 1886, *OC*, 10, p. 446.
23. Ibid., p. 447.
24. Ibid., p. 448.
25. Ibid.
26. Ibid., pp. 448–9.
27. Ibid., p. 449.
28. Ibid.
29. Ibid.
30. Letter to *La Nación*, dated 16 May 1886, published 2 July 1886, *OC*, 10, p. 451.
31. Ibid., p. 452.
32. Ibid.
33. Ibid., pp. 452–3.
34. Ibid., p. 453.
35. Ibid., p. 454.
36. Ibid., p. 455.
37. Ibid., p. 456.
38. Letter to *La Nación*, dated 3 June 1886, published 15 July 1886, *OC*, 10, p. 469.
39. Letter to *La Nación*, dated 2 July 1886, published 15 August 1886, *OC*, 11, p. 17.
40. Letter to *La Nación*, dated 2 September 1886, published 21 October 1886, *OC*, 11, p. 56.
41. Ibid., p. 57.
42. Letter to *La Nación*, dated 28 September 1886, published 14 November 1886, *OC*, 11, p. 83.
43. Ibid., p. 84.
44. Letter to *La Nación*, dated 3 October 1886, published 7 December 1886, *OC*, 11, p. 91.
45. Letter to *El Partido Liberal*, dated 16 January 1887, published Mexico City 1887 (no more precise date) and in *La Nación* 14 April 1887, *OC*, 11, p. 139.
46. Ibid., pp. 139–40.
47. Letter to *La Nación*, dated 15 March 1887, published 4 May 1887, *OC*, 11, p. 171.
48. Letter to *El Partido Liberal*, dated 9 May, published 1887 (no more precise date), *OC*, 11, p. 207.
49. Letter to *La Nación*, dated 15 March 1887, published 4 May 1887, *OC*, 11, pp. 172–3.
50. Ibid., p. 174.
51. Ibid., p. 178.
52. Letter to *La Nación*, dated 10 April 1887, published 21 May 1887 and in *El Partido Liberal*, 1887 (no more precise date), *OC*, 11, p. 184.
53. Letter to *La Nación*, dated 17 August 1887, published 29 September 1887, *OC*, 11, p. 269.

54. Letter to *La Nación*, dated 3 September 1887, published 9 November 1887, *OC*, 11, p. 285.

55. Ibid.

56. Letter to *El Partido Liberal*, dated 22 September 1887, published 1887 (no more precise date), *OC*, 11, p. 311.

57. Letter to *La Nación*, dated 13 November 1887, published 1 January 1887, *OC*, 11, p. 334.

58. Ibid., p. 335.

59. Ibid.

60. Ibid.

61. Ibid., p. 338.

62. Ibid., p. 339.

63. Ibid., p. 343.

64. Ibid., p. 344.

65. Ibid., pp. 348–9.

66. Ibid., p. 349.

67. Ibid., p. 356. Our retranslation of Martí's Spanish version of Black's words.

68. Ibid. Our retranslation of Martí's Spanish version. Cf. Matthew X, 16.

Appendix:
Krausism

The main source of Martí's ideology seems to have been the philosophical system known as Krausism, which greatly influenced several generations of liberal Spanish intellectuals right up to the Civil War of 1936. It had its apogee, however, in the period 1857–74, that is, between the time of its public introduction in Spain and the overthrow of the First Spanish Republic. Martí evidently imbibed it during his first Spanish exile, over the years 1871–74, when he was a university student. Martí's exact relation to this doctrine is given in his second notebook, corresponding to this period. There we read, under the heading KRAUSIST LANGUAGE: 'Krause is not all true. It is simply a simplifying, dividing, Spanish language which I wield and use because it seems to me to be the most suitable for bringing out (expressing) my ideas' (*Obras completas*, vol. 21, p. 98).

Krausism was the neo-Kantian philosophy of the German Karl Friedrich Krause (1781–1832) brought to Spain by the Professor of the History of Philosophy at Madrid University, Julián Sanz del Río, who presented it publicly in his inaugural lecture for the 1857–58 academic year. In 1860 Sanz also published a free adaptation of Krause's *Urbild der Menschheit* (1811), which he entitled *Ideal de la Humanidad para la vida*. Krausism claimed to be a complete philosophical system, although its Spanish exponent admitted not understanding completely all its tenets.

The essence of Krausism is summed up in the description 'harmonic rationalism'. It stressed the ultimate harmony of the universe and the brotherhood of man, who by an ever fuller exercise of his reason was progressing towards a realization of these two truths. In the words of the principal student of Krausism, Juan López Morillas, on whose book *El Krausismo español* (Mexico, Fondo de Cultura Económica, 1954) this appendix is based, 'the German philosopher identifies the ideal of socio-political perfection with the ideal of full religious awareness. The coming of a better world is the result of the rational understanding of the idea of God and the divine order'. He then adds that here there shows a great similarity with the doctrines of the fourteenth-century German mystics, especially Meister Eckhart, to whose 'ingenuous pantheism' a 'longing for social harmony based on the foundations of Christian ethics was closely linked' (pp. 18–19, our translation).

147

The fount of all being is, for Krause, the *Wesen* (or Absolute Entity, God), from whom emanate the two finite essences, Nature and Spirit. Individual man partakes of these two essences in his body and intellect, respectively. Krause dissents from Kant, however, on one very important point. Kant believed that we could only know *phenomena*, not *noumena* (or things in themselves), through our reason, whereas Krause thought that ultimate harmony (the Absolute, God) could be perceived by reason. Indeed, it was reason's task to reveal the Harmony beyond apparent chaos. Man himself, in López Morillas' paraphrase, was 'the perfect synthesis of the two finite essences of the universe, (. . .) the highest finite essence to have come from the hand of God' (p. 36).

Krausist ethics (with which we are mainly concerned here) have as their object the study of the extent to which the greatest good (an attribute of God) is realized in the human being. Man must fully develop his moral potential (cf. Kant's categorical imperative). Evil was not ultimately a reality, since it was only due to ignorance or blindness. As for the relationship between God and the world, 'The world is not outside God (. . .), nor is it God himself, but has its being in God and through God' (p. 39).

History is the process whereby man discovers the 'self-determinings' of the divine essence, which, as far as man goes, consist of the development of man's intellectual and moral faculties. Man's 'gradual return to unity with God, the supreme aspiration of the human individual, is the real content of history' (p. 41). This seems a Hegelian addition.

Man has already passed through two historical stages and is at present embarking on a third, that of his maturity. The first is that of primitive man, the second corresponds to man's youth, when monotheism loses its religious content and becomes mere convention or poetic myth. The last, present, stage is when 'man turns his eyes on himself and discovers in the intimacy of his consciousness the image of the one God, the creator and regulator of life' (p. 44). Man now feels 'capable of interpreting the fundamental cohesion which lies at the root of the chaos of his life'. 'What is called "human dignity" is the realization by man of his essential integrity', through 'the notion of a superior Consciousness, one and the same, infinite in time and space, which serves as a support for and bond with all finite beings. The discovery of the unity of his own consciousness leads man, in short, to the discovery of the unity of God' (p. 44). This 'God' is not the monotheistic God of Christianity, which was but a stage in man's self-perfectioning, and in fact itself had been the cause of wars and other forms of strife.

Only with the disappearance of 'spiritualist monotheism', which had 'degenerated into a theocratic and static interpretation of society', and the 'awakening of the scientific spirit' does man reach the understanding that he is 'a combination of nature and spirit, and that the full life requires the harmony of these two essential elements' (p. 47).

Man was meant to live in harmony with his fellow men, and a true society 'must be organic and act in pursuit of the same goals' (p. 81). Man is still the battlefield between 'nature' and 'spirit'; this is the sign that a truly organic society does not yet exist. The root cause of man's troubles 'is not in the family, in the State, or science, or religion, but rather in each individual man, clinging to that man's individual consciousness' (p. 82). For this reason the individual is the starting point for all enquiry about and reform of the world. Man must be educated in the clear knowledge of his destiny, so that he behaves at all times as if on each and every one of his acts depends the salvation or perdition of the human race.

According to a younger disciple of Sanz del Río, Francisco Giner de los Ríos, the founder of the Institución Libre de Enseñanza, responsible for the formation of so many great Spanish intellectuals prior to the Civil War, the goal of the evolution of humanity is 'a religion without dogmas, or mysteries, or miracles, or revelations, based on the conviction that reason in itself is enough for a knowledge of God' and that 'the recognition of God and of his absolute properties is the only religion worthy of humanity' (p. 161).

Krausism, therefore, is an off-shoot of Christian philosophy which, having passed through the rationalist filter of Kant, has acquired a greater degree of confidence in reason than Kant himself, in true nineteenth century fashion. It has also acquired a rather Hegelian theory of history as progress and eventual return to the Godhead. Naturally, the Catholic church condemned Krausism, and Sanz del Río was deprived of his chair at the university by a decree from the pious yet profligate Queen Isabel II, obviously acting under the influence of the notoriously illiberal Pope Pius IX. Many liberal catholics, however, nauseated by the peculiarly reactionary nature of the Church of that time, ended up by embracing Krausism in Spain. Amongst its adherents were many freemasons (such as Martí himself). Indeed, Krause himself had been a leading light in German freemasonry.

As far as day-to-day conduct went, the Krausists were expected to practise a certain austerity; many of them dressed in black (as did Martí), to emphasize the seriousness of their mission. Sanz had called on them to form a 'spiritual priesthood', and no doubt Martí's elevated tone owes much to that demand. The importance the Krausists gave to education, again, seems in part to explain Martí's own interest in the subject. Moreover, this education concerned the body in conjunction (or symbiosis) with the soul. The Krausists were the first people to stress the need for physical fitness and contact with nature in Spain. Martí, as already noted, hated the big city and loved the countryside. Lastly, Krausism shares, in German idealism of the late eighteenth and early nineteenth centuries, a common origin with North American Transcendentalism, the principal of whose exponents, Ralph Waldo Emerson, Martí much admired, as he did Walt Whitman, another Transcendentalist.

Brief Chronology
of Martí's Life

28 January 1853: Born in Havana, first son of Mariano Martí, a sergeant in the Royal Artillery Corps and a native of Valencia. His mother was Leonor Pérez, born in Santa Cruz de Tenerife, Canary Islands.

Educated in various schools in Havana, including the San Pablo College run by his future mentor, the Cuban patriot Rafael María de Mendive. Secondary school education begun in the Havana Institute, 1866.

1869: Writes pro-patriot articles in *El Diablo Cojuelo*, a newspaper started by his schoolfriend Fermín Valdés Domínguez. Brings out *La Patria Libre* (one issue) in support of the same cause (the Cuban rebels who had begun their revolt against Spain in 1868). Here he publishes his drama *Abdala*. Mendive imprisoned. Letter found in Valdés Domínguez' house accusing a schoolmate of going over to the enemy and joining the Spanish Volunteers. Martí and Valdés Domínguez detained and imprisoned.

1870: Martí sentenced to six years hard labour. Released after six months because of illness contracted in the quarries of San Lázaro, and sent to the Isle of Pines to recover.

1871: Deported to Spain. Publishes in Madrid *Political Imprisonment in Cuba*. Enrols as a student in the Central University of Madrid.

1872: Valdés Domínguez joins him in Spain, and he and Martí decide to go to Zaragoza to study.

1873: First Republic proclaimed in Spain. Martí writes *The Spanish Republic and the Cuban Revolution*. Enrols in Zaragoza University.

1874: Completes his B.A. in Law and Philosophy and Letters. Leaves Spain and makes a tour of Europe, visiting Paris. Sails for Mexico.

1875: Arrives in Mexico (Veracruz), and in Mexico City is reunited with his family. Starts to publish in the *Revista Universal*.

1877: Back in Cuba, travelling under a pseudonym. February, leaves for Guatemala. Appointed Professor of Literature and History of Philosophy in the Central Normal School in Guatemala City. In love with María García Granados. 20 December marries Carmen Zayas Bazán, a Cuban woman, in Mexico City.

1878: Leaves his teaching post in Guatemala because of dislike of President Barrios' dictatorial methods. Back in Havana. Refused permission to work as a lawyer. Son José Francisco born.

1879: September. Arrested in Cuba for conspiracy. Deported again to Spain. After a stay in France, sails for New York.

1880: Arrives in New York in January, and later made Interim President of the New York Cuban Revolutionary Committee. Starts publishing in English-language journals such as *The Hour* and *The Sun*. Friendly with the American intellectual Charles A. Dana. 28 November, his probable natural daughter María Mantilla is born, from a liaison with his Cuban landlady Carmen Miyares de Mantilla.

1881: Arrives in Venezuela. Writes in the newspaper *La Opinión Nacional*. Publishes the *Revista Venezolana*, in which appears an article on the poet Cecilio Acosta, a deceased enemy of President Guzmán Blanco. Martí forced to leave, 28 July.

1882: Back in New York. Publishes a book of poetry, *Ismaelillo*, dedicated to his son. Starts to write chronicles for *La Nación*, the prestigious Buenos Aires newspaper.

1884: Named Uruguayan Consul in New York, a post which he leaves to dedicate himself to new anti-Spanish plans. 20 October, breaks with Máximo Gómez and Antonio Maceo, because of Gómez's high-handed attitudes with regard to the revolutionary movement.

1887: Translates *Ramona*, the pro-Indian novel of Helen Hunt Jackson. Disillusionment with United States after the executions of the Haymarket Martyrs.

1889: Writes articles in defence of Cuba after hostile articles in the American press. Publishes the first numbers of *La Edad de Oro*, a magazine for children. Panamerican Congress, which Martí influences in defence of Latin America.

1890: Founds *La Liga*, with Rafael Serra, an association for the promotion of Cuban and Puerto Rican blacks and mulattoes. Named Argentinian and Paraguayan consul in New York. Named Uruguayan representative to the International Monetary Conference in New York.

1891: Draws up final report in the Conference, hostile to North American aims. Publishes his *Versos sencillos*, New York. Gives up his consular posts to dedicate himself to the coming anti-Spanish campaign. Arrives in Tampa, to speak at a benefit for the Ignacio Agramonte club of Cuban exiles. Makes two important speeches outlining his aims regarding the new Cuba. Tampa Cubans approve Martí's *Resolutions* for the formation of the Cuban Revolutionary Party. Goes to Key West, to meet other Cuban emigrés.

1892: 14 March, first number of Martí's newspaper *Patria*, founded to promote the revolutionary cause. 10 April, founding of the Cuban

Revolutionary Party. Visits to several cities in the United States to further the cause of Cuba. Visit to Haiti. In Santo Domingo to see Máximo Gómez. Haiti again, Jamaica.

1893: Back in New York, Martí completely given over to the movement, which means constant journeys to visit Cuban supporters, including another trip to Santo Domingo, and one to Costa Rica, to see Antonio Maceo.

1894: Cuban tobacco workers' strike in Key West. More journeys, inside the United States and abroad, including Mexico.

1895: Fernandina plan fails, after a Cuban collaborator reveals its details. 29 January, order for the uprising to begin in Cuba given. 30 January Martí sails for Haiti. In Santo Domingo with Gómez. *Manifesto of Montecristi* proclaimed, 25 March, outlining the aims of the Cuban insurrection. 11 April, Martí's small expedition reaches Cuba (Playitas). 2 May, letter to the *New York Herald*. Interview with Maceo in La Mejorana, where Maceo opposes Martí's plans for an assembly of delegates, and bitter words are exchanged (5 May). Martí falls in battle with Spanish forces, after Gómez has ordered him to stay in the rearguard, 19 May 1895.

Brief Bibliography

1. *Obras Completas*, Havana, Editorial Nacional de Cuba, 1963–5, 27 vols.
This is the main souce for the author's investigations. The bias of the present book is towards Martí as an intellectual phenomenon. In other words, the writer's starting point has been to examine the workings of Martí's mind in its evolution. The enormous mass of secondary material, constantly spawning more secondary material, has tended to swamp the primary source of information on Martí's ideas which is constituted by his actual writings.
2. *Selected secondary sources*
 Martínez Estrada, Ezequiel. *Martí revolucionario*, Havana, Casa de las Américas, 1967. Second ed. 1974.
 Martínez Estrada, Ezequiel. *Martí: el héroe y su acción revolucionaria*, Mexico, Siglo XXI, 1966. Third ed. 1972.
These two volumes by an Argentinian scholar now deceased are invaluable for the mass of information which they offer. Their drawback is the rather hagiographical tone they adopt. However, they are perhaps the principal general secondary source on Martí. Martínez Estrada had planned three volumes for his work, but for some reason only two have appeared, dealing with, in the author's own words, Martí's 'personality, the man' (*Martí revolucionario*), which is volume one of the complete work; then volume three (*Martí: el héroe y su acción revolucionaria*). The middle volume has not yet made an appearance. According to Martínez Estrada, it was to be entitled *'The social and political doctrine: the Apostle'*. Martínez Estrada died in late November 1964, having perhaps left part 2 in an incomplete state. (Even part 3, although published, is possibly incomplete.)
 Ibarra, Jorge. *José Martí, dirigente político e ideólogo revolucionario*, Havana, Editorial de Ciencias Sociales, 1980.
One of the best books to be published on Martí, by a contemporary Cuban historian. Ibarra has no truck with those who try to make Martí a socialist before his time.
 Cantón Navarro, José. *Algunas ideas de José Martí en relación con la clase obrera y el socialismo*, Havana, Editora Política, 1980.

A book of the same invaluable ilk as the previous work, a hard, un-squeamish evaluation of Martí's views of and relation to the working class and socialism.

Rodríguez, Carlos Rafael. *José Martí, guía y compañero*, Havana, Editora Política, 1979.

Of the same standard as the two above books. A good short, general guide to the fundamentals of Martí.

Fernández Retamar, Roberto. *Lectura de Martí*, Mexico, Editorial Nuestro Tiempo, 1972.

A very useful series of essays on various aspects of Martí by a well-known Cuban literary intellectual.

Mañach, Jorge. *Martí el Apóstol*, Madrid, Espasa-Calpe, 1942, a reprint of a book originally published in 1933.

A well-known biography of Martí, slightly ironic, by an old-time Cuban bourgeois intellectual. Some unsubstantiated material.

Gray, Richard Butler. *José Martí: Cuban Patriot*, Gainesville, University of Florida Press, 1962.

A largely superseded work.

Kirk, John M. *José Martí, Mentor of the Cuban Nation*, Tampa, University of South Florida Press, 1982.

The latest book on Martí to emerge from the United States. Much recycled information and waffle. The writer declares his 'neutrality'.

González, Manuel Pedro. *José Martí, Epic Chronicler of the United States in the Eighties*, Chapel Hill, University of North Carolina Press, 1953.

This book's author is one of the most honest of Martí scholars.

3. Anthologies of Martí's writings in English

Onís, Juan de, ed. *The America of José Martí: Selected Writings*, New York, Noonday Press, 1953.

This book has been largely superseded by the following:

Foner, Philip S., ed. *Inside the Monster: Writings on the United States and American Imperialism by José Martí*, New York, Monthly Review Press, 1975.

Foner, Philip S., ed. *Our America*, New York, Monthly Review Press, 1977.

Index

LATIN AMERICAN AND CARIBBEAN TITLES FROM ZED BOOKS

Fidel Castro
THE WORLD CRISIS
Its Economic and Social Impact on the
Underdeveloped Countries
Hb and Pb

Donald Hodges and Ross Gandy
MEXICO 1910-1982: REFORM OR
REVOLUTION?
Hb and Pb

George Beckford and Michael Witter
SMALL GARDEN, BITTER WEED
The Political Economy of Struggle
and Change in Jamaica
Hb and Pb

Liisa North
BITTER GROUNDS
Roots of Revolt in El Salvador
Pb

Ronaldo Munck
POLITICS AND DEPENDENCY IN
THE THIRD WORLD
The Case of Latin America
Hb and Pb

George Beckford
PERSISTENT POVERTY
Underdevelopment in Plantation
Economies of the Third World
Pb

Tom Barry, Beth Wood and Deb
Preusch
DOLLARS AND DICTATORS
A Guide to Central America
Hb and Pb

George Black
TRIUMPH OF THE PEOPLE
The Sandinista Revolution in
Nicaragua
Hb and Pb

George Black
GARRISON GUATEMALA
Hb and Pb

Cedric Robinson
BLACK MARXISM
The Making of the Black Radical
Tradition
Hb and Pb

Teofilo Cabastrero
MINISTERS OF GOD, MINISTERS
OF THE PEOPLE
Hb and Pb

Chris Searle
WORDS UNCHAINED
Language and Revolution in Grenada
Hb and Pb

George Brizan
GRENADA: ISLAND OF
CONFLICT
From Amerindians to People's
Revolution 1498-1979
Hb and Pb

Maurice Bishop
IN NOBODY'S BACKYARD
Maurice Bishop's Speeches, 1979-
1983: A Memorial Volume
Hb and Pb

Carmelo Furci
THE CHILEAN COMMUNIST
PARTY AND THE ROAD TO
SOCIALISM
Hb and Pb

Latin American and Caribbean
Women's Collective
SLAVES OF SLAVES
The Challenge of Latin American
Women
Hb and Pb

Miranda Davies
THIRD WORLD — SECOND SEX
Women's Struggles and National
Liberation
Hb and Pb

Margaret Randall
SANDINO'S DAUGHTERS
Testimonies of Nicaraguan Women in
Struggle
Pb

Bonnie Mass
POPULATION TARGET
The Political Economy of Population
Control in Latin America
Pb

June Nash and Helen Icken Safa
(Editors)
SEX AND CLASS IN LATIN
AMERICA
Women's Perspectives on Politics,
Economics and the Family in the
Third World
Pb

David Stoll
FISHERS OF MEN OR FOUNDERS
OF EMPIRE
The Wycliffe Bible Translators in
Latin America
Hb and Pb

James Petras et al
CLASS, STATE AND POWER IN
THE THIRD WORLD
with Case Studies of Class Conflict in
Latin America
Hb

James Millette
SOCIETY AND POLITICS IN
COLONIAL TRINIDAD
Hb and Pb

Sue Branford and Oriel Glock
THE LAST FRONTIER
Fighting for Land in the Amazon
Hb and Pb

Michael Kaufman
JAMAICA UNDER MANLEY
The Failure of Social Democracy
Hb and Pb

Gabriela Yanes et al
MIRRORS OF WAR
Literature and Revolution in El
Salvador
Hb and Pb

Richard Harris and Carlos Vilas
(Editors)
NICARAGUA: THE REVOLUTION
UNDER THREAT
Hb and Pb

Enrique Medina
THE DUKE
Memories and Anti-memories of a
Participant in the Repression
Pb

Roxanne Dunbar Ortiz
INDIANS OF THE AMERICAS
Self-Determination and Human
Rights
Hb and Pb

Mario Hector
DEATH ROW
Hb and Pb

Charles Edquist
CAPITALISM, SOCIALISM AND
TECHNOLOGY
A Comparative Study of Cuba and
Jamaica
Hb and Pb